MW00440354

Ma Doula

With Blessings!
Stephanie

Author with one of her many babies.

Ma Doula

A Story Tour of Birth

Stephanie Sorensen

NORTH STAR PRESS OF ST. CLOUD, INC.
St. Cloud, Minnesota

Copyright © 2015 Stephanie Sorensen
Cover image © iStock/Getty Images

All rights reserved.

ISBN: 978-0-87839-821-8

First edition: June 2015

Medical Disclaimer: This book is not intended as a substitute for the medical advice of your midwife, obstetrician, physician, pediatrician, lactation consultant, or other care provider, but rather is meant to supplement, not replace, your primary health care person(s). The reader should regularly consult with one of the above care providers in matters relating to his/her health or your baby's health, particularly with respect to any symptoms that may require diagnosis or medical attention. This book has incorporated "best practice" guidelines as much as possible and encourages all parents to continue to research the subjects discussed here as new studies are continually being done both here in the U.S. and abroad.

Printed in the United States of America.

Published by
North Star Press of St. Cloud, Inc.
P.O. Box 451
St. Cloud, MN 56302

www.northstarpress.com

"All over the world there exists in every society a small group of women who feel themselves strongly attracted to giving care to other women during pregnancy and childbirth. Failure to make use of this group of highly motivated people is regrettable and a sin. . . ."

~Dr. Kloosterman
Chief of OB/GYN,
University of Amsterdam, Holland

Dedication

I wish to honor the memory of Dr. John H. Kennell, who died on August 27, 2013, at age ninety-one. When Dr. Kennell was a hospital pediatrician in the 1950s, newborns were typically whisked away within minutes of delivery, washed, weighed, blood-tested, and plunked into bassinets under the nursery's fluorescent lights. Their mothers were not permitted to hold them for twelve hours, sometimes longer. Dr. Kennell liked to say that " . . . it was the full-throated complaints about this state of affairs" by his patients that led him to undertake a research project in the 1960s that helped change the world on which most newborns now open their eyes. The babies of the world thank him!

"If a doula were a drug, it would unethical not to use it."
~John H. Kennell

Table of Contents

Preface

My husband and I were living in Pennsylvania in the mid-to-late 1970s when I first helped Amish women give birth in their homes, often by lamplight. Most of the births were uncomplicated. However, I soon realized I didn't have the training, knowledge, or experience to help as much as I wanted when births didn't go as planned.

I did discover, though, that I had the temperament, patience, compassion, curiosity to learn, and not just the desire but a passion to be a part of what I still consider to be the most momentous events on earth. In the following years I became a licensed midwife, a childbirth educator, a lactation (breastfeeding) consultant/educator, then a birth doula. Most importantly, I became a mother of five, including twins, and eventually a grandmother.

My own birth journey began when, after years of infertility testing, I became joyfully pregnant. Though there were several books on the market in 1980 about raising children, there wasn't much about giving birth. When I discovered the first edition of *Spiritual Midwifery* by Ina May Gaskin, I devoured it. *I can do this,* I thought. And I did, giving birth to my almost-ten-pound Abraham without drugs, in a little hospital birthing room before the doctor even arrived. We went home six hours later.

I wanted to do the same thing when I became pregnant again. We knew it was twins before the doctor did. I scheduled my own ultrasound to convince him. Though protocols were beginning to change, the only way I could deliver them in Minnesota in 1982 was in an operating room after being prepped for surgery. They said they would let me try to have a natural birth—but it terrified them. So I called Ina

May Gaskin for advice and she invited me to The Farm Midwifery Center in Summertown, Tennessee. I moved to Tennessee that autumn and had a beautiful experience birthing two healthy babies. One weighed seven pounds, fifteen ounces; the other was seven pounds, seven ounces. Their births were filmed (See *Twin Vertex Birth* in Resources) and the video has been used as a teaching tool for many years.

After our twins we had two more babies, three years apart. They were both unassisted home births. Though I had planned to have a midwife both times, they didn't make it in time because though I thought I had planned well, I forgot to calculate how long it would take the midwives to reach our small log home in rural Wisconsin.

By the time we had five children I had taken a few courses and began to seriously think about become a licensed midwife. It all came together when I received a Bush Leadership Fellowship in 1989, which enabled me to complete an internship in midwifery at a freestanding birthing clinic in El Paso, Texas, which also served the neighboring city of Ciudad Juárez, Mexico. It allowed me to complete the final requirements needed to take the state midwifery boards that same year. I received my midwifery license in 1989.

Fast forward to 2010. We had just returned to Minnesota after living in England for several years. Our children were grown and on their own. I was in my fifties and knew that I did not want to work in a hospital or clinic as a midwife where I would be assigned two, three, or more families per shift and would have to leave them at the end of my

shift. I also did not want to take my midwifery board examinations all over again, which could take up to two years of preparation. I wasn't sure it would be worth all the work; besides, I was not too keen to learn all the new electronic charting and the rocket science monitoring systems now in place since I left.

Stephanie with her twins.

I looked up my old mentor from long ago and we put together a plan to bring some of my credentials current by taking a few continuing education courses. Several months later I was ready to look for work teaching childbirth education classes and as a lactation consultant.

One day I was taking some Somali women on a tour of a free-standing birthing center to show them some of their options in this country. The director asked for my phone number should they need a teacher in the future. A month later, on the eve of the Fourth of July, with every room in the birthing center full, I received a call, begging me to come in as an extra pair of hands to help them out.

I was soon hired as a childbirth education teacher, lactation educator and consultant, and birth assistant, working under one of the other midwives. It was great fun and an honor to be back in birth work. During my year there I also became certified as a postpartum doula and was able to help couples at home, too, after their births. Soon I became a birth doula, which allows me to accompany a woman to the hospital when her labor begins and stay with her for the whole birth. I don't have to leave at shift change. I don't have to be concerned about the paperwork or if the machines are working properly. I don't have to leave to be with another family.

Being a doula is my dream job. In the last few years I have helped moms of every size, shape, color, almost every religion under the sun, first-time moms, fourth-time moms, moms who wanted no drugs, at least one who wanted an epidural in her eighth month of pregnancy, uncomplicated vaginal births, C-sections, multiples, breech—almost every scenario you can imagine. Two decades ago I lost count after helping with my two-hundredth baby. I am still honored and humbled when I can witness each magnificent, mystifying miracle of birth.

"Natural childbirth has evolved to suit the species, and if mankind chooses to ignore her advice and interfere with her workings we must not complain about the consequences. We have only ourselves to blame."
~Margaret Jowitt

Introduction

I'll briefly explain the similarities and the differences between a mid-wife and a doula. A midwife is a medical professional who has gone through extensive training, education, and supervised clinical experience before being licensed. Midwives can perform gynecological exams, orders tests, and prescribe some medications. Depending on state requirements, they can deliver babies in homes, birthing centers, and hospitals, with or without a physician's participation. They practice under the particular state's protocols for low-risk births.

Doula, pronounced DOO-la, originated from the Ancient Greek word meaning "servant to women," a non-medical person who assists a woman, her partner and/or family before, during, and after childbirth, providing information and physical and emotional support. A doula is not considered a medical professional, though we hope we're seen as a part of the birthing team.

As I see it, my job as a doula is primarily to listen to the moms-to-be, and to be their personal advocate for their wishes for their births. I can help them decide what they want and do not want during their pregnancies and deliveries. I can help them write a birth plan, though I cannot and will not make any decisions for them but I will support them should they have to change course.

I need to listen and understand who this woman before me is and ask myself, *What is she thinking? How far does her understanding go? What does she want to try? What is she saying just to please me and what does she really want? What are her fears?*

I am called upon to be perceptive, discerning, compassionate, intuitive, maternal, and empathetic. A doula is truly a teacher, guide, coach, sister, mother, and friend all at once. My bag of tools means nothing if I haven't made her feel respected and trusted. I don't need to earn her respect or trust here. I need to make her feel safe so that she can access her own wisdom and inner power to the best of her ability.

I need to make her feel that she was a smashing success after she gives birth, that she did her very best and succeeded. I want her to say "We did it!" and not, "I couldn't have done it without you."

And then I must find the right words to help her connect with her new baby if she doesn't automatically fall in love with him. Not everyone does. It can take time.

All of this takes experience. Doulas learn from each and every birth they attend. Our moms teach us. I believe we become more humble in the face of such power and grace, not more knowledgeable or self-assured as time moves on. I feel like I know less now about the vast mysteries of birth and how nature and creation works than when I began this journey.

I always want to know more. I was blessed with a gigantic curiosity. Throughout my life that curiosity has enticed me to travel the world and learn as much as I can about the humans that inhabit our planet. When we moved back to Minnesota, I starting working with many different immigrant communities who have chosen the Twin Cities, Minneapolis and St. Paul, to be their home after escaping devastation of many kinds in their home countries. I've worked with students from all over the world who have come to our universities to study. I also work with teenagers who have no support from partners or families and married yuppies who are followed to the hospital by entourages of anticipatory grandparents-to-be, aunts and uncles, and best friends. I work with non-profit organizations and with private clients.

In the following birth stories you will read about several of them. Though they may differ in education, customs, cultures, religions, beliefs, ideologies, sophistication, and maturity, they all had one thing in common: a desire for a healthy baby.

I hope this book encourages those of you who are on the path to becoming doulas to continue down that path. I hope others of you will think about becoming doulas, even if you never entertained the thought before. We need you. We need compassionate, giving hearts. In the end it isn't about knowing about massage or herbs or a bag of tools. It is about love.

To those of you who are becoming parents, I hope this book gives you courage and confidence, knowing there are women who are ready to accompany you on your journey to the land of birth.

At the front of this book is a medical disclaimer. Since almost no one will read it, I want to make a one thing clear in non-legal language. This is not a how-to book and should not be read as such. Though there is information, it is not meant to be comprehensive or complete.

The names of people, places, and other identifying facts have been changed throughout the book to honor each family's privacy unless specific permission to use their names has been given.

Rules, regulations, laws, and protocols differ between birthing centers and hospitals, from one hospital and another, city to city, county to county, and state to state. It's important to know what your options are, whether you're a mom-to-be or someone thinking about becoming a doula.

As my friend and colleague Liz Abbene of Enlightened Mama says, "It is important to ask questions because if a woman doesn't know what her choices are, she simply doesn't have any."

"The whole point of woman-centered birth is the knowledge that a woman is the birth power source. She may need, and deserve, help, but in essence, she always had, currently had, and will always have the power."
~Heather McCue

A Note to Grandmothers and Grandmothers-To-Be

My editor emailed me after she read the manuscript, "As I was fin-ishing today, I couldn't believe my thought: 'I want two do-overs!' I think I was allowed to get out of bed once to go to the bathroom when I was laboring with my first baby for thirty-six hours (Chicago, 1978). I don't remember being allowed out of bed during my second (twenty-four hours—Maine, 1981). I didn't know there was an-other way to give birth other than on my back and in stirrups. I can't believe how much has changed."

Yes, grandmothers, birth protocols have traveled lightyears from what it was in your childbearing years. My first baby was born in 1980, and I can name dozens of things that have changed since then. Not all changes have been good. We have a paradox here. We have more knowledge and know-how than ever before. We can look into a baby's heart on an ultrasound at only twenty-weeks' gestation and detect prob-lems. We can save twenty-one-week old babies who will grow up with-out the side effects we saw only a decade ago due to the lack of technologies that are now in place today.

But we can also do more C-sections than ever before and introduce more interventions than anyone could have dreamed of, which can and sometimes do come with their own sets of unimagined complications. Now we have an entire subculture of new parents revolting against the space-age medical world we have invented—though with all good intentions—and going so far in this rebellion as to insist on having their babies at home, unassisted by any level of any kind of birth professional.

What many of us wish for and are working toward isn't a compromise. We are simply asking, "What have we lost in the confusion that we should have kept (now called 'best practice'), and what can we learn from how human mothers were meant to give birth?" Yes, C-sections and other interventions are there to save mothers and babies, and there are times and circumstances for both, but now that we have seen the ravages that have been wrecked on both sides of the pendulum, can we all just be a little humbler (and respect Mother Nature more) and find a way to agree and better serve the next generations —our future?

"Anyone who thinks women are the weaker sex never witnessed childbirth."
~Anonymous

Chapter One

"Now You Are Our Sister"

In the late 1970s and '80s I volunteered through Macalester College in St. Paul, Minnesota, to work with the Hmong refugee population when they began arriving in the Midwest in the late 1970s. That was at the end of the Vietnam War era. The Hmong had assisted U.S. troops in the jungles of Laos and incurred the wrath of the communist Pol Pot regime in doing so. I learned to speak Hmong (never mind that I had flunked French two years in a row in high school) and acted as a liaison in the Minnesota justice system, in hospitals, and at funeral homes.

I immersed myself in the Hmong culture, attempting to find ways to make their assimilation less painful, if possible. I marveled at the resiliency of an entire society uprooted by war and replanted half a world away from the only home they had ever known.

Our family remained intertwined with our Hmong friends over the ensuing decades. Our children grew up with their children, also becoming bilingual, which greatly surprised the Hmong. I tried to explain that while I was calling landlords and bill collectors, teaching English classes and scheduling appointments for everything from prenatal exams to visa and citizenship hearings on their behalf, that their grandmas were watching my kids and constantly talking to them in Hmong. I said I was not surprised they picked it up. I pointed out that if I were to keep one of their babies for any length of time and they heard only English, they too would speak mostly English. That met with a decidedly negative response. I was firmly told that Hmong babies are born knowing Hmong. I couldn't convince my new friends otherwise. Over the years we have laughed and cried together, birthed their babies and buried their elderly, often casualties of the war that continued to rage inside of them in spite of the fact that they were here in the U.S., thousands of miles away from the carnage.

When we moved back to Minnesota from the U.K., we saw the amazing transformation that had taken place with the arrival of over 70,000 African immigrants in Minneapolis and St. Paul. I was intrigued. That winter I began researching what I needed to do to update my credentials but found I had lots of time on my hands. I wanted to rediscover this global market I had returned to.

I heard about a Somali marketplace that had opened. I thought it might be a good place to start to learn about these people who I had never had a chance to know before. I found very quickly that they were as curious about us as we were of them. Every day for the next weeks and months, I took a bus over to Karmel Mall. After a few weeks I was on a first name basis with some of the grandmothers who "manned" the little stalls at the mall. I asked one woman named Fadumo how to say "midwife" in Somali. Now I could introduce myself, but some Africans spoke Arabic, or Oromo, or Amharic or Swahili. I couldn't tell yet by their dress who was from where, Jordon or Kuwait, Egypt or Pakistan, Somalia or Kenya. It turned out that many stopped in other countries on their long journey away from their war-torn countries. Some settled down temporarily and moved on once they had enough money to try to catch up to relatives who had the good fortune to be in the U.S. I even met some Somalis who spoke no English but were fluent in Swedish! They had been offered only Swedish visas when they approached the consulates to escape from Somalia.

Fadumo and I became close friends. Also a grandmother, her little stall boasted beautiful fabrics from around the world, including wedding robes, matching *hijab* and underslips, perfumes, jewelry, henna kits for decorating women's hands, arms, and feet for special occasions, an assortment of tea sets, and drapery and carpets for transforming an

American apartment into a true Muslim home. I found a Somali-English/English-Somali dictionary for the times we hit a wall trying to communicate something to each other. We spent hours asking each other questions about the other's culture and other times just compared what we planned on cooking for our husbands that night.

Fadumo had been a licensed massage therapist while her family lived in Nairobi. I found her a book on baby massage, which she pored over for weeks. At lunchtime she would often order a platter for two from the mall's halal restaurant and bring it back to her little stall and, sitting on the floor on a carpet, she would teach me how to eat goat meat and spaghetti Somali-style with my hands, or I should say, with my right hand, since the left hand is reserved for unclean things, not for eating. Over the next few months, more often than not, we would both end up reduced to giggles. She had never had to teach a grown woman how to eat!

As I continued to visit her, I was approached by several students who asked if I could proofread their college homework. I gladly did, having learned some editing and proofreading while working for a Hmong newspaper years earlier. Soon I had a handful of students asking for help with their papers.

One woman, Halima, who was studying for her master's degree in economics, told me she was expecting baby girl number four! She laughed when she told me she only makes girls and that they hadn't figured out yet how to make boys. I asked if her husband was disappointed or if in their culture he could take another wife in order to produce boys. I knew that in the more orthodox or Hassidic branches of Judaism, after a proscribed number of years, a man could divorce his wife and take another if she had not produced children for him, and I knew of similar customs in other countries, so I was concerned. Halima said he couldn't blame her or be unhappy with her because it is Allah who chooses what kind of baby to send couples. They are taught to be grateful for whatever gifts He sends, so no, her husband would not be sad this time. Then she asked me if I would be her doula. I was honored.

We continued to meet over the next months, discussing diet among other topics. Unfortunately, many Somalis have adopted our SAD diet, the Standard American Diet, packed with fats and calories and few nutrients. Their former culture had a wonderful diet full of fresh fruits, vegetables, meat, and very little dairy or wheat. Many now eat the white bread, pastries, cookies, candy bars, snacks, soda, and other nutrient-deficient junk foods they find at their neighborhood stores and fast-food restaurants. Their lifestyle, of course, is no longer one of nomads or camel herders who worked hard to eke out a living off an arid land, and now are often sedentary much of the time. This is taking its toll: diabetes and obesity are now rampant in their community.

Finally one night Halima called to let me know she was on her way to the hospital. We had both been so excited about this baby's arrival and the day had finally arrived. I got to the hospital as the nurse was checking her. She was five centimeters already! This wasn't going to be long. Between contractions, or rushes, as I now call them, Halima introduced me to her mother, Ubax, an elderly aunt, Deqo, and her sister Sahroh. All were dressed from head to toe in wraps of one sort or another. Men were not especially welcomed at births. This was women's work.

Halima wore a hospital gown instead of the traditional robes, though she still wore two headscarves. We were quite a team, breathing together, the grandmas happily catching up on gossip in one corner, Halima walking around the room, then trying to sit on the birth ball (a rubber exercise ball) for a while. I like getting moms up and out of bed because gravity helps babies move down the birth canal. Sitting on a birth ball not only keeps things progressing, but often aids in turning a baby into the optimum mother-baby face-to-face position for birth. Babies who begin labor "sunny side up" have a harder time and often will not turn making the descent-down-the-birth-canal stage harder. Some babies are turned halfway between the two presentations, with the head in an "acyclic" position (turned to the side), which often holds things up, literally. Lying in bed can actually slow labor down or even stop it in some cases. By being on a birth ball not only does gravity help, but a mom can rock her hips side to side and in a spiral or circular motion, which greatly aids in engaging the baby's head properly. When that happens and the baby's head molds to fit the birth canal it also helps slowly stretch the walls of the vagina, which can in turn prevent tears.

Things were going smoothly with short naps between the rushes. Then Halima started shivering. I assumed it was transition, but when the nurse took her temperature, we saw that it had shot up. She continued to shiver as I piled on warmed blankets. *Darn it,* I thought, *and just when everything was going so well.* The doctor ordered blood tests right away and started an IV with antibiotics "just in case" the fever was a sign of infection. The doctor started suggesting interventions should we not be able to get the fever down. Within half an hour the baby's heart rate jumped up, too, and more interventions to speed things along were offered.

Halima and I had agreed that in the event the staff offered treatment options as we went along in the birth, she would suggest she have a few minutes with her family to discuss any suggestions first. It was time for that. The nurses and doctor all left us to deliberate. Halima again made it very clear that she did not want drugs and certainly not a C-section unless things looked too risky. I explained that I could not decide what was best for her, but that an infection could get nasty, that the IV was not a bad idea, and that she could probably ask for a little more time to see how things worked out. She agreed with this plan and let the nurses know. She started to drink more juice to help with the fever and build up her strength. She continued to dilate, which was good. The next check told us she was at seven centimeters. Then we were alone again.

She started to feel better. I had peeled back the blankets, was sponging her down with lukewarm washcloths, and brought her cup after cup of juice. Suddenly she said she wanted to push. I was surprised and thought it was just the pressure of the baby moving down, but when she yelled, "I am going to push!" I knew nothing was going to stop her. I rang for the nurse and she came into the room.

When this nurse had taken a blood sample earlier for the lab, she hadn't put enough pressure on the site when she removed the needle and blood had spurted all over the bed and the floor. The grandmas clicked their tongues and shook their heads: not a good nurse. Now she sauntered back in, saw the black curly-headed baby crowning, and whipped on a pair of gloves. Actually, she only managed to get one hand covered, which she used to support the baby who was coming out. She held her other hand above her head so as not to become contaminated, I guess, and left the baby lying in a puddle on a Chux pad. I could tell the baby wasn't breathing, and in slow motion wondered, *Who is going to do something?* I grabbed the end of the sheet and started wiping off the baby girl's face and rubbed her down to get her to breathe. I lifted her up with both of my ungloved hands as the nurse stuck a bulb syringe into the baby's mouth with her one gloved hand and we both moved together over to the warmer, which had been turned on earlier. I continued to rub and the nurse kept suctioning for the next few seconds, which felt like an eternity. The baby started pinking up by then, though I didn't think she was really breathing well yet just as the NRP (neonatal resuscitation program) team ran into the room and started to work on the baby, who cried within the next few seconds. The doctor was there in time to watch Halima push out the placenta. The second, or pushing, stage had lasted less than five minutes.

Things finally settled down and Halima was happily nursing her fourth little girl, whom she named Maryan. I was standing next to the bed just taking it all in, so very thankful that everything turned out okay. The grandmas were talking quite loudly at this point so I asked Halima what they were saying. She listened for a minute and told me, "They are saying they wished they had had a doula at their births!" I found out that they had spent most of the waiting time retelling the stories of their own births, even when Halima was trying to rest. She told me later that even their woman-chatter was comforting at the time.

Then the grandmas came over to where I was standing and started stroking my arms and my shoulders, then my head and my hands. Without moving a muscle, I asked Halima under my breath, "Halima . . . uh . . . what are they doing?"

She explained, "They say you are like a holy person who has made the pilgrimage to the Haj in the East, and you love us and treat us like your own family. Now you are our sister."

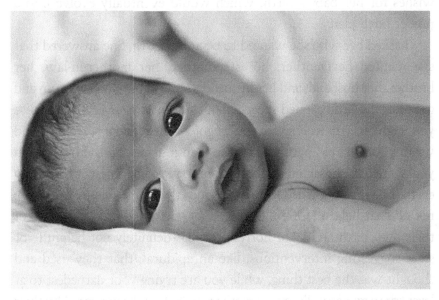

"Around us, life bursts with miracles—a glass of water, a ray of sunshine, a leaf, a caterpillar, a flower, laughter, raindrops. If you live in awareness, it is easy to see miracles everywhere. Each human being is a multiplicity of miracles. Eyes that see thousands of colors, shapes, and forms; ears that hear a bee flying or a thunderclap; a brain that ponders a speck of dust as easily as the entire cosmos; a heart that beats in rhythm with the heartbeat of all beings. When we are tired and feel discouraged by life's daily struggles, we may not notice these miracles, but they are always there."
~Thich Nhat Hanh, Vietnamese Zen Buddhist monk, teacher, author, poet, and peace activist

Chapter Two

Sometimes It Does Take a Village

I was filling out Tiana's paperwork as I signed her up for our doula program. At the same time, I was gathering information about her wishes for her baby's birth, which would eventually evolve into a proper birth plan.

I asked her who she wanted to be at her birth. She answered that she wanted her mother, her stepmother, her mother-in-law, her brother, her husband, and her husband's sister. I put my pen down and gave her my little canned speech about not inviting everyone because you might end up feeling like you've got all these people watching and waiting for you to "perform" rather than just making the birth room yours, making it a sacred space wherein to welcome a new little soul to earth. I have also learned from experience that sometimes relatives are not all that helpful. Often, during labor, they will start telling all of their own birth and labor horror stories—definitely not helpful—or start suggesting interventions, like an epidural, that they used and thought was the best thing, while you are trying your darnedest to at least try to go naturally. Some mothers-to-be have been begged by their own mothers or best friends or mothers-in-law to please let them be there for the birth, and if moms-to-be aren't assertive enough to say no, soon the entire congregation is attending the birth.

I had my say, for what it was worth, and finished up the paperwork. That done, we watched the DVD called *Doula* that I like to have first-time moms see because it shows diverse families, what they wanted for their births, and how a doula tries to create the birth experience the parents want. There are home births with siblings present;

8

home water births with dad in the pool, too; hospital water births; hospital medicated and un-medicated births; au *natural* births and moms dressed in their own clothes; unplanned Cesarean births and planned C-sections.

Thinking she was empowered with all this information, I ended our first meeting and encouraged Tiana and Zion, her husband, to read as much as possible and suggested checking out some of the videos on my resource handout.

Our next couple of meetings went well as we got to know each other. Zion asked insightful questions about birth and labor and was really getting "charged up," as he put it, for his son's birth. Tiana was less vocal. I wondered if she was just plain scared, because most of her answers to my questions about how she was preparing for their baby were all, "Yes," "No" or "I dunno."

Then as week thirty-eight was quickly approaching I gave her a sample birth plan and suggested she change it to fit her expectations. She never worked on it, which was okay, but I had been hoping she would take a more active role in her birth. I did learn that her mom had four very fast natural births, so she thought she would try that. We were at her thirty-ninth week appointment when she asked if she should just show up at the hospital on her due date and wondered how they "start it up." The midwife we were seeing that day laughed and said, "Remember when we went over the signs of labor starting? Well, we wait until your body tells us it is ready. You will see some spotting, though that doesn't always have to happen first, or your water breaks, or you have contractions that don't go away when you try to rest."

Tiana thought about that a minute and then frowned. "You mean I gotta wait for that? It ain't just gonna all be over on my due date?"

Whoops. I thought we had been preparing better than that. Tiana was still in high school and at one appointment had told me about the birth classes the school also held for young moms, so I had thought she had plenty of childbirth education, but I was wrong.

The midwife patiently went over the basics of early labor again and reassured Tiana that it was all perfectly normal and that often first babies decide to arrive after their official due date, which is in fact only a guess date. There is no magic formula to predict when each baby will be born.

"Shit!" was her response. Tiana was tired of being pregnant. She was tired of heartburn and swollen ankles, uncomfortable nights and constipation, all normal side effects of pregnancy. She had been all geared up for this pregnancy to be done with on her due date, which was now one week away. Her mother was going to come up to be with her on that day and needed to go home shortly afterwards. Tiana got dressed and left, a very unhappy mom-to-be.

When I worked at a freestanding birth clinic where we didn't have drugs even if our moms wanted them, every single woman who chose to birth there had done her homework, had read every book on the market, viewed every YouTube video out there on birth, had interviewed every midwife within a 200-mile radius, and was ready for just about anything. The problem was not convincing them to birth naturally or be willing to go through a twenty-four- or thirty-six-hour first-stage of labor; there the problem was convincing them that when we see meconium or another serious complication, it is time to consider transferring to the hospital.

A week later I met with Tiana again. As soon as the midwife came in the room and started to measure her belly, Tiana asked if she could schedule an induction. The midwife asked why.

"I want this baby to come while my mom is here."

"I can't do that. Your baby will come when he is ready," her midwife replied.

"But if I am really overdue you could induce me, so why can't you now?"

The midwife tried to explain that there has to be a good reason to induce babies and that her mom being here for a short time wasn't one of them. This did not sit well. Tiana left shaking her head while Zion practically danced out of the clinic, singing a little made-up rap, "I'm gonna be a daddy, YES! I'm gonna be a papa . . ."

That night I got a call from Tiana asking if there was anything she could do to bring on labor. I explained that she could ask the midwife what she thought about what we call "stripping the membranes" where, if her cervix has started to dilate, the midwife can sweep a finger around the cervix while gently separating the bag of water from just inside the cervix. Sometimes this will trigger the uterus into thinking it is time for early labor. I also told her how I had gotten on a bike one day and rode for an hour up and down a dirt road when my twins were due and it worked. She asked about Pitocin. Again I said that there had to be a true medical reason to induce. I also encouraged her to keep in touch with her midwife, who might have other suggestions or tricks up her sleeve.

Well, the guess date came and went. Then two days later, at 4:00 a.m., the phone rang. Tiana was having contractions! I asked her to call the midwife and let me know what she said. She called me back and said they wanted her to wait until she had contractions five minutes apart for two hours. She told me they were already unbearable. I suggested she get in a hot tub or shower and keep me posted. An hour later I received a text that she was on her way to the hospital. I was off, too.

The hospital she had chosen had a triage unit where moms first go to be assessed. Too often women enter the hospital in very early labor and are encouraged to return home, where they can labor in familiar surroundings, resting and eating until labor is truly established. In triage the baby and the contractions are monitored and if everything looks good they can be reassured that they are doing well, that labor will pick up exactly at the right moment, and they should not be discouraged.

The midwives assured Tiana that her body was getting ready, that this was all perfectly normal for a first-time mom, and that her baby sounded great, but that early labor could go on for another day and they really thought she would be more comfortable at home. Zion, however, was not phased. He was dancing around the room singing another original rap about his son whom he couldn't wait to meet.

Tiana's stepmother, Imani, was helping her dress to go home when we all heard a tiny wet *splat.* Tiana looked down and exclaimed, "Ewww!" There on the floor was her mucus plug and water was running down her legs, filling her slippers.

"That's so damn grossss!" was her next expletive.

I laughed and said, "Your water broke! Congratulations! See? Your body knows exactly what to do."

Her reply, as I grabbed some gloves and paper towels to wipe it up before anyone slipped was, "Ewwwgross!"

Imani steered Tiana into the bathroom to clean up as I cleaned up the floor, skirting Zion as he tiptoed around the room humming his little song. I told the nurse that it appeared Tiana's water just broke. She went back to the nurses' station and got a test swab to confirm that it indeed had. By the time Tiana was dressed, the contractions had picked up appreciably and the nurse put her back on the monitor. No one was going home. We were going to have a baby.

Soon we were in a proper birthing room. I got a birth ball and filled a pitcher with ice water. Zion had texted his mom and sister and before I knew it I was being introduced to Alexi, Naveah, Jayla, Kiara, Tiana's sisters Trinity and Onieda, and cousin Melida. Then her brothers arrived. As we got settled and hung up coats and collected more folding chairs from the other rooms, I found a quiet corner and parked on an exam stool to update my paperwork. Everyone got comfortable while Zion wrestled with the lounge chair, trying to figure out which knobs to pull to turn it into a daybed. He was ready for a nap, having been up since 3:00 a.m. I poked around the cupboards in the room until I found some sheets and a pillow and helped him make up the bed.

As relatives continued to arrive and greet one another, I tried to get near the bed. I wanted Tiana to know that everything was going really well. The contractions were picking up and their baby sounded wonderful. I reminded her to breathe slowly and remember to relax her face, throat, then shoulders and legs. I massaged her hands during the next contractions and then as her mother-in-law took over the hand massages I moved down to her feet. She said that all helped her relax. During the next hour Tiana asked to just be allowed to rest in bed. She was tired.

At shift change I wiped the whiteboard in the room and updated it with our new nurse's name, the new midwife's name and under the title "Goals" wrote, "Have Baby Boy!" I invited Tiana's sisters to fill in the rest of the box marked "Companions." They managed to squeeze all fourteen names in the box.

One of her cousins busied herself with Tiana's make-up. She wanted her to look her best for the pictures they all planned to take. The cousin suggested only above-the-waist photos before the baby came and maybe a few as he was crowning. Tiana wasn't sure about that. They continued discussing pictures while Tiana had her eyebrows sculpted. Lip gloss completed the process. I noticed how relaxed she was while being made up, no complaints about the contractions or rushes. Hmm.

Suddenly about six cameras started clicking and flashes started going off, now that the star of the show had on her make-up. It looked like a scene on the news of some diva rock singer as she steps out of her limo onto the red carpet at the Grammy Awards. I had been wondering when her midwife would comment on the sheer number of people in the room, and now she did.

"Maybe you can put away all the cameras and phones for now, at least until the baby is born, so we can work around the bed and help Tiana relax." She was very diplomatic.

I sat next to the bed and encouraged Tiana through each rush. After another hour she asked how much longer this could go on. I explained that for a first baby we expect about one centimeter of dilation every hour, or sometimes every two hours. I also said that she would feel a whole lot better doing anything other than being on her back in bed. We finally helped her up and she walked down the long halls with Zion. I demonstrated, with his cooperation, how to lock her hands behind his neck and hang that way during the rushes and that moving her hips from side to side and in a spiral or circular motion would also help the baby move down.

After one lap around the fourth floor she was back, heading for the bed. I grabbed the birth ball and firmly but gently suggested she stay upright awhile longer sitting on the birth ball at the edge of the bed, which I raised up to her shoulder height once she was seated. I positioned a pillow in front of her on the bed so she could really rest in between rushes. After awhile, though she admitted the birth ball had helped, she asked about pain medication. I suggested she call the nurse and discuss her options together. The nurse told her it was still pretty early in the labor, and strongly urged she try a hot bath. They discussed this back and forth for a while until Tiana agreed to try it. Once she was ensconced in the tub with the lights out and tiny pin lights glowing around the edges of the tub, she relaxed. I got a pitcher and slowly poured a little stream of water over her belly. After a few minutes, I asked Zion if I could show him how to do it. He bounded in, humming a new little tune, and quickly got the hang of pouring a steady stream of water over Tiana. They stayed like that for almost an hour. When she got out the nurse checked her. She was at three centimeters—not too fast, but definitely progress. We tried the birth ball again and I had Zion behind her on a chair rubbing her lower back with a massage ball. I assured her that back pain was a good sign that her baby was moving down into her pelvis. He was still sounding wonderful when the nurse intermittently checked his heart tones with a Doppler.

While Tiana was in the tub the sisters had gone down to the cafeteria and returned with covered plates full of eggs, sausages, biscuits, and toast and passed those all around. Another sister came back with a tray of coffee in paper cups. They knew how to feed a crowd. *This group knew how to "do family,"* I thought as I watched in wonder. I had also been figured into the breakfast count, bless their hearts!

Another aunt came in during breakfast and announced that since it was such an auspicious day, the day of their little man's birth, she had gotten lottery tickets, the scratch-off kind, and passed them around. Someone was sure to get lucky today, she explained.

As breakfast was wrapping up, Zion went around the room picking up all the paper plates and cups and generally tidying up the room. About that time Tiana asked one of the nurses if they might have an even larger room available. The nurse left to check and soon came back saying that one other mom had just gone home and they had called housekeeping to clean it right away. Within an hour we moved into our new, bigger, temporary home.

Sometime around five centimeters, Tiana decided she wanted an epidural. When the anesthesiologist arrived, I took the lead and announced that we all had to leave so he could set up. I promptly escorted the crowd into the hall, where the conversations continued about who was bringing what for the family's Thanksgiving dinner.

Around 5:00 p.m. another aunt appeared with her two daughters. They were toting bags of fried chicken, dinner rolls, bottles of soda, chips and . . . Halloween candy. A few minutes later I left Tiara's bedside to get more ice water. On the way out the door I passed several cousins and brothers, all big macho guys, with Zion in the middle, still happily humming. Each had a lollipop in his mouth.

Only a few minutes later the nurse announced that Tiana was ten centimeters and we were going to set up the bed for the delivery. With his mouth full of chicken, Zion looked at me with a pained expression and asked, "Now? I can't even eat fried chicken?"

I laughed and said, "I think Tiana needs you over here just now."

Zion gulped down some more chicken and stood by Tiana's head, wiping his fingers off on a napkin before he reach for her hand. I was by the head of the bed on the other side, showing her how to hold her legs behind her knees. The baby warmer was turned on and the sterile pack of instruments was being unwrapped at the other end of the bed. About eight ladies were lined up behind that, cameras and cell phones ready. I looked over this scene and thought, *What is wrong with this picture?* I left Tiana's side and walked to the end of the bed and suggested that the ladies might want to stand closer to the windows to give Tiana a little privacy at the end of the bed where the nurses were helping her position her legs on two trough-like stirrups. The epidural had rendered her legs numb and as heavy as tree trunks.

I returned to my position and encouraged Tiana during the next rush. She did not have an urge to push because the epidural blocked any sensations there, but the midwife was ready to offer directions from down below where she was now stationed. I was too far up near the head of the bed to see what was going on down there but could tell from the midwife's responses that things were going very well and she could see the baby's curly black hair even after just the first push. I whispered to Tiana that she could rest for a bit and when the midwife said to push, I would help her take a deep breath, then let it out as the contraction built and, with another deep breath, put her chin down to her chest, hold it . . . and . . . push . . . and again . . .

The baby's head was out. Just like that. It was the shortest second stage of labor in a first-time mom I had ever seen. The midwife said the same thing. Another push and all of him was out. The ladies had migrated once again to the end of the bed in those few minutes (it was nearly impossible to keep the paparazzi away) and the flashes started again amidst crying and hugs.

I looked up to see Zion wiping his eyes and shaking his head in disbelief. One lady moved over nearer to me and said, "I am twenty-nine years old and I have never seen a birth before. This is so awesome!" It really was.

I whispered into Tiana's ear, "You did it! I knew you could! You are amazing and I am so very, very proud of you!" She was crying, too. As soon as Zion cut the cord, the baby was put onto Tiana's chest and a fresh warm blanket was laid over him. She instinctively held him there with both hands and, seeing his warm little bum sticking up under the blanket she proceeded to pat it with both hands. She couldn't say anything yet but just looked over at me beaming. Tears rolled down into her ears. Her make-up was still perfect.

The family continued taking pictures from every angle, including the end of the bed where the midwife was waiting for the placenta. I don't know how I could have managed crowd control any better. Tiana seemed completely unperturbed by it, so I just let her lead the way. I had let her know early on that she could tell me if at any point she wanted me to thin out the audience and send a few people out but she said it was all good. She had such an amazing family and support network. They were really good at this.

The next day I emailed a friend/RN/aspiring Certified Nurse Midwife (CNM) in St. Paul, asking her what her hospital's policies were when it came to families. She wrote back: "Our hospital does not have a specific number, but leaves this to the physician and nurses' discretion. If the room is big enough, and the family is respectful, we can allow many people to stay. If they have a big family, I try to lay a ground rule early on that only two or three people fit in the room, and appoint a gatekeeper (another family member) to do crowd control. There have been times we have needed to invent a unit-wide rule for the sake of getting obnoxious and unwelcome family out of the room, but only if they are truly interfering or causing a safety risk—there are even times we have had to call security to control a crowd for us when there are twenty family members trying to take over a room. If we can't get a bed past them out to an OR, or a neonatal crash team into the room, it's not safe and they need to move. If they are making unhelpful comments or being rude to me or any of the identified birth team, I'll boot them."

She continued, "I once had a teen mom where I was certain that the six people she had identified on her birth plan to come would cause me grief all day. They were loud, discussing sports or their own births, and kept repeating untruths about birth and reproduction. I resolved that I would need to thin the crowd as she moved to active labor. But then her friends and family moved to interact with her, every one of them taking a task and becoming the most beautiful team of doulas I have ever witnessed. They all stayed as the baby was born, and they were sensitive and respectful, aware of the space the physician and I needed to work, and quietly efficient! Loved it!"

Another friend wrote back saying, "Each hospital sets its own number. Here in New Jersey it is five. You know the saying: the more people in the room the more dysfunctional the family."

While Tiana was being cleaned up and wrapped in pre-warmed blankets and her baby boy was nursing like a real pro, I packed up my things from all around the room, quite ready to catch up on missed sleep. The room had thinned out appreciably and I assumed the family had started going home. I was wrong. It was time to eat again. They all came back in, this time toting submarine sandwiches for everyone. As I prepared to leave after hugging everyone goodbye, I made my way down to the hospital lobby. One group of brothers and boyfriends of sisters and cousins who were not with the sandwich crowd were just coming back into the hospital as I reached the front doors.

"I thought you all left," I said.

Zion answered for them, "No, we just went out for a smoke."

I couldn't help it. I hugged him goodbye and whispered in his ear, "I hope you can give this up—smoking—it's not good for your baby. Even second-hand smoke is really dangerous, you know."

All I got was a half-hearted, "I know."

The next day the crowd was smaller. One of the aunties was changing the baby's diaper. I mentioned that I had just run across a new gadget for babies that they had to see. I got out my phone and showed the website for a soft little cover (a Pee-pee Teepee; see resource section) that can be put on a baby boy's penis while his diaper is being changed to protect his clothes and the changer's from any unexpected geysers. They thought it was the funniest thing they'd ever seen.

I finished up my paperwork and hugged Tiana goodbye. I would miss her and her big, loud, loving family.

"It's not just the making of babies, but the making of mothers that midwives [and doulas] see as the miracle of birth."
~Barbara Katz Rothman

Chapter Three

A Christmas Baby

It was Christmas. My husband and I had gone to the midnight service extra early to hear the special hymns and carol singing. It was beautiful and inspiring. The crèche at the church was stunning; it was close to life-size, camels and all. Christmas has always been a special time for me.

When we finally got home and crawled into bed at 2:00 a.m., I gave thanks for all that was well with the world, especially our deliciously cozy featherbed, and was quickly sound asleep. Soon I was dreaming that the phone was ringing. Why didn't it stop? It just kept ringing. My husband nudged me. I rolled over and looked at the clock: 4:00 a.m. The phone continued to ring.

Why would someone call me now? Oh, duh. I am a doula. But none of my moms-to-be was due for two more weeks at the earliest.

I picked up the phone. "Hello?"

The caller was laughing! I didn't like this joke. "Isn't this funny?" the voice giggled.

"Um, not really," I answered.

"I'm gonna have a Christmas baby!"

"Who is this?" I demanded, still half-asleep and thinking it was a prank call.

"It's Shannon, and our baby decided today is The Day. I don't believe this! We're on our way to the hospital."

"When did it start?" I asked as I leaped out of bed with a sudden spurt of adrenaline and ripped a clean outfit from the closet.

Usually I have my clothes laid out on a chair in the order I would put them on during the general time of any upcoming births. I'd have my bag by the door with my ID tag on top and a sticky note above the lock on the front door reminding me to bring a snack, my watch, my cell phone, charger cord, and purse. I have arrived at too many middle-of-the-night births missing one of these essentials.

I asked which hospital they were going to. A pencil and notepad live under the phone by my bed to write it down immediately. I don't trust my brain to register correctly, especially when I've had little sleep, and this night was definitely one of those.

Sleep or no sleep, it is always an honor to be invited into a family's most intimate moments and witness the miracle of birth once again. And this miracle would be happening on Christmas!

This was Shannon's third baby, so there was no time to waste. I tugged my clothes on with one hand while still holding the phone with the other, the usual litany running through my brain at the same time: *coffee, filter, mug, lid, creamer, sweetener, spoon . . .*

Shannon, her husband Aaron, Eloise, their toddler, and sometimes her older sister Lilli were always early for our appointments. Shannon even brought her mom along once. I enjoyed our visits and looked forward to their birth. Her two previous births had been plagued by high blood pressure. Combined with that, Shannon was living with Ehlers-Danlos Syndrome, which complicates not only pregnancy but daily life. A side effect is hypermobility, when joints over-extend. People with joint hypermobility syndrome may experience many difficulties. For example, their joints may be easily injured, be more prone to complete dislocation due to the weakly stabilized joint and they may develop problems from muscle fatigue as muscles must work harder to compensate for the excessive weakness in the ligaments that support the joints. Hypermobility syndrome can also lead to chronic pain and disability. As her pregnancy progressed Shannon needed to use crutches just to walk. Her pain continued, growing worse in the final two months. A scrupulous organic diet helped to stave off the worst complications. Shannon had thoroughly researched everything that is known about this disability and the benefits of the right diet and certain supplements.

Shannon was dealing with the contractions quite well when I got to the hospital forty minutes later. She was up and walking around the room with Aaron's support, but she didn't feel she could go further, not even down the halls. A birth ball also helped since she could be upright, letting gravity move her baby down. During the next hours, as she steadily dilated, she ate and drank and combined short rests on the bed with time up on the ball or in a chair. While she rested we used a peanut ball, which is like a birth ball but shaped like a giant peanut. When she lay on her side, I would put the peanut ball between her knees. It is large enough that the upper leg that is draped over the top of the peanut can hang up and out over the side of the bed. The lower leg is brought up, bent at the knee as high as is comfortable. This position opens the pelvis as wide as possible in a lying position to facilitate the baby's continuous descent. Every half hour or so, Shannon would roll over to her other side and we would replace the peanut again. Her blood pressure was creeping up during this time, possibly because of the added pain she was experiencing in her expanding joints, along with the contractions of labor, so her nurses suggested staying in bed if possible to help keep the blood pressure from rising any higher without medications.

Shannon began dilating quickly and by 10:30 a.m. she was able to push. Nora Jane was born after a short second stage with perfect Apgar scores. We didn't really need those numbers to tell us she was finally, happily, here, though she seemed to register otherwise with her lusty cries. And then, before she was weighed or the cord even cut, she held up one pudgy little hand, thumb up, seemed to contemplate it for just a second, and then popped it in her mouth, sucking contentedly. That was a first for me.

I stayed long enough to celebrate this very special baby (who turned out to weigh nine pounds, eleven ounces) with her parents and made sure she was nursing well. There was no problem there. She had already made up her mind that today she was going to feast.

"Many western doctors hold the belief that we can improve everything, even natural childbirth in a healthy woman. This philosophy is the philosophy of people who think it deplorable that they were not consulted at the creation of Eve, because they would have done a better job."
~Dr. Kloosterman

Chapter Four

An Amish Birth

On my way home from the hospital, I thought back to another birth I was honored to witness. When we lived in Wisconsin in the early 1980s, I attended several Amish births. The Amish don't use modern farm equipment, electricity, or indoor plumbing, and also don't have telephones, much less computers, email, iPods, or other gadgets. So when a baby announces his or her imminent arrival, the mother has to first locate Pa somewhere on the farm, get the children to Grandma and Grandpa's "*doddy haus*" (the grandparents' apartment, usually attached to the farmhouse), find a teenage neighbor to agree to do the morning or evening milking that day, and have Pa go to the nearest friendly "English" (non-Amish) neighbor to use their phone to call the midwife or doctor.

Emma and Joel were expecting their seventh child. She had experienced easy births with the others and remained in good health throughout this pregnancy. She had carried the baby to term, he was growing nicely, she took good care of herself, understood good nutrition, kept her house clean and tidy (one of the things I observe when I consider a family's suitability for a homebirth) and was excited that they had been blessed with yet another baby, though they didn't know if it was another little "dishwasher" or "wood chopper" yet—the terms they used when announcing a new baby girl or boy to their Amish family and friends.

I carried a primitive kind of pager back then and had the dads call me as early as possible when things started up. The Amish settlements stretched for over fifty miles in all directions. There were perhaps half a dozen of us covering this area who often assisted at these births.

When Joel's call came one sunny day about noon, I quickly called my husband David, who helped me pack up our five children so he could drive me to the Lehmann's farm. When we got there Emma had everything all arranged—the farm and kids were all taken care of, she had washed the dirty dishes, the bed was made up with a plastic sheet under fresh linens, with another full set under that for after the birth, and she was walking around the house in her homemade nightie and slippers, grinning from ear to ear and blowing little puffs of air along with the contractions while Joel was nervously trying to work on a jigsaw puzzle she had assigned to him (to keep him busy and occupied, I suspect).

She walked around for a while, sipping juice and taking short trips to the outhouse every hour or so. The bedroom had a freshly painted commode by the bed so she wouldn't have to leave the bedroom after the birth for ten days. A nightstand was set up with everything she would need to care for the baby and herself: diapers, a diaper pail, baby clothes, sanitary pads, and an oil lamp.

Things slowed down around four in the afternoon. I suggested she use the time to nap, but she was all business and suggested using "the combs." I had never heard of this so she showed me the pressure points along the base of my thumbs, which she said can be stimulated to help with contractions. She made two fists around two small hair combs and, sure enough, she got the contractions going again in no time. About an hour later she made a beeline for the bedroom, had Joel light a kerosene lamp and hold it up for me, and propped herself up on the bed, though I could not detect by her breathing that things had picked up that fast, but after a couple more rather sedate, lady-like puffs, she started pushing. Before I could dribble oil on my hands to support her perineum, out barreled an eight-pound wood chopper who promptly howled his arrival. Leave it to efficient Emma! They hadn't really needed me at all. They knew exactly how to do this.

Joel cut the cord, then picked up and held his baby while I helped deliver the placenta, which in Amish tradition would be buried under the eaves of the house. Then Joel spoke for the first time all day. He told me how with their first baby he had been so afraid of poking him with a pin while diapering him that when he finally finished and tried to pick up the baby he found him stuck to the bed—he had pinned the diaper to the sheets!

Joel looked down at Emma and said in his slow drawl, "Well, Ma, what should we name him?"

Emma said, "Oh, Pa, I dunno. What do you wanna name him?"

He replied, "Well, I dunno."

After seven kids, surely they knew how to do this, I thought.

After a minute or so he added, "Maybe we should get the hat."

Handing Baby Boy back to Emma, Joel got his black Sunday hat from its peg in the kitchen by the woodstove and set it on the bed. Then he cut up little pieces of paper and they both wrote down their favorite boy names, folded them, and dropped them in the hat. I still didn't know where this was going.

Then Joel picked up the baby and gently put a little hand into the hat. When he did, the baby's hand opened up as his arm was extended and then shut into a fist when it touched the bottom of the hat. He was supposed to pick his own name!

His father pried the scrap of paper out of the tiny fist, opened it, and announced, "His name is Elmer!" They both positively beamed at each other then, a long loving look into each other's eyes.

Elmer could never blame them for the name if he didn't like it. He had chosen it himself.

"For far too many women pregnancy and birth is something that happens to them rather than something they set out consciously and joyfully to do themselves."
~Sheila Kitzinger

Chapter Five

A Circus of a Birth

Fast forward a few decades across the border in Minnesota. It was more of a circus than a birth. Bah's family had recently emigrated to the United States from Southeast Asia. As was normal in their culture, her parents had married at fifteen; life expectancy in their experience was about forty-five. Bah was foruteen.

The family slept on homemade platforms at home, squatting on the floor to play cards, like in the old country. Gold *jos* papers were stuck to the walls to placate any bad spirits that might be lingering there.

Bah (not her real name) called me late on a Friday night to tell me that she was having contractions and wondering if it was time to go to the hospital. I offered to go to her home and hang out with her until it was time to go. She agreed.

The contractions weren't very strong and by 4:00 a.m., now Saturday, they had petered out. They stopped altogether after a breakfast of whole fried fish, eggplant soup, and steaming piles of rice. I went home after breakfast, suggesting she rest and call me when the contractions were three to five minutes apart for a whole hour or her water broke, whichever came first. The call didn't come until 11:15 that night. She wanted me to come.

Bah's mother had given birth to nine full-term babies. Three had died simply because no one knew how to resuscitate them at birth. Her last baby was born shortly after they arrived in the U.S. She didn't understand English, her labor stalled, and she ended up needing interventions that terrified and traumatized her. In the end, she jumped off the

bed—IVs and all—and gave birth to her baby while squatting in a corner, surrounded by doctors and nurses screaming at her.

When I arrived back at their home, Bah's mother told me that no
one was to touch her daughter—no internal exams, IVs, Pitocin, medications, C-section, and no men, including male doctors. Understandably, she was projecting her fears onto her daughter. I told her we
would try to labor at home as long as we could, though I couldn't promise what she was asking.

Though Bah spoke English, her mother still did not. I had learned
a bit of their dialect over the years, which helped a lot. I explained to
Bah that her labor was going really well and she and her baby were
healthy. We stayed at her home until things picked up about 2:00 a.m.,
now the third day.

I settled Bah and her mother into the hospital room and went out
to brief the nurses. The head nurse wanted to know why Bah's mother
hadn't been able to resolve some of her issues in counseling. I explained
that she was from another part of the world where they don't talk
about these things, and certainly not with strangers.

The staff left us pretty much alone. After awhile the nurse asked
if she could check Bah's dilation. I told Bah's mom very simply that the
doctor wouldn't come to deliver the baby if she wouldn't allow a check.
She said okay, but only one finger, and very gently. The nurse agreed.
(Normally a vaginal bimanual or two-finger exam is done to track the
progress of the cervix's dilation from zero to ten centimeters.)

Bah was at eight centimeters. Great news. Though pretty worn
out having now been up two days and two nights, I was surprised how
well she was doing with the pain. Labor was slow but not unusual for
a first baby.

An hour later an aunt showed up with an herbal potion that she
claimed would speed things up. The doctor didn't want to speed things
up, especially since waiting can allow the baby's head to mold well and
stretches the mother naturally, but they insisted. So Bah drank the brew,
which immediately started coming back up. I got to hold the bag. Just as

she was getting cleaned up another aunt came and proclaimed that the reason her baby wasn't coming was because she ate sweets and made her baby too fat. As soon as I could, I whispered to Bah between contractions that her baby was just the right size for her, not an eight- or nine-pounder, and her labor was going really well and how very proud I was of her.

Great Aunt showed up next and told Bah that her baby wouldn't be born unless she apologized to her parents for the times she talked back to them. She apologized. They gave her more brew.

Then—I swear this is all true—three chubby middle-aged tribal pastors arrived, sent by the baby's father's clan, to pray over her. They walked in the door without knocking, looking like the Three Stooges in pinstriped suits that were too big for them. I asked Bah if I should send them away. She said they could come in for just a minute. They trooped to the bed, laid their hands on her head and prayed, on and on, through at least two contractions with Bah trying valiantly to hold still. Finally I said, "Amen!" and physically ushered them out, thanking them profusely: "Ua tsaug rau koj heev npaum li cas. Sib ntsib dua"—"Thank you so very much, bye bye." Then I got a door sign directing all visitors to check in at the desk first and closed the door.

Finally Bah was ten centimeters and could push. Between the next two contractions she leaned into me and whispered, "No more babies. Never!" It took another hour but her little boy was born, crying right away. Grandma told us she would hold him first because the placenta wouldn't come out if Bah held him, so we wrapped him in warm blankets and she held him after she cut the cord. She cried when she cut the cord and thanked us. I had tried to involve her as much as possible, hoping this birth might help heal some of her memories.

So Grandma was holding the little guy, who wouldn't be officially named for a couple of weeks (the bad spirits might hear his name or hear someone say how cute he was and could take him away.) At this point, Bah started bleeding a bit too much and promptly fainted. An IV was started while another nurse massaged her uterus to control the bleeding.

Grandma had a total meltdown, threw the baby onto the lounge chair, and started shrieking not to touch Bah. The doctor had me explain hemorrhage and what they needed to do but Grandma was beyond reasoning with. She called the clan elders on her cell phone to hold a *palaver* (confer) and take her side. In their culture, no major decisions are final until the clan ministers have been consulted and pass down their decisions.

In no uncertain terms I told them that there were mothers dying in China after childbirth every day because they don't know these procedures! At this point the doctor and nurses were all vigorously nodding. Finally, we got her to stop yelling. I helped Bah get the baby latched onto her breast properly, which would help the uterus clamp down and reduce the bleeding further, and he started nursing. Things settled down.

The next day I went back to the hospital to figure out the next step. In their tradition, a mother can't return to her family after birth; she is "unclean" for thirty days. We wouldn't want to incur the wrath of the bad spirits, but she couldn't go to her boyfriend's family either, because Child Protection was involved and wouldn't allow it. The baby's father, who was only fifteen, had a hearing scheduled that month; he was charged with statutory rape because Bah was under fifteen, the cutoff age for a "consensual relationship" in the U.S.

I had heard of another family in a similar predicament. They had built a hut in their backyard for the new mother and baby, probably something they had done in Southeast Asia, but this was in the middle of a Midwestern winter and, of course, the courts got involved then, too.

Bah's doctor wouldn't discharge her unless she was okay with whatever arrangement we could get the family to agree to. Finally, Mother Teresa's nuns at the Missionaries of Charity shelter agreed to take Bah and her baby.

We had all learned a lot about cultural differences.

"However much we know about birth in general, we know nothing about a particular birth. We must let it unfold with its own uniqueness."
~Elizabeth Nobel

Chapter Six

Due Dates or Guess Dates

O ne of my clients was told she was overdue and was becoming in-creasingly nervous, but unless a baby is conceived by artificial or in vitro fertilization, or the couple chart basal body temperatures and see ovulation occur, it is almost impossible to predict the exact date of conception and then calculate the due date.

We are actually changing the term from "due date" to "guess date." In the past, doctors have induced babies rather routinely that were still not showing any intention of coming out in their forty-first week. They were worried about things that might happen when babies are truly overdue and their placentas are no longer working at 100% capacity, but babies who "cook" until forty-two weeks are more often than not per-fectly healthy and do very well. Babies are mature and viable, as we say, after thirty-seven weeks, though they do even better if they arrive during their fortieth week. So, without knowing a true guess date, babies have been induced far too early due to miscalculations and it becomes apparent that they are even premature, not at all overdue. The medical community is taking a new look at induction at this time, with good reason.

Jeannie called me the day after she reached her forty-week guess date. That morning she had seen her doctor, who had insisted that they go ahead with an induction the following day and possibly a scheduled C-section. Her doctor cited the reason was that the baby "appears rather large." Jeannie had given birth to two other children but the doctor was worried about a host of "risk factors" surrounding post-date babies. Jeannie's first baby had been born by C-section, though baby number two was a successful VBAC (Vaginal Birth After Cesarean) at only twenty-eight weeks. Another baby, a beautiful little girl, was born in 2010 but was also very premature and did not survive.

When she called, Jeannie was crying, understandably upset with all that the obstetrician had laid out for them the next morning. She had gone home and told her husband and asked him what they should do. Lonnie's answer was, "Call Stephanie. She'll know what to do." So she was on the phone asking for advice and much-needed support.

It is important to explain that as a doula I do not make decisions for anyone. I don't tell them which is the best of all the options they are offered, but I will help them explore the possibilities and give them as much information as I have or call someone else if I don't know. She asked if there was anything they could do to encourage labor and avoid being induced.

I told her that they could have sex, for one. It has worked for some moms. The thought is that the male hormones assist with "turning on" labor, and that orgasm simulates blood flow and the uterus often follows suit. Sex can be quite comfortable if your partner is behind you while you are lying on your side. Being on top of him may not feel quite as good if the baby is well engaged low in the pelvis. Foreplay alone is another option. Nipple stimulation (also with help from a willing partner or available toddler who is still nursing) often works. Rolling your nipples manually or using a breast pump has also been suggested. It has been long thought that being "turned on" is what got the baby in there in the first place and that there is a place for it here, too.

Some women have tried the notorious castor oil cocktail, which works by stimulating the bowel and in turn, if irritated enough, triggers a response by the uterus, and thus labor. Some practices do not advocate this method at all. A mom-to-be could become quite ill and not go into labor anyway. Riding a bike or taking a drive on a long dirt road has supposedly worked on occasion, too.

"Stripping the membranes" is when a midwife or doctor separates the cervix from the bag of water by sweeping a finger around the baby's head just inside the cervix. It also tips off the hormones that labor should soon follow but that can only be done if the cervix is dilated one to two centimeters already.

An Amish friend of mine told me her method when I was "overdue": "You get in your buggy and go visit a friend and that will start labor, rather than sitting at home hoping." I guess lifting three or four little kids up into a buggy, riding along bumpy back roads and then lifting the kiddies back down at the friend's house, with all the snacks and coats and all, and hauling myself up and down on the buckboard would have worked for me.

Instead of suggesting a buggy ride, I said to Jeannie, "You should take some quiet time and connect with your baby. Tell her it seems to be time and you don't want a C-section or any drugs, for that matter, so maybe you two can work out some kind of a deal." She agreed and thanked me and promised to call the next day.

The phone rang at midnight. Jeannie and her family had spent a quiet day at home together, took a nap, and then went to a barbeque at a friend's house. Just as they finished eating, *Wham!* The contractions started on their own. She was euphoric, but told me they were going to head right to the hospital because she didn't think there was time to go home and pick up her baby bag first.

The nurse was checking Jeannie when I got to the hospital. Six centimeters already! We gave high fives all around.

Then she told me one of the strangest stories I had ever heard. While they were settling down for their nap earlier in the day, she was talking to her baby, connecting as she fell asleep like I had suggested. She had a dream, describing it as "totally real." In the dream she was talking to her baby, whom they were planning to call Camilla, and the baby was telling her, "Well, actually, I'm not coming out unless you agree to name me Veronica. No way!"

So, in Jeannie's words, "I said, 'Okay, anything you want. You got it,'" and the dream ended. They told their other kids about it and all agreed that Veronica it would be, though they had never given that name a thought.

Then Veronica's older sister said, "It should be Veronica Jordan. I am sure." Jeannie and Lonnie looked at each other and decided that their kids seemed to know a whole lot more about it than they did, so Veronica Jordan it would be.

About half an hour after the nurse checked her, Jeannie said she was feeling a bit "pushy." The nurse checked again and she was ten centimeters. The nurse ran out, crashing into another nurse coming into the room and both raced to get the room set up with a warmer, instrument tray, and all the other paraphernalia that is part of a hospital birth these days.

I helped Jeannie focus on breathing and get into a comfortable squat on the bed while Dad picked up all the coats, the birth ball, and clothes strewn around us. In the rush, someone asked if the doctor had been called. She hadn't, until just then. Jeannie and I just grinned at each other. Another doctor was on the floor and quickly gowned up and stood at the end of the bed, hands ready to catch. As the little head crowned, Jeannie's doctor rushed into the room, and the other doctor stepped aside so she could catch the rest of Veronica Jordan as she slid out. It was all and more than we could have wished for.

An interesting aside is that another baby girl was born to a family down the block from Veronica's house about the same time. They did not know the family but found out later that they named their baby Camilla.

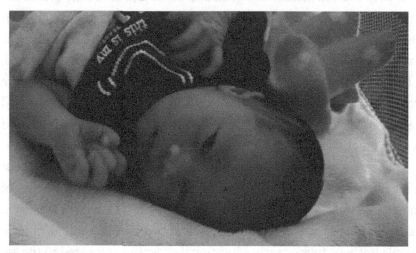

Veronica Jordan.

"Women's strongest feelings [in terms of their birthings], positive and negative, focus on the way they were treated by their caregivers."
~Annie Kennedy & Penny Simkin

Chapter Seven

Everybody Loves . . . Babies!

My Ethiopian mama was on her way to our last appointment. I usually see ladies four times before their guess dates. Our plan was that I would go with Farhia to her birth, helping her labor at home first. I would see her at home again for the final postpartum visit, usually two days after the birth. She was expecting her first baby, a girl.

When she arrived she told me that her iron had been low in spite of taking iron pills. I took the opportunity to discuss nutrition. Her diet was very good, full of fresh fruits and vegetables, but I reminded her that liver and red meat is also good and beans and dark leafy greens are just as beneficial. I told her about a recent study that found that even those who eat an iron-rich diet might need to include some dairy at each meal, which in turn helps the iron bond and be better assimilated. I told her that yogurt, kefir, milk, cottage cheese, and ice cream were good choices. I also suggested prunes and prune juice, which she had never heard of, so I got out the prune juice and she discovered she liked it very much.

Then we watched the movie *Everybody Loves . . . Babies*. Without a lot of words, this award-winning film clearly shows the benefits of maternal-infant and parent-infant attachment. The babies shown in poorer countries actually seem happier and become more confident little people without toys or early educational programs compared to the babies in the Western cultures who have every advantage but appear bored, frustrated, and whiny. I use this film in my childbirth education course to point out the blatantly different styles of parenting across cultures and the resultant levels of bonding.

Filmmaker Thomas Balmes offers a glimpse at the first phase of life in this film that follows four newborn babies through their first year of life. Ponijao, Bayar, Mari, and Hattie were born in Namibia, Mongolia, Japan, and California, respectively. By capturing their earliest stages of development on camera, Balmes reveals just how much we all have in common, despite being born to different parents and raised in different cultures. What is not said, however, is that all the toys, gadgets, enrichment classes, and numerous other choices presented by parents, actually don't make our babies smarter, more self-assured, or more prepared for life.

The converse appears true: babies in the so-called "Third World" are simply part of the family or society's ongoing continuum of daily survival and work. They aren't singled out for special baby activities, or coddled, and seem to have greater self-esteem and are more independent earlier than Western babies (and less work). Likewise, in her recent book, *Parenting Without Borders: Surprising Lessons Parents Around the World Can Teach Us*, Christine Gross-Loh repeatedly points out how our Western views and models of parenting actually undermine the self-esteem we are hoping to instill in our children.

Next I met with a couple expecting twins who heard about me from another couple who hired me as their doula for their twins' birth. I hadn't met them before, so this was just a consultation or information session with no obligations. Couples actually should interview several doulas before they find one that is right for them, and I encourage them to do so when they come to meet me.

I like to start a first appointment with a beautiful little DVD that the Childbirth Collective in Minneapolis produced in 2012, called *Doula: A Documentary* by Emily Rumsey. It tells better than I could what a doula is and isn't. It presents a look at water birth, home birth, hospital birth, and C-sections.

Since this couple was expecting their first babies, I offered to show the DVD of my twins' birth with Ina May Gaskin at The Farm, filmed in 1982. They had lots of questions, actually the same questions I had over thirty years ago when I found out I was carrying twins and realized that the whole land of birth as I knew it with a singleton two years earlier had suddenly changed. We visited for over an hour.

My next appointment was with a Somali mom at her home in the housing projects that have been dubbed "the Cages." It is thirty floors of tiny airless apartments with only one elevator as access, which is known to frequently break down. I have never tried walking up thirty flights of stairs; I hope I never have to. It was like a scene right out of *Rachel and Her Children* by Jonathan Kozol.

Fatima was one of my clients the year before when she birthed her fourth little girl. Her youngest, Hikmet, was now eight months old and the continuum bonding that her mother practiced was obvious. A bright, inquisitive baby who was never far from her mother, little Hikmet enjoyed life as it was meant for babies. She had no need to cry for what she wants. Her earliest cues were noticed and answered, whether it be for food, affection, or the need to be changed or kept warm. I was visiting to drop off a breast pump and show Fatima how to use it, though I hoped she was able to put off going back to work for a little longer.

I let Hikmet initiate a visit to my lap when she was ready to explore beyond her mother's safe bubble. Continuum babies will tell us when they are confident enough to wander beyond the safe place that is their right. Then they will venture further and further away, secure in the fact that a parent will be there when they have the need to check back in again. Continuum babies actually become very independent little people earlier than babies who were separated shortly after birth and forced to sleep in a crib or cradle and self-soothe themselves during intervals throughout the day.

When I got home after my last appointment, I remembered I needed to call a client's clinic on the other side of town. I had seen her the day before for a prenatal doula visit and was shocked at the enormous amount of swelling that hadn't been there when I saw her the week before. She assured me she was seeing her doctor later in the morning, but I wanted to let her provider know of my concern. My client's English wasn't all that great. She could speak some English, but Amharic, her native language, doesn't always translate well, especially with medical terms. As a doula I don't do anything clinical that her provider does, but I could let the provider know when I noticed something that may have literally been lost in the translation.

Also, she wore a floor-length *hijab* or robe that completely covered her legs and ankles, potentially hiding any problematic swellings. She also told me she stopped taking her prenatal vitamins and extra iron because of constipation. I told her to be sure to let her midwife or doctor know this too, so they could discuss it. I suggested making a list of questions before going to the appointment so all of her concerns could be discussed.

My last appointment of the day was with a first-time mom, also a recent immigrant to the U.S. She couldn't attend our breastfeeding class so I offered to visit her at her home and go through the material with her. I enjoy this class very much. I wish I had even half the information we now have when I was nursing my babies in the 1980s and '90s. La Leche League was available for support groups or by phone, but we didn't know then what we know now about latch, positioning the baby(ies), cracked nipples, or many of the basics.

In my breastfeeding classes I first like to show *Breastfeeding: the Why-to, How-to, Can-do* videos. Each one runs about twenty minutes and is packed with information that is presented in a confidence-building way.

For my classes I made my own demo breast out of an old white t-shirt. I dyed one piece of t-shirt cotton in tea water overnight, and another piece in a brew of cocoa and coffee. Without rinsing them I dried and then ironed the two swatches to set the colors. I sewed and stuffed the main tea-dyed "breast" and then hand sewed on the darker coffee-and-cocoa-dyed "nipple."

My cloth breast comes in handy when demonstrating things like how to make a "sandwich" of your nipple to help a newborn latch on. It also shows clearly what Nature had in mind: the darker nipple and areola is actually a "bull's-eye" that your baby can see and is therefore directed toward as his first destination after birth. I can also demonstrate massaging and expressing that will come in handy should a mom become engorged.

Next I bring out Tofiq (pronounced: toe-FEEK), my anatomically correct seven-pound boy baby doll that I use to have parents practice nursing positions. When we were having our babies two and three decades ago, many of us did not know that they should be lying on their sides to nurse and not flat on their backs with their heads craning around to reach the nipple. We didn't know how to keep them nursing when they fell asleep or how to burp or not burp them. We didn't know about the side-lying position, crossover hold, cradle hold, or football hold. I can also demonstrate baby-led or baby-initiated breast crawl and latch with Tofiq. He has also been bathed to show how to safely bathe a newborn.

Finally it was time to go home and make dinner. It was a long but satisfying day in the life of this doula.

"A healthy woman who delivers spontaneously performs a job that cannot be improved upon."
~Aiden MacFarlane, author of The Psychology of Childbirth

Chapter Eight

A Just-In-Time Belly Cast

M iruts came in for her last prenatal meeting before her due date. We offer belly casting as part of our doula services at Everyday Miracles for our expectant moms and I had reserved the belly cast room for Miruts.

Everyday Miracles in Minneapolis has been my employer the last few years. About thirty doulas of several nationalities meet moms and their families in the offices for prenatal classes, yoga, car seat and baby-wearing clinics, and general support, especially for low-income mothers. Our doulas are Hispanic, Somali, Hmong, and a melting pot of Americans who see women from the whole Twin Cities metro area and attend their births at any of the hospitals in the area. As doulas we also follow up with postpartum visits to ensure they are doing well and that mom and baby are getting the hang of breastfeeding.

I am not sure when the art form called belly casting came into being. It can be one way to help an otherwise overwhelmed young woman bond with her baby before birth. Some call it taking pride in their changing body or "bonding with their bump."

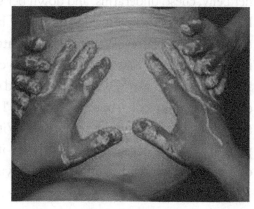

Part of the job of a doula is to emotionally support a mother-to-be and help her fall in love with her baby if she isn't already in love. Numerous distractions can threaten to obliterate this fragile connection. A young

woman often has to face questions of employment, schooling, even where she will live with her baby. Relationships often become brittle as the reality of a baby sets in. The responsibility for a new little person can affect all the different parts of a woman's life.

Sometimes our job is to try to find ways to gently steer attention back to this connection or bond with her baby. We try to find ways to celebrate the life that is growing within each new mother. One way is to create a belly cast toward the end of her pregnancy. It is also a chance for the doula and the mom to share some special time together before labor and delivery. We will be working together once labor starts and will need to know each other quite well to work as a team.

When we create a belly cast we first put a tarp down on the floor to catch any drips. Then the mom takes off her blouse and bra and coats her belly, chest, underarms, and down her sides with Vaseline or lotion. Plastic wrap is tucked inside the top of her skirt or pants to protect them from the plaster. We use plaster-coated gauze sheeting that comes in strips, the kind that was once used to cast broken limbs. After dipping a sheet into warm water it is layered on until her whole belly and chest up to her collarbone is covered. I usually lay on two layers, smoothing out any wrinkles as we go. Within ten minutes it dries and pulls away from her skin. We gently lay it down on the tarp to finish drying while she washes off with fresh warm water and soap.

Many women paint their belly casts. Some decorate them with henna patterns. Others bring their belly casts to their baby showers and have everyone write wishes or blessings on them. The possibilities are endless.

Miruts was not due for over two more weeks, so I was surprised when her husband Tamirat called me at 5:30 a.m. two days after we had done her belly cast. He was quite upset as he explained that his wife was bleeding and they had called 911. I asked if she was having any contractions and he said no, none. I asked if it was just a little blood, like spotting or a bloody show, and he said no, the blood was all the way to the bathroom and back again and on the bed. I stopped breathing. All I could think of was, *Why them?* Then he told me that the 911 dispatcher had told him that bleeding is normal at birth, but he kept insisting this was an emergency. Since his English is limited they thought he was just an anxious father and had tried to reassure him. I learned later that when the ambulance finally arrived (they took their time) the paramedics were absolutely mortified and flew into action.

Miruts and Tamirat had come to the U.S. less than a year before from Ethiopia, seeking a better future for their children. They were learning English and working hard to assimilate. I had really enjoyed getting to know this little family and had looked forward to this baby with them the last few months.

I raced to the hospital, praying the whole way. I've often wondered if we can alter a divine plan, if such a thing exists, by prayer, but this was one of those times I was certainly going to try. All the causes of early bleeding were racing through my mind—placenta abruption (also called simply "an abruption") was uppermost. That is when the placenta begins to detach from the inner wall of the uterus before the birth of the baby. Sometimes just a portion of it comes off, causing bleeding, but the remaining part is still able to deliver blood and oxygen to the baby through the umbilical cord. Should it completely detach from the uterus, oxygen is cut off and the baby cannot survive. It is one of the causes of a stillbirth. Another possibility was placenta previa, where the placenta has attached to the uterine lining near or over the cervix itself, close to the opening of the uterus. A more remote possibility was a uterine rupture, in which there is a tear in the uterus at a weak spot, though this is more common, although still rare, when there has been a previous C-section, and the strength of the contractions stress that area. That can also cause bleeding, even hemorrhage.

At that point, all I knew was that I was scared, more scared than I had been in a very, very long time, and I could hear Tamirat's fear too. When I arrived at the hospital Miruts's midwife was watching the baby's fetal heart tones on the monitor by the bed. They checked out okay, which was a huge relief. The monitor also showed us contractions coming at regular intervals, though Miruts wasn't feeling them yet. The midwife then checked to see if Miruts was dilating, which produced a fresh gush of blood, not a good sign. The midwife left to call the obstetrician on duty while I tried to tell Miruts that the baby still looked good and that they had done the right thing coming in so soon. She was not panicking up until then, but the midwife leaving to call the doctor alarmed her and she started crying.

When the doctor first came in he reviewed the readout from the monitors and agreed that the baby was still doing fine, though the heartbeat was fairly unchanged throughout, what is called "non-variable." He ordered an ultrasound, hoping to get a look inside the uterus and maybe find a clue as to what was going on, but the baby appeared to be toward the front of the uterus, covering a posterior placenta, meaning it was attached to the back wall, or closest to the mother's back, which made it impossible to view. Due to this, he also couldn't tell how high or low it was.

The doctor suggested breaking the bag of water. His rationale was that it would inform him further if the baby was feeling stressed, in which case he might consider a C-section if baby was not okay, or we could continue to wait a bit longer.

When babies are not doing well, or are feeling stressed, as might happen when less oxygen is being delivered to them, they often poop in the water before birth and the amniotic fluid turns greenish, or sometimes has dark particles. Artificially rupturing the bag of water at this point could also possibly help hasten labor along. The doctor explained that the baby needed to be born sooner rather than later today, and though the baby looked fine at that point, he was continuing to weigh his options. He could do an emergency C-section, but the risks of major surgery were a serious consideration, especially when the mom was bleeding already. A vaginal birth was still the ideal option and might pose less of a threat to the baby and mother.

This doctor was weighing the pros and cons minute by minute and I could visibly see his concern. He spoke about using Pitocin should the contractions not pick up or the baby's status changed. But first he went ahead and broke the water—a simple procedure the mom doesn't feel. An amnihook, a sterile plastic probe, is used to snag the amniotic sac. A small hole will allow the fluid to seep out a little at a time if the baby's head is not entirely engaged. Care must be taken to not be too aggressive, which could tear a larger hole in the bag, allowing for a more forceful gush of fluid and the potential of bringing the umbilical cord down with it, which could conceivably pinch off the flow of oxygen to the baby before birth.

Usually we don't like to see this or any other intervention used, and the parents could have refused it, but in this case and at this time it seemed warranted. These are tough decisions. Many have planned an unmedicated natural birth and never even entertained a thought otherwise.

When births don't go as planned—remember, we never have complete control over our births—and parents find themselves on a totally different "planet," I am often asked what I would do in their case. I pull out my "Welcome to Parenthood" talk, which goes like this:

"Welcome to Parenthood! You must find out what is right for you, not me, not the doctor or midwife, not your mother or mother-in-law. You must go into your hearts and together find out what is best for you, for your family. You'll make lots of mistakes in the next eighteen years or so. This is only your first test. You can't ask anyone else what to do. You have to decide this one for yourselves. You will know. And we will support you."

Fortunately, Mirut's fluid was clear, indicating that at the moment, at least, her baby was not exhibiting signs of stress. At that point Tamirat asked to see me in the hall. He was beside himself with worry. Their first baby had been born in Sweden the year before as they waited for visas to enter the U.S. The birth had taken place in a birthing room with a midwife, a natural birth lasting only five hours. This birth process was very different and he was losing it.

First, he didn't understand why he wasn't being consulted on every decision that was being made, and he didn't understand why a C-section was being mentioned at all. In his country, he told me, an elder, or at least a husband, would be consulted by the doctor, and the patient was rarely advised on all the aspects of her condition, partly to spare her worry or concern but also because she might not be in the best position to make decisions.

I explained that in the U.S. we have innumerable laws giving the patient complete rights over her own body and, subsequently, her own treatment. Only when she agrees to it is her husband or partner or family brought into the discussion. His English was adequate, but he was trying to bridge the whole cultural barrier. I was able to go over each point that the doctor was concerned about until Tamirat was satisfied that everyone really was trying to find the very best course of action for his wife and baby.

Very soon after, the contractions picked up, which often happens after the water breaks, triggering a hormonal response in the brain. This was a good sign, and the baby continued to tolerate the stronger contractions very well. I couldn't give Miruts juice or even water since they were still leaving the Cesarean option open as a possibility, but I did succeed in getting her nurse to give us some ice chips, which was better than nothing at this point. Miruts was breathing well with the contractions and getting up to the bathroom. She was dilated to five centimeters the next time the nurse came in and the bleeding seemed to have slowed down—all good news.

The nurse left us alone at this point. She had other patients and, of course, could follow the monitors back at the nurses' station should anything change. The next time she came in she surprised us when she announced that the cervix was now at eight centimeters. It had only been about half an hour since the last check. She scurried out to let the doctor know. I took one look at Miruts and knew she was already thinking about pushing. I hit the nurses' light on the bedrail as I put on a pair of gloves and sure enough, Miruts took a deep breath and gave it all she had with the next contraction. I helped her slow down her breathing just a bit as the nurse ran in. She started to put on a glove as the little head crowned. I picked up the other glove she had dropped on the bed and held it open and she shoved her hand into it, barely in time to catch a very plump little baby. The doctor walked in just then and, seeing that the baby had been born, stayed in the doorway. I saw the nurse trying to unwrap the cord, which was around the baby's arm and chest so I moved in and held the baby by the hips so she could unwind the cord. At the same moment the doctor came up behind me and gently told me to hold the baby's hips even higher, which I did, basically turning the baby head-down, which would drain any fluids, extra blood included, before she took a breath. Then the doctor gave the nurse the umbilical clip and hemostat clamps and handed the scissors to Tamirat. Most of this had taken place in complete silence.

At that moment, the baby let out a huge screech. When he heard his baby, Tamirat started sobbing, relieved that his wife and baby were out of danger. He blinked back tears as he cut the cord. Then the nurse turned to him and asked, "Well, what is it? A boy or a girl?" Earlier, I had clued-in the nurse that they didn't know the baby's sex, and I thought it would be nice if we left it to Dad to announce.

"It's a girl," he proclaimed.

With the advent of sophisticated ultrasounds today, it's rare that we don't know the baby's sex, so when this happens I let the father or partner have the honor of making this announcement. I did this with one couple from Kenya. The midwife had caught their baby and in one fluid movement plopped it onto the mom's stomach. All the father saw was the backside of their baby, but thought that was enough. He started dancing around the room yelling, "I have a boy! I have a son!" He even called relatives in Kenya with the announcement during the next twenty minutes or so. Finally, the mother asked me to take the baby so she could sit up and get cleaned up and when I did, I noticed something. I nudged her and whispered, "Look here," and she laughed out loud. They had a girl! The dad had never seen a baby girl, it turned out, and just assumed baby boys looked like that, from behind at least. He had to call Kenya back.

Miruts's placenta followed right away with a little more bleeding. It was over. We all breathed a huge collective sigh of relief. Tamirat went from kissing his brave wife to thanking the doctor and nurses, to crying and kissing his wife again. Of course the nurses offered to weigh the baby right away, but we had already discussed this and put in the birth plan that they preferred to just bond and put off everything else for a couple of hours. I find that nurses are generally relieved when they hear this; it takes the pressure off of them to hurry through the list of things they are required to do before the end of their shift. They simply chart, "Mom refused" and are off the hook. The next shift has the whole day to fit it in.

Miruts and Tamirat needed time to take everything in. It had been intense. It was only three hours from the time they had come in by ambulance. This labor was even shorter than their first baby's had been. A fast labor like that, called "precipitous labor," can be very overwhelming, especially for the mom. We wrapped her in warm blankets and I got some juice for her. Finally she could drink. She would need to replace all the blood she had lost and regain her strength. She was soon feeling much better and talking to her sweet little girl. Tamirat checked again as I replaced the baby's damp blankets and hat with fresh warm ones and confirmed that they indeed had another girl. Little Selam would be pleased to have a baby sister. They named her Negasi. I think we were all still stunned that she was here and that she and her mommy were okay.

Tamirat asked if I would stay with his wife while he went home for clean clothes and to get the car. He had come with her in the ambulance and didn't have their hospital bag or other items. We relaxed and ordered a huge breakfast that was delivered shortly. Miruts told me she was actually feeling good, even after such a traumatic morning. Tamirat soon returned with roses and a big pink balloon with "IT'S A GIRL!" written on it, and a teddy bear "for Negasi to give to Selam when she visits" he explained. And then he handed me a small brown bag with organic dates and a soy milkshake from a nearby co-op. I was stunned! He had remembered what I had carried with me and ate a month earlier when we met over the lunch hour for a home visit.

The next day I went back to the hospital. We again talked about the birth. They were trying to process all that had happened. It takes time to take it all in and consider how it could have been different (it couldn't, really) or better (we were very, very fortunate).

During our prenatal visits I often brought my laptop along and shared some of the DVDs I have on baby-led breastfeeding, labor, or natural birth. The last one I had shown Miruts, which was filmed in Brazil, was about a midwife there who has discovered a way to foster the gentle birth continuum with her method of gently bathing newborns. It really is amazing. The midwife slowly submerges the day-old baby while running water over his head, until only his nose is above the water. His ears, eyes, and body are under water and each baby in the video seems to really like it and becomes very calm, then closes his eyes and actually goes to sleep. I had been introducing this to new mothers and have had the same results with each and every newborn baby. Miruts was anxious to try it, so we did, right there in the hospital the second morning. Just like in the video, her baby loved it, closed her eyes, and actually went to sleep while floating in the tub! Some of the nurses asked to watch us bathe Negasi and I am sure it was a first for them, too. Gone are the days that we subject newborns to the bed bath, scrubbing them from head to toe with a rough, damp washcloth, taking extra care not to get the umbilicus wet (never mind that it was submerged in water for the last nine months, anyway) or their ears (ditto). We patted the umbilical stump dry and didn't put anything else on it.

As in the video, Miruts massaged her baby slowly with almond oil while still on her towel. She enjoyed that, too, though she decided it was time for lunch—now!—so we wrapped her in a dry blanket without any clothes and got her mom dry and back in bed, also without a gown (she had climbed in the bath first). Negasi fussed until she was latched on and then blissfully went back to sleep. She even smiled for us at that point.

Think about it: we are the only mammals who dress our babies after birth. We are also the only mammals who ask ourselves, "Where will my baby sleep?" and "What should my baby eat?" Last year I found a wonderful talk by my favorite U.K. midwife, Carolyn Flint, who said that we " . . . should go home, if we aren't already there after the birth, and take all of our clothes off, and all of our baby's clothes off (nappies or diapers allowed) and go to bed for fourteen days with our little mammal." Just consider, this gives mom time to recover and rest; baby can establish a good milk supply by nursing on demand; bonding is optimum when there is uninterrupted skin-to-skin contact; and the family can bond in the sacred space they have created in their bedroom.

Britain's best-known midwife, Caroline Flint. (Photo © Do Book Company.)

"We are made to do this work and it is not easy . . . I would say that pain is part of the glory, or the tremendous mystery of life. And that if anything, it's a kind of privilege to stand so close to such an incredible miracle."
~Simone Taylor

Chapter Nine

Ma Doula

We weren't sure what she was trying to say. I was making a belly cast of her mama's incredibly beautiful eight and a half-month belly and had invited Moriah, Dakota's little five-year-old, to join us. Moriah hopped off the chair I had designated for her and asked, "Ma Doula, can I do that?" then "Ma Doula, I wanna help." So I told her where to smooth out the plaster and gave her the job of holding up the gauze strips before I dipped them into the warm water to soften them.

"Ma Doula, can I have a belly cast, too?" she asked. I told her she could when she was bigger and there was a baby in her tummy.

Then her mom said, "Baby, what's you keep callin' her?" Moriah ignored her mom, too engrossed in smoothing out microscopic wrinkles in the gauze as I laid it on, layer upon layer. Dakota and I let it go and kept chatting about finally getting to meet her son and how stressful the time had been, especially since she and Moriah were homeless.

Dakota and Moriah had moved to Minnesota from Mississippi to be closer to family and friends, but had not been able to get an apartment in time for the birth.

"Ma Doula, how do I get this stuff off ma hands?" Moriah asked. I directed her to gently rub them together in the bowl of warm water until it all came off.

"Ma Doula, do I get tah paint it, too?"

Dakota had had enough. "Girl! What's youz callin' her, anyway?"

Before Moriah could answer, it dawned on Dakota. Talking to her mother and sisters on the phone earlier that day, and several times earlier in the week, she told them that she was "goin' tah see ma doula." Moriah thought it was my name!

I could hear Mary and Debby, my supervisors, giggling from their nearby offices every time Moriah called me that. It is ma new nickname at work: Ma Doula.

"I've learned that people will forget what you said, people will forget what you did, but people will never forget how you made them feel."
~Maya Angelou

Chapter Ten

Bonding

*Z*oë was a very courageous single mother. She called me sometime during the night on a Friday, one day after her guess date. I rarely look at the clock anymore when the phone rings. My night is over no matter how much or how little I've slept, so I let the adrenaline take over. I am blessed with being asked to attend yet another miracle. I am grateful and a bit in awe each time, even after thirty years. It is actually the most important event at this moment in the entire universe, and I get to see it.

Instead of the clock, my eyes automatically look to see whether or not I laid out a clean set of clothes on the chair the night before and that my packed bag is standing by the door.

Zoë's contractions, or rushes, were strong enough that she couldn't sleep, but nothing else was going on. Her water had not broken. Zoë's visit with her midwife the day before confirmed that she was starting to dilate. The midwife was concerned that the baby didn't appear to be very big and might not have grown in the last couple of weeks. She ordered an ultrasound, during which the technician guessed the baby was about six and a half pounds and said that all looked well in there. There was also some concern that Zoë's blood pressure was slightly higher than they would like. Zoë's midwife had already started talking about inducing her should her blood pressure stay too high, or if the baby appeared to have stopped growing and might do better outside rather than in at this point.

I told her that it sounded like this might be the night and encour-aged her to try to sleep, even if she just dozed. I told her that if she slept and the rushes went away then we would know it was just early labor. If they picked up and became more regular or her water broke, then we'd have the real thing. I also advised her to let her midwife know about the rushes and to let me know if the midwife wanted Zoë to go to the hospital yet. I went back to sleep and didn't hear anything from Zoë the rest of the night, so I assumed things had settled down.

I texted her about noon and she replied that the rushes were still very sporadic but she was visiting friends and walking a lot. Later that night she called asking if she might be seeing the mucus plug, or bloody show, which I confirmed. I told her it was all completely normal and that she should try to nap and to keep eating.

Finally at 10:00 p.m. Zoë called to report that the rushes were about five minutes apart and that she couldn't keep it together alone at home anymore. I suggested she call her midwife and to let me know if she would be going to the hospital. I offered to hang out with her at home, too, if she wanted to do that. She called back within minutes and said they wanted her to go to the hospital. She suggested calling me after she got there to see if they really were going to keep her or send her home. A bit later she called again and said she was at three centimeters but that her blood pressure was high and they wanted to keep her and monitor it. I was on my way.

During the night the nurses had her stay in bed, hoping her blood pressure would come down. It did for a little while, but then when the rushes got more intense it rose again. We tried different positions in bed that might help the baby labor down even if she was not able to walk around. Sitting up in bed cross-legged, on all fours, on her knees with her arms resting on the raised head of the bed, and lying down with a peanut ball between her knees were all used to encourage the baby's descent.

Finally she got to eight centimeters around dawn. We were able to move to the tub at that point, which Zoë said felt wonderful compared to the bed, but even after more than two hours, she was still at eight centimeters. The midwife suggested breaking her water to help the baby's head press against the cervix, hopefully encouraging the last two centimeters. There was some meconium in the water, so at the midwife's insistence, we went back to the bed and the monitor to see if baby was okay. The fetal heart tones were not ideal, so they watched them for a while. The blood pressure was still too high for comfort, but the midwife was quite relaxed and didn't suggest any interventions, which surprised me. Most of the other hospitals I have worked at would have been talking about a C-section at that point if not before. As a doula it is not my call, so I shelved that one.

The nurses' shift changed. New nurses fluttered in and out of the room. By 8:30 a.m. Zoë had been up two nights and three days and announced that she was done in. She asked for something for pain or something that would let her rest for a while. The nurse called the anesthesia department and set up the room for an epidural. I got Zoë up to go to the bathroom and suggested she stay there for a bit. Sitting on a toilet is an ideal position to labor in, and she felt better being up so we hung out there. When she returned, the anesthesiologist quickly ran through his list of dire side effects, had her sign the consent form, and then sped through the screening questions. At one point he asked, "Normal blood pressure?" and since Zoë was in the middle of a rush, the new nurse answered for her, "Yes."

I was surprised and hesitantly added, "Um, no." He turned to the nurse, who explained that it was high when she came in but it was fine now. I was shocked, knowing that it was higher than any protocol that was in place when I was still a practicing midwife, so I ventured out again, though I still thought perhaps I was mistaken, and said, "Well, actually, it is not normal. It has not come down. The last one was in the 150s."

The nurse huffed; the doctor looked at her and back at me, quite befuddled. Then he said, "Okay, let me see the [monitor] strips then." He carefully unfolded the strips from the previous night and noted the elevated numbers and announced, "No way!"

The nurse looked too and said, "But no one told me!"

It obviously got missed during the shift-change report. She should have been alerted but wasn't. I wasn't overly upset; I knew we were all part of a team wanting the best for Zoë and we needed to look out and cover for each other. The doctor ordered a blood test that would tell him if she was indeed pre-eclamptic, which could be quite serious. I knew she wanted some pain relief so I asked him if he could recommend something while we waited for the blood tests to come back, which I knew could be quite awhile. He suggested fentanyl along with another drug for the blood pressure, which the nurse ran to get. Zoë was still trying to work with the rushes and trying to follow my breathing but was very impatient at this point for some kind of a break.

The fentanyl didn't do anything. Zilch! I had never seen that. It usually helps women relax almost immediately and some people actually feel rather happy or even goofy on it. I tell them that I promise not to repeat anything they might say, since it is known for its somewhat drunk-like-inducing properties. It doesn't take away the pain, but it does take the edge off for an hour, or sometimes two, and then can be given again if needed.

But this time we had to work with each rush just like we had been doing. This was a first for me. We both concentrated on staying connected and I reminded her to rest between each contraction. While we kept dealing with each rush and then resting, the doctor left, the lab people left, and the nurses all filed out, leaving us alone.

Looking back, I wonder if her full bladder had slowed things at eight centimeters or if just getting up and sitting on the toilet at that particular time did it, but as soon as the room was cleared (taking with them all the concerns and negative vibes) Zoë went back to the bed and announced she wanted to push. I completely trusted her instincts on this one, even though she was supposedly only eight centimeters five minutes earlier. I suggested just some tiny nudges on the next rush. She tried that and I could see the baby's long black hair.

I called the nurse, who hit the "Come all" button on the wall as soon as she saw it, too. Two more pushes and the baby was on the bed. Zoë reached for her, crying and overcome with joy. Baby's cord was too short to let her be lifted up to Zoë's chest, but as soon as it stopped pulsing the midwife cut it and baby was with her mama. She nursed shortly after, without anyone even showing her how. Little Jazelle was six pounds, five ounces, and nineteen inches long, not overdue at all. Her fingernails were not long and she had plenty of vernix, the creamy coating that prevents babies from turning into little prunes from living in water for nine months. It is a waxy white protective substance cov-ering the skin of a fetus, short for "vernix caseosa." Some have sug-gested we collect, encapsulate and patent it, using it instead of diaper ointments and lotions. It really is an absolutely amazing substance—nature's own recipe. Jazelle's little ears were still stuck flat against her head, another sign of prematurity, or in this case, not being "overdone." Overdue babies' ears often stick out and the placenta will also show signs of aging if truly overdue.

We had worked out a birth plan ahead of time that stipulated she would like to be with her baby for at least two hours after the birth. After that, any care would be done on the bed and her baby would not be removed to the warmer or nursery. So that is what we did. We just hung out and got to know Jazelle.

Zoë hadn't been able to eat during the night, which is unfortu-nately still standard procedure for labor and delivery units, especially when they have concerns like meconium or high blood pressure, which puts the mom on a fast track to the possibility of a C-section and moms can't have any food in their stomachs for that, so it is pretty common to have to switch to ice chips and water when interventions first appear in the conversation. Needless to say, Zoë was ready for a couple thou-sand calories; after all, she had just spent as many calories as she would have running a marathon. We called down an order for just about everything from the breakfast menu, which arrived a short time later.

I finally got ready to go. I packed up my tea lights, massage tools, snack boxes, and juice bottles and hugged Zoë goodbye. I whispered in her ear, "You got the natural birth you wanted in spite of everything. I am so very proud of you!" We agreed to get together again as soon as she got home.

I left another happy motherbaby couple. We are actually beginning to write "motherbaby" as one word. Stop and think about it: they have been one for so many months and that bonding continuum should be ongoing during the next weeks and months. Our babies are not born mature enough to be without us at all. They are totally helpless, far more vulnerable than any other baby mammal at birth. Zero separation is what Mother Nature had in mind. We should listen to her.

Have you ever wondered why we as humans have such large brains? It's obvious: we are smarter than any other animal. But our babies are more helpless than other mammals at birth. Have you ever wondered why? Part of the reason is that, yes, we are the most intelligent species, but our babies are born unprepared for survival. Our brains grow so fast before we are born that, if they kept growing until the rest of the body caught up and was as mature as, say, a calf is at birth, our heads would be far too large for the birth canal. Since our brains are so advanced, they grow faster in the first year than the brains of any other species. If we waited another four to five months to deliver our babies, their heads would be too big to fit our frames. So Mother Nature had a toss-up: make mothers' hips even bigger than we have now (horrors!) or have babies born sooner than they are, in reality, ready. Thus they are not as mature as other little mammals and do need us constantly, even more than the offspring of other species.

Nature knows this. Babies know this. Do adults? We don't act like we know it. Nature knew also, by the way, that baby elephants would not survive if they couldn't walk and keep up with the rest of the herd shortly after birth. They would be eaten by other animals if left behind, so elephant mamas are pregnant for two years or until baby Babar can walk! And we complain about our nine months' gestation.

Our babies are just about as immature at birth as our foremother Lucy's were over three million years ago. Consider cave mama Lucy (who currently resides in the Ethiopian National Museum in Addis Ababa, Ethiopia), whose babies had to be carried, and in constant contact with her, twenty-four hours a day for at least two years or until they could walk. He (I am just guessing it was a first-born son) had constant skin-to-skin contact, was in constant proximity for eye contact with his mother or whatever member of the clan his mother was interacting with throughout the day, at an adult's eye level, incidentally, not lower as in a crib or stroller where faces suddenly appear to loom above his and just as quickly disappear. He nursed on demand. He had no need to cry. A grunt or his reaching for a breast would be enough of a sign. His mother had enough time connected to him that she could easily "read" any signals coming from him. He listened to his mother interacting with others all day long. We don't know when she began speaking directly to him, though. Perhaps it began when he spoke first, having listened to adult speech and figured out how it worked.

We now know that bonding is reciprocal. Even into the twenty-first century, however, we can read books written by some authors who still consider bonding a mother-led phenomenon, whereas it is actually reciprocal. When a baby searches his mother's face, he is seeking her gaze in return. If her gaze is not there more times than it is there, she is giving him a clear message that this is not how we humans interact, though she gives him no alternative solution. When he reaches out to touch her, he expects his hand will be held or caressed. When he first coos, a rewarding sound from his mother will encourage more early speech.

When parents are engaged elsewhere, mentally or literally—interacting with a cell phone or texting, for example—and those overtures from their babies are ignored, it too is a message: he isn't being answered. Perhaps his voice may be the best way to communicate after all. He'll have another try at it first: cry louder, perhaps, to get the needed response. He'll do something, anything, to get attention. In Lucy's day, bonding was essential for survival. Had she put her babies down, they would have been mauled or eaten. And we would not be here today.

I visited Zoë a couple of days later and didn't recognize Jazelle. I had only seen her while she was still nursing, before she had been cleaned up after her birth. They both looked great. Zoë had support from her family and friends and was still floating on cloud nine. She could not believe how intense and how incredibly amazing Jazelle's birth was.

Mothers-to-be can watch dozens of videos about birth and read all sorts of books but nothing really prepares them for the experience. I told her I knew she could do it and that now she knew it too—she could do anything. It was a very empowering experience for her. She will need that inner strength to raise her baby girl on her own.

"The effort to separate the physical experience of childbirth from the mental, emotional and spiritual aspects of this event has served to disempower and violate women."
~Mary Rucklos Hampton

Chapter Eleven

Nature Makes No Mistakes ... Or Does She?

My mantra has always been "Nature makes no mistakes," so how could I understand this birth? Perhaps we are not meant to know all of nature's secrets in this life. Maybe it will be given in the next. I can't explain what we witnessed. I can only wonder.

Leslie and Fred's first baby had died at five months' gestation. It was a nightmare, finding out that their baby was no longer living, having to say goodbye, but still deliver him.

There was little explanation as to why it happened, but in the process of sorting out what little they did know, several chronic medical concerns with Leslie's health did come to light and those were what she could focus on and improve. Thus began their journey into holistic and alternative medicine, which enabled Leslie to regain her health.

It had been a huge learning curve, but a much needed one. Physically, she was now in a better place than she had ever been, caring for herself and addressing issues she had tried to ignore for decades. But five years later, she was still not pregnant. She and Fred figured they were not meant to have their own children in the usual way and decided to adopt. Surely there were babies out there who were waiting for a family, their family.

They had also put in their time at a university fertility clinic. They took tests and tried scopes, dyes, charting, sex-on-schedule, everything medicine could offer or could think up, but nothing worked.

And then Leslie was pregnant. The biggest hurdle was to hope without setting themselves up for that raw disappointment again. It was inevitable that they would hold their breaths every day, every hour, until they got past the sixth-month mark this time. They tried not to put too much stock in hoping for a successful pregnancy, but at the same time, anyone in their situation is going to hope.

But as her belly grew and the days moved into months . . . six . . . then seven . . . and eight . . . they hesitantly allowed themselves to become excited. The "what ifs" never went away completely, but it seemed that Someone had indeed smiled upon them and this baby was meant to be with them. They knew it was a boy and promptly named him. They found a doctor they felt they could trust who would work with them on their terms. And they decided to hire a doula.

I received an email one morning asking if I was available that week to interview with them. I said I was very interested and sent along the link to my blog so they could get to know me a bit before we met. Leslie, Fred, and Leslie's mother, Alice, read several of the stories I had posted on the blog, many of which are now included in this book.

I agreed to meet Leslie later that week at a nearby coffee shop. We hit it off right away. We asked each other lots of questions and talked and, before we knew it, two hours had passed. I told her that she could let me know the following week either way and explained that I would email them a contract to go over should they wish to continue with me. We hugged goodbye and she assured me she would be in touch.

We got together the following week, this time with Fred and Alice. We talked about what services I could offer and went over what a doula does and does not do. Then we watched *Doula: a Documentary*, to give them more information about the options available.

Our last prenatal appointment finally arrived. This was it. The next time I would see them would be in the hospital. We were excited, nervous, and very encouraged that this little guy had made it this far. And he wasn't tiny, either. The doctor guessed him to be around eight pounds. He also began to question Leslie's ability to birth such a big baby. He ordered a further ultrasound and explained to the couple that Leslie had a narrow pelvis. The doctor knew they wanted a water birth and definitely a natural, unmedicated birth, but now he felt he had to share some of his concerns. He was absolutely willing to let her try a vaginal birth but wanted to prepare them should they run into true cephalopelvic disproportion (CPD), a dynamic that indicates that the size of the baby's head is different from the size of the pelvis and signals a lack of the proper relationship between the two factors. CPD occurs when a baby's head or body is too large to fit through the mother's pelvis, despite allowing ample time to mold. Her baby had also been breech, or head up and feet or butt-first before the last appointment, but then it was confirmed that he had indeed turned around all on his own. I had told Leslie that I had complete confidence that her body had grown this baby and would now also know how to birth him.

During the next week Leslie was feeling contractions on and off, usually picking up in the evening, though none progressed into a real labor pattern. We talked by phone daily. My main job was to remind her that she would not always be pregnant. I encouraged her to eat, rest, and take walks and I told her I knew he would come . . . on his birthday. I told her I had no doubt. Then she had another prenatal appointment on Friday.

First it confirmed the baby was still head down. Good baby. Because of the combination of some of the medical issues they were dealing with, the doctor explained that he was not comfortable waiting for labor to start after the due date. He felt he should intercede in the next few days, citing some very valid studies that said the placenta will sometimes not do very well given the concerns they were dealing with, and he was not willing to wait until problems presented themselves. He scheduled an induction for the following Wednesday evening. He proposed first using a prostaglandin medication to ripen the cervix. It would be inserted and left there for twelve hours, preferably while Leslie slept. Then on Thursday morning Pitocin would be used to encourage contractions, and labor, hopefully, would kick-in soon thereafter. (In some rare cases the first medication alone is enough to turn labor on.)

I did not know it at the time but Leslie had quite a track record for being one of those rare cases where nothing that came next was ever written in any textbook. Her mother and Fred were going to stay overnight with her in the hospital Wednesday night and I would join them by 8:00 a.m. unless, of course, they wanted me to come earlier. By 3:00 a.m. Leslie was having some really good rushes about five minutes apart. She had been only one centimeter dilated when they put in the prostaglandin the night before. They wouldn't check her again until they removed it at 8:30 a.m.

I arrived shortly after 6:00 a.m. and helped her with her breathing. We breathed together, "slowly . . . in . . . now out . . . relax your shoulders . . . relax your jaw . . . You are doing great!" I was excited too. This was the real thing. We were going to see this little big guy soon. Leslie was doing amazingly well hour after hour. She could write the book about relaxing in labor.

At 8:30 a.m. the nurse checked her—still one centimeter. I told her that I wasn't at all discouraged. This was not a normal labor—yet. It was an induction. All the different parts had to come together in order to progress to the next stage. She needed to eat now, rest, visit the bathroom, and walk. I showed Fred how to support her with the next rush and sway or dance from side to side to help her baby move down. She had been working so hard with the contractions, I was a bit mystified.

The next time the nurse checked her she could not feel the baby's head. Had he slipped up further from the pelvis? She wasn't sure. She called the doctor, who recommended starting some Pitocin to try to strengthen the contractions and hopefully start her dilating and moving into active labor.

Four hours later the nurse found the cervix to still be at one centimeter. This wasn't going anywhere. Then Leslie said, "I just heard a pop. My water bag broke!" We continued breathing and trying to relax, one rush . . . at . . . a . . . time. The nurse returned with an ultrasound machine and proceeded to try to map out where the baby was. She went back and forth and up and then down with the gooey wand. We were all watching, hoping to get a good look at him. She finally gave the wand to another nurse, who started scanning higher up this time. As she did, I saw the baby's head clearly silhouetted. I blurted out, "He's breech!" The nurse simply nodded and wheeled the machine out into the hall, the other nurse following close behind. While I grabbed a towel and wiped off her sticky belly, Leslie started sobbing.

The Pitocin was stopped and her doctor was called. When he arrived he said he was as surprised as the rest of us. He was not prepared to offer a vaginal birth now, especially since he was already wondering about the size of the pelvis. He was also surprised that, in spite of the water bag having broken, somewhere in the last few hours it appeared the baby had turned around. Again. Why would he do that? He said that the chances of that happening were far less than three to four percent. Leave it to Leslie to be off the grid.

Looking back on this series of events, I can only wonder, did he at least try to engage his head and, finding it wasn't possible, decide to attempt to come feet first? Did he have any idea that the first option was simply impossible? Do babies have some kind of innate ability to conform to the particular circumstances? Does nature adapt? Did She make a mistake this time? Or was this part of some divine, exquisitely intuitive plan?

Because her membranes had ruptured, we were past the point where the doctor could try to turn the baby. He had actually been thinking on the drive to the hospital that he would offer that as an option (good man). He also did not realize until he arrived that the contractions were still continuing to intensify, even with the Pitocin stopped. He discussed the options remaining to the couple and together they decided on a Cesarean section, not the water birth they had so carefully planned. All those hours writing a birth plan, the long weeks of hoping, months of planning, hours watching water births on the Internet—all culminated in this moment when all control was removed from their hands. We were all crying at his point—Fred, Alice, Leslie, and me. How could we get back to focusing on their precious baby about to be born?

I gently tried to tell her she would be holding her little one soon. I assured Leslie that she had done a valiant job and could not have done more. Two nurses returned and went into action. There was a whole list of protocols now to run through: papers to sign, shaving her lower belly, drinking the antacid cocktail, etc.

I had noticed throughout the day how connected Leslie and her mother were and decided to bring up the subject then about who would go into the operating room with her. The nurse had tossed two sets of scrubs onto the bedstand and I told Fred that we needed to get ready. While the anesthesiologist was talking with Leslie, I took her mother aside and asked if she would like to go in as her doula.

She jumped at the idea. She was about to see her first grandchild being born. There very well might never be another chance like this one. I told her if anyone questioned her, she should say she was a doula in training, besides being her mom. It worked.

I have always gone into the operating room with my clients when they needed a C-section. I have been able to make sure that the baby is brought sooner, rather than later, to his mama to hold or even nurse. If there isn't a partner with her, I make sure we get some good pictures and let Mom know how her baby is doing while he is on the warmer until he can be with her. Afterward, it is important to talk about what happened and why. It is hard to process the chain of events sometimes. Often a woman feels like she has somehow failed if she needs a C-section and I want to have this discussion to reinforce the fact that she was a total success and that she did everything in her power to birth her baby but that certain things happened and we had to deal with them as they came up.

I remind her that this is now the land of parenthood, where there are curves in the road, there are exceptions to every rule, and even our best-laid plans are apt to be foiled in the blink of an eye. This land is not always very fair, or forgiving, and we cannot see the future. As one wise woman once said about the land of birth, "Meconium happens."

So I didn't go into the OR, but used the time to clean up the room and grab some food. Leslie would be returning to the same room after only an hour in recovery. I prayed too that it would all be okay. I was anxious to meet this little man who had such an unorthodox way of coming into the world. I had never seen anything quite like it before, even after more than thirty years in birth work.

Finally, Alice came back to the room, absolutely radiant, followed soon after by a nurse wheeling the baby in. I took one look. He was beautiful and he was huge! He weighed in at ten pounds, seven ounces. Leslie was soon brought back with the proud dad. It was over. We hugged all around, crying happy tears this time, so relieved that everyone was here safe and sound. Every time I looked at the baby I marveled at how this had all played out. Could he have known he would not fit head first? What would this birth have looked like in Tanzania or Zimbabwe? Or even if he had been born in the last century here in this country? Would either of them have survived? I continued to ponder these things in my mind as I got ready to leave later that evening.

But he was here and healthy, and his parents were very relieved and happy. And exhausted. Before leaving I reminded Fred to protect mother and baby in the next few days and not let her get overwhelmed with visitors. I told him in no uncertain terms that the space around her was sacred and it was his job to protect it; their families could descend upon them next week, or better yet, the week after that, but not now. He agreed and gave me a big hug goodbye.

"There is a secret in our culture, and it's not that birth is painful. It's that women are strong."
~Laura Stavoe Harm

Chapter Twelve

"Can I Keep Her Forever and Always?"

I never thought we would "click" at all. Everything was wrong from our first appointment. China complained about how awful pregnancy was. She accused her baby of hating her—why else would he kick her so much? She told me she was having this baby with the wrong man. She confided that he was a loser and she hated him; he couldn't even find them decent housing. They were homeless and camping out at his sister's house.

If she blames her baby for her discomfort now, what will labor look like? I wondered. *And she says she wants a natural birth.*

Then after the hospital tour that OB patients were offered she called to tell me that the hospital was all wrong. She could not, would not bring her baby into the world in such a depressing place—I had to find her a better hospital. They didn't even have pictures in the rooms! I thought, *Sweetheart, you're not gonna care what's on the walls when the time comes.*

I called my supervisor at that point, asking for some wisdom. Was I the right doula for this client? Would she be happier with someone younger? Debby told me she wouldn't choose that particular hospital either, saying, "It *is* depressing."

Okay. I'd keep her.

I started going to prenatal visits with China. I needed to get to know her better. I gave her the phone numbers for some of the birthing centers throughout the city. She visited one that was absolutely gorgeous, but they were not a nonprofit and subsidized their medical assistance payments from low-income families by charging an additional $300 in cash up front. I told her I would find a place for her.

I called some of the other birth centers and found out that most did not take transfer clients after their thirty-fourth week. I knew I could probably get her into the midwife program at a local public hospital, but imagined she would be turned off by their "public" image. It is often seriously overcrowded, usually very loud, with standing room only in the emergency waiting room no matter what time of day or night it is. I called them and asked for the labor and delivery charge nurse. I explained who I was and what I was hoping to do for China. She explained that it was too late to transfer, but she actually knew who I was from some of the births I had been to there and asked if I would hold while she checked with the floor supervisor. She came back on the line and told me that if I could get China to the clinic the next day they would take her. I asked if I could also tour the labor and delivery area with her and silently hoped that their "better" rooms would be unoccupied so she could see them.

The next hurdle was getting her there. Medical Assistance will provide a taxi for medical appointments but only if scheduled two days in advance. I don't drive so I was trying to figure out how to get her there in the morning. They were staying with her boyfriend's sister in a suburb where the buses only run once an hour. It had been below zero all week with wind chill factors in the thirty-below range. Buses were out. I called Medical Assistance's transportation number and told them that one of my clients had to get special emergency clearance to get next-day rides from here on out until she delivered. They actually approved her if I would arrange the rides for her. Great! It worked.

The next day we were in a tiny cubicle waiting for the midwife. China must have gotten out on the wrong side of the bed that morning because the first thing she did when the midwife came in was demand that she be induced! She said she was sick of being pregnant and miserable, couldn't eat or sleep, that her baby hated her and kicked her on purpose, and that she would only stay if they got the delivery rolling . . . today!

The midwife listened and, skirting the issue completely, asked if China would kindly jump up on the table so we could hear her baby.

The midwife and I both gushed about how wonderfully strong her baby's heartbeat was when the Doppler was turned on. China just kept griping. I had had enough so I said to her, "You know, I have had ladies in the past year whose babies couldn't move like yours can. I even had one baby who was born with half a heart. You have a really healthy baby, and I am really looking forward to seeing him, too!" The midwife was nodding her agreement the whole time.

We finished with the appointment and the midwife explained that it was not their policy to induce labor without a good medical reason, such as when the mother has preeclampsia or diabetes. China grouched a bit more but realized the two of us were not going to be moved on this one.

We walked through the midwives' labor and delivery side of the hospital wing then, starting with a huge open room, almost a suite, with a birthing tub, private bathroom, little refrigerator and, yes, pictures on the walls. We saw two more rooms, decorated sparsely but pretty. They passed her royal highness's inspection. Whew! I thanked the midwife profusely and we left to wait for the return taxi.

Talk about an attitude! Maybe she was feeling so very helpless being homeless and without support that she had decided to demand her rights to the tiniest things that perhaps she could have control over. She was twenty-three going on twelve.

Then it dawned on me—I would gain her confidence with love. The expression, "Kill them with kindness" came to mind. I would lay it on so thick she wouldn't know what hit her. I would smother her with kindness. I couldn't imagine how else we would be able to work together through this birth. I knew she didn't have a clue how hard it was going to be. And I didn't want to see her fall apart before she even got into active labor and had to actually work to birth her baby.

My supervisor suggested I show China a book from our library called *Bonding With Your Baby Prenatally*, which I had brought along. I gave it to her as I hugged her goodbye that morning. It was almost Christmas.

The following week I collected all sorts of baby clothes and wrapped up a beautiful new scarf a friend had just given me. I already had four

others so I thought it was just the right thing to give her. My old heroine Dorothy Day once said that, "The extra coat hanging in your closet
actually belongs to the poor." I decided this must apply to scarves, too.

The following week I was given donations to give to some of my
mothers, so I started another care package for China. She was charmed,
to say the least. And we even got along well enough to talk about a
birth plan and her wishes. That was better, but when I asked if she
wanted her boyfriend in the room at all she said, "He is gonna be there
the whole time and see what he did to me!" Oh dear, not a good reason
to add him to the birth plan.

The next week she called me demanding induction. I very calmly
explained that she was only at thirty-six weeks and that I would find it
really sad if her baby had to stay in a NICU (intensive care unit for
newborns) and couldn't go home with her after he was born. I told her
that the next couple of weeks would ensure that he was really healthy,
and that at this point his lungs were not mature yet and might need
extra help breathing should he come out now. She backed down. I told
her to call me anytime and stay in touch.

A Korean graduate student in my apartment building was moving
out about that time and asked if I could find takers if she gave me some
nice but used clothes she couldn't take with her. China was just as petite
as Song Jung. I looked in the box when I got it back to my place. I never
would have been able to afford the cute sweaters and dresses, even designer
lingerie from Victoria's Secret! It was a huge success. I had found China's
weak spot! She absolutely shivered and then squealed with delight as she
unfolded each layer from the box. We were definitely buddies—at last.

One evening in her thirty-eighth week China called to ask if she
might have lost her mucus plug and described what she was seeing. I
agreed that it sounded like it and congratulated her. I cautioned her that
though her body knew exactly what to do and would certainly kick into
gear on her baby's exact birthday (which, of course, only he knew), it
could still be several more days. I advised her to just keep doing whatever
she had been doing—resting, eating, watching movies, and walking.

Two days later she called again, screaming that she couldn't sleep all night and she couldn't do it anymore, that her back was killing her and she was nauseated, and so forth. I was quite excited that this might be early labor. I was really looking forward to meeting this baby. I told her to eat and rest and call me if things changed or she got regular contractions. I also told her to call the hospital and let the midwives know. They might want to check her. I hung up and went back to our supper. By the time we were washing the dishes a very hysterical China called to say she had been on the phone with her grandma when her water broke. What should she do? I suggested she call the hospital, then let me know what they said. I knew they would want her to come in, but that wasn't my call as a doula. I made her promise to let me know.

Yahoo! We were going to have a baby! I realized then how much I really cared about China. She was the same age as one of my own daughters and I really wanted to see her succeed, to be a good mom and get her life back on track. It wasn't until I stopped judging her and started listening that I realized how very hard she really had it: parents on drugs, foster homes, you name it. I had to hand it to her, though— she told you what was on her mind and she wasn't bashful about letting you know how she felt that day. There was no guesswork at all—you got the whole story whether you wanted it or not.

When I arrived at the hospital, China was almost two centimeters, ninety-five percent effaced, and her contractions were picking up. This was it. The midwife confirmed that her water had broken. China wanted to rest for a bit so she lay down and closed her eyes. All of a sudden she rang the nurse's button and sat up. When the nurse came in China announced that the room she was in wasn't the room she had seen on the tour of the unit the week before. That room was pink. This one was an ugly tan. I tried to ignore this comment, but she wasn't going to let it go. She dug in her heels. She threw on a robe and said she wanted to check out all the other available rooms. The midwife took a deep breath and said, "Okay," as she led the way.

We walked into each of the other six rooms and then backtracked through each one of them once again, China leading the way with all of us in tow. She settled on a pink room and, climbing up on the bed, ordered us all to go get her stuff and bring it in.

The rest of the afternoon and evening was uneventful. She was dilating about one centimeter every two hours and the baby sounded great. It was slow, but not unusual for a first baby. By four centimeters China asked the nurse about getting something for pain. The nurse reviewed all of her options and China chose a low dose of an IV drug to take the edge off but not make it impossible to get up or get into the tub. In the end it barely helped and wore off before an hour was up.

It also affected the baby. His heart rate flattened out to a low 100 to 110 beats per minute, which isn't all that great. When China asked for more, the nurse suggested an epidural, but she really didn't want that if she could possibly avoid it. I backed her up and pointed out that the baby didn't do too well with the first drug and that I wasn't encouraging her to get more. I suggested she try the tub at this point, got her a cup of cranberry juice and filled the tub. She really liked it. I had been telling her that being flat in bed was not the best position to labor in. In the tub she found a real rhythm on her own. I was surprised and told her how well she was tuning into her body and finding a way with each rush as they rolled in on her.

Eminent author and doula Penny Simkin talks about the Three Rs: relaxation, rhythm, and ritual during labor but I had never seen someone find it on her own in exactly this way. It happened when I was breathing with her during a rush and her head bent down and leaned forward and rested on my knees. I automatically ran my fingers through her hair from the back of her neck and then gently pulled her hair back toward me. We did it a few more times and I asked if that helped at one point and she just purred, "Uh huhhhhh," so we kept doing it. She changed position after awhile and with each rush ran her own hands down her neck, and rocked gently forward until it passed. For the rest of the labor she found a rhythm to add to the breathing, which I found fascinating. She had tuned into some inner strength that I had not seen before and just went with it.

Suddenly, in walked the grand matriarch of her family, Grandmama, in flowing black and purple layers of some kind of robe, antique silver earrings, and a spotted leopard hat to top it all off. Regal is a modest description. She blew me away! As she glided into the room she set out bags of goodies for all of us. She had thought of everything: granola bars, bottled spring water, snacks, and cookies. Then she looked over at China and beamed, saying, "You are so beautiful! You are a goddess! You are doing this sooooo well!"

She proceeded to unpack a huge bag of baby blankets, baby clothes, baby socks, baby shoes, all brand new and all blue! Then she turned once again to China and said, "You can't have any more kids 'cause this all broke the bank!"

China was back in bed and with the next contraction the Dowager Empress stood by and breathed with her. Then she brushed her hair and massaged her neck. I was still sitting there in awe. All this loving on China really got things going. Soon she was saying she couldn't do it anymore and needed an epidural now! I knew she was at least nine if not ten centimeters. I explained that this was transition, the end of the very longest part of labor, that she was doing so, so, sooo well and that we would help her with each rush until she could push. I said she should rest in the few minutes in between rushes, which she did. She trusted me by now; we were finally a really great team. I let Grandmama coach her all she wanted and hung back a bit. The lady was truly stellar.

China tried a hands-and-knees position and then went back to sitting up cross-legged. I asked the midwife if they had a squatting bar, thinking that it might be just the right thing, and it was. China leaned into it, threw off her hospital nightgown and pushed! Two more pushes and she screamed. The midwife assured her she was doing it perfectly and she could feel the baby's head. I tried to help her reach down to feel the baby's head crowning but she shook my hand away, grabbed the bar once again and pushed her baby out onto the bed. Still squatting, she picked him up and held him to her chest. He gurgled a tiny cry and then let loose. He was tiny, perhaps all of six pounds, but sure had a huge set of lungs. We helped her so she could lay back on the pillows as I piled them up behind her. She studied her beautiful little baby as he blinked back at her and then said, "I love you so much!" We let him do the breast crawl and latch on his own when he was ready. He was on within twenty minutes.

The next day I visited China one last time. I sat and held little Baby Boy (who didn't have a name yet) while China filled out the evaluation form I have to give all mothers. When she was finished I took it and stuffed it right away in with the other papers in my bag and hugged her goodbye. I whispered in her ear, "You know, my love, now you can do anything!"

She looked me straight in the eye and answered, "Yeah, I can do anything!"

I pulled out the paperwork later that evening so I could finish my report and mail it the next day. As I was stapling the papers, I read the evaluation page. One question asked, "Overall, how would you evaluate the usefulness of having the doula present?"

The ratings went from "1: More harm than good" to "5: Was a big help." China had written "10." Then I saw her comment: "I love my doula. Can I keep her forever and always?"

"The most precious gift we can offer anyone is our attention. When mindfulness embraces those we love, they will bloom like flowers."
~Thich Nhat Hanh

Chapter Thirteen
An Unplanned Natural Birth

I was given a new referral, a mom whose obstetrician was concerned about a big baby. The midwives at her clinic had referred her to an OB because, besides the big baby, Ayana had serious diabetes. This was her second pregnancy and she was due in a week and a half. The OB suggested an induction. We were now on a high-risk track.

Many of the women at this clinic are recent refugees from Ethiopia. All of us in birth work want to make their experiences of pregnancy and birth in their new country a positive one. We have all read everything we could about cross-cultural medicine and tried to learn from the earlier mistakes when they first began to assimilate in Minnesota. One of my favorite resources is the book *The Spirit Catches You and You Fall Down: A Hmong Child, Her American Doctors, and the Collision of Two Cultures*, a brilliant and timely work by Anne Fadiman. All the universities and medical school programs in Minnesota now offer and require courses that concentrate on helping us understand the barriers facing diverse immigrant communities in our state, which include, especially, cultural and linguistic challenges.

I met with Ayana, who did not speak English, and learned through an interpreter that she had not attempted to get prenatal care until her eighth month even though she had state-funded insurance to cover her throughout. Coming from a district in Ethiopia that didn't have a medical facility, many in her community were unaware of the concept of preventive medicine and how it can help pregnancies and affect outcome. During our first visit I explained the role of the doula prior to and at birth. Through an interpreter she said she was delighted to have so much help as her own family was not in the U.S. She had few female relatives here and her husband had said that his job would be to watch little Omar, their very energetic two-and-a-half-year-old boy, while she was in the hospital. It is a pretty universal assumption in traditional African societies that birth belongs to the realm of women and that men are not especially welcomed.

One father from Cameroon recently took the time to sit me down and patiently explain that African men don't like to see their wives "like that," meaning sweating and pushing their babies out, and that we would do well in America to explain this to our husbands and perhaps they would respect their wives more and there would be far less divorce. I didn't agree or disagree but just listened and said, "Oh, uh huh. Hmmm," my pat answer when our cultures clash but I don't see any point in trying to correct what I perceive as error quite yet. Perhaps later there would be an opening to discuss this. He wasn't ready. And since I wish to continue working with families from cultures other than my own, I have learned that I get a lot more mileage coming to this work with respect and humility than attempting to confront my perception of the differences. A very wise, timely saying from the last century that I believe is attributed to Chief Seattle says, "Do not judge your neighbor until you walk two moons in his moccasins."

We would begin preparing Ayana's baby's birth now, however late in the game. I often meet with women at their clinic appointments. I get a lot of "no shows" if I schedule our meetings outside of other commitments. I am not sure why, though I can guess that with small children, in a new country, and with the language barrier, plus learning the bus system if they don't drive, meeting with a doula, or midwife for that matter, isn't on the top of their to-do list. Just getting to English class, getting the groceries home, and picking up a kindergartner after school is mind-boggling enough for many.

At our first meeting I showed Ayana the *Doula* DVD, which is perfect for the population I serve: not only are there women of color having babies in the film, but there are home births, hospital births, footage of C-sections, water births, hands-and-knees births, and mamas picking up their own babies at birth. Equally important (though I am sure that the women who made this beautiful film may not have realized it) is that my mothers can see women in America giving birth completely *au natural*, some wearing nighties, others with their partners in the tub with them— the options are endless. This is important because I want them to know that the birth room is their space, that they will own it, and that they can do whatever they instinctually need to do to birth their babies. They don't need to worry that there is a certain way they have to conform to, like they have to do every single other day in American society. In the birth room they can literally let their hair down—or their *hijab*.

After we watch the movie I often wonder at the look of awe I see. This has opened up a whole new world of possibilities to many of these women. They are being put in charge of something for the very first time since coming to the United States and I articulate it this way: "This is your birth. It is your body and your baby. I will not be making any decisions for you but I will support you throughout your birth. I will not leave at shift change when you get new nurses and often a new midwife or doctor. I will be your advocate for whatever your wishes are." This is a scary prospect to some. It is exhilarating to others. For every one of these women, though, it is a new concept. They are in charge. They are often liberated by this one experience alone.

The next step is to write a birth plan. I give them a sample plan I wrote, suggesting they edit it, completely rewrite it, or throw it out and tell me what they want it to say instead. The interpreters at the clinic help us with this, too.

The birth plan is one page long. I have seen templates for birth plans on the Internet that are nine pages or more. From my experience, no nurse or doctor will sit down and read anything longer than one page. They don't have time, and I do not want them to just skim over it. Since it is part of my job to greet anyone who comes into the room, I immediately introduce myself and then invite them to read our birth plan. It sets the tone that says this lady knows what she wants and has definite ideas. It says that she has wishes and choices and implies that because I respect that, we expect they will, too. It sends a powerful message, I believe, not adversarial but focused on her.

Mom-to-be and I usually talk about each entry on the birth plan and what each option means. After we write it, I go through a little exercise I learned in my own doula training. I suggest she look at her birth plan and if she absolutely had to, decide what ten items she would keep and which would she be able to let go of. Then, which five? And then all but one. We don't have absolute control over how our births will go; it is our first test in the journey of parenthood and deciding what is best for our family, not for our mothers, our midwives, our best friends, or doulas. I believe there is a greater dissatisfaction with our births when we cast our birth plan in stone and then feel like we failed if we weren't able to do everything the way we had planned.

This is a sample birth plan I like to start with.

Sample Birth Plan

- I would like my partner to call our doula at: (phone number) when labor starts. I want to labor at home as long as possible. He/she will also alert our midwife/doctor at: (phone number).
- Who I want in the room: I want my partner and my doula in the room with me at all times. If any residents or students wish to attend our birth, please check with me first. If anyone else arrives at the hospital, please ask me first if I would like them present.
- What I want: I want to walk, use the birthing tub, birth ball, etc., and move as much as possible during labor. I want to eat and drink and wear my own clothes and not be offered pain medication. I will ask for it if I need it.
- What I don't want: to be asked what my pain level is. I will ask for medication if I need it.
- I don't want nurses shouting to push or counting out loud. I want to push with the urge and work with my doula during this stage.
- I do not want continuous monitoring but prefer a portable Doppler.
- I do not want the bag of water to be artificially ruptured.

• I do not want an episiotomy. I would rather tear. I would like my doctor/midwife to use oil on my perineum to help with stretching.
• When my baby comes, I want to hold him as soon as possible.
• Please delay cutting the cord. Then I would like my partner to cut it.
• I want my baby on my chest and to let him initiate breastfeeding. My doula will work with us on baby-led breastfeeding.
• I want him weighed and measured and any care done while on my bed after about two to three hours of bonding.
• I want my doula to help me give my baby his first bath in our room before we leave the hospital.
• I do not want our baby going to the nursery at all. We will room-in.
• I do not want him given formula, sugar water, or pacifiers.
• I want vitamin K and eyedrops given after he has been with me for about two to three hours. I want to hold him for the Vitamin K injection and later also for the PKU test. (The Vitamin K shot helps with any blood clotting issues, and the PKU test screens for an amino acid disorder that is rare, though disastrous if missed.)
• I will sign a waiver that I am/am not giving my baby _____ vaccine at this time.
• I will go with my baby to have his hearing screening done.
• I want to bring my placenta home.
Thank you in advance for your help and consideration!

Ayana's doctor scheduled an induction for the following week. Spiking sugar levels and insulin were his main concern. Also, her first baby had been only six pounds but this baby was much bigger.

Ayana and I met at the hospital and walked up together. She told me she had just decided on a name, Sisay. She said that in Ethiopian it means "an omen of good things." When we were settled I filled out the whiteboard in her room: baby's name, mom's name, doula, interpreter, etc. The Amharic interpreter who came that day was one of the most amazing women I have ever met. Belem had left Ethiopia and moved to

New Delhi, India, six years earlier, all by herself. A traditional Muslim woman, she earned a master's degree there in business administration before moving to the U.S. She took a course in medical interpreting and got a job with an agency that serves Minneapolis hospitals. This was my second birth with her as an interpreter and we were both delighted when we saw each other again. I had been emailing her and encouraging her to continue her education. Together we are looking into midwifery programs for her. We desperately need women like her in the birth community. She has a heart the size of Texas and is a natural from all that I have seen.

The induction started out slowly. There were mild contractions and Ayana was dilated to two centimeters for the first two hours. I was glad they encouraged her to eat and walk around. By early afternoon the contractions had stopped. It was time for a snack and a nap. The doctor came by and suggested trying some Pitocin next, which Ayana agreed to. The rushes picked up slowly and finally we thought they had gotten into a nice pattern when the nurses saw that they were actually coupling, or coming two at a time with longer rests in between. That occurs when the rushes are neither very effective nor helping the cervix to dilate, so the Pitocin was stopped. The doctor thought Ayana should rest, have supper, and then suggested using a medication called Cervidil that would help ripen the cervix so that either contractions would establish themselves, or if they had not by morning, then the Pitocin might be more effective. Ayana thought this all sounded okay, though it was not in her birth plan. I was glad the doctor was not being more aggressive and actually rather reserved from what I had seen in other hospitals.

By morning Ayana felt much better. Her contractions were regular, though weak. Pitocin was started again. Pretty soon we were in business: four centimeters and she wasn't laughing at my jokes anymore. This was active labor—serious business. We walked and danced a slow version of a belly dance with me humming along while we bonded with the walls up and down the four halls framing the unit. I suggested different positions: hanging while holding onto my shoulders, leaning into the wall, squatting by the bed, sitting on a birth ball, and hands and knees. We tried the tub for a while, but Ayana liked walking best. Every time we completed a four-hall lap we would go into her room for a potty stop and another full cup of juice. (I am a serious pusher, of juice that is, and not the sports or calorie-free electrolyte versions. This mama is running a marathon here and needs both natural sugars and calories.)

We didn't need a nurse to check to know she was opening up. The rushes were closer now and Ayana asked for an epidural. I explained some of her other options, but she had had an epidural with her last birth and had written it into her birth plan this time. Although I would love for every mom to explore natural birth, I have a strong commitment to support each one in whatever way they feel is best for them. I can only hope that they will gain strength and confidence with each birth and perhaps consider using less conventional methods in the future. They know I am there for them unconditionally and will not criticize their choices or continue to push in a direction they have decided is not what they want. So I let her nurse know that she was asking for the epidural. She called the anesthesia department with the request and set up the room for the procedure while we continued walking and drinking juice, since I was pretty sure they would not let her drink once the epidural was in place. It is usually ice-chips-only at that point.

Fifteen minutes later Ayana asked when the anesthesiologist was going to come. The nurses assured her he was on the way. Half an hour passed and we were doing some pretty heavy-duty breathing now. At one point I looked over at the nurse who shrugged her shoulders, looking baffled, too. Where were they? Ayana was obviously miffed at this point; she had not planned on this at all. I kept telling her how strong she was and how well she was doing. I helped her rest between the rushes but when each one crept up on her again and then quickly intensified, she repeated her little mantra: "When? When? WHEN?!" Finally another nurse came in and very apologetically told us that the anesthesiologist had been called away to an emergency C-section and would come as soon as possible. I silently wondered why only one anesthesiologist was in the hospital, but I didn't want to do anything to further disturb our routine at this point, so we continued breathing and resting. The interpreter and I knelt on each side of Ayana, who was sitting in a rocking chair.

All of a sudden she stood up and said she had to go to the bathroom. She had just been to the bathroom so I knew this was the beginning of the urge to push. I was surprised that our interpreter could also read the signs (I knew she was cut out for this business!) and quickly instructed Ayana to sit on the bed where we could help her better. As we got her more comfortable I hit the nurse button and said as quietly as I could, "We are thinking about pushing in room 350." Sure enough, with the next rush Ayana flashed a look of panic at me and then took a deep breath—as I did—and pushed. And pushed. The doctor ran into the room between two nurses, who were wheeling in the warmer and instrument cart. Another push and we could see lots of Baby's head. Another grand push and she was born.

Ayana looked down and just sobbed as she reached for her baby, who was already crying. We got them comfortable while we waited for the placenta. Ayana's look of absolute shock sent Belem into a gale of giggles. I told Ayana how amazing she was. It was obvious that she couldn't believe she had actually birthed a baby without any medication. We told her it showed how strong she really was.

I found out the next day at our postpartum visit that she is a single mom. Recently divorced, her ex had offered to watch their son when she went to the hospital but had no intention of helping her further. In some larger cosmic plan I believe this birth was meant to be this way to prove to Ayana that she is capable of anything. I think she can now agree, too. I stayed for two more hours to marvel at how beautiful little Sisay was and her newly empowered mother.

"Sometimes the only thing that makes a woman's pregnancy high risk is her choice of a care provider."
~Anonymous

Chapter Fourteen
Birthing a Birth Plan

Searching "Birth Plan Templates" on the Internet will garner a myriad of styles, types, varieties, and different interpretations, some good, others not so good, and a few that are downright bad. Throughout my career I have developed what I call my "rule of thumb" for birth plans.

No one will read anything longer than one page. Don't even think of it! One website boasts "Everything you'll need . . . " You're supposed to fill in the blanks and then print out all nine pages. No one will ever read all of that.

When I am working as a doula I tell the family that part of my job is to be a gatekeeper at their birth. When any new nurse or resident walks in the room, it is my duty to intercept him or her and introduce myself, "Hi, I am Stephanie, Jane's doula, and this is our birth plan." That way everyone in the room is hopefully on board and it sends a message that Jane has done her homework and this is important to her.

When a mom sends me her birth plan I check it over and make any suggestions if I wonder about something, like, "Don't you want to have the baby with you during any exams?" Sometimes I will suggest adding a point or two, or perhaps omitting outdated practices, like being strapped into stirrups. I want to be sure I am clear about her wishes. It isn't necessary to repeatedly write, "But in an emergency . . ." or "If a C-section is recommended," because the mom will be the first to know and be consulted if there is a concern.

We need to stay positive and not write in every dire intervention. Yes, we will educate ourselves about what might happen and our options, but we don't need to expect every such horrific outcome.

Another reason to learn about interventions and what options you will have should events warrant is because if you don't understand what your rights and options are, then you really don't have any choices; you have decided that you trust the doctor or midwife enough to allow yourself to go into default mode and will do what they feel is best.

A study was done in the U.S. that asked mothers to rate their birth experiences in relation to their birth plans. Mothers (and partners) most dissatisfied with their birth experiences were those who expected every point to be honored by all present at all times. They felt their document was almost cast in stone, and then thought they had "failed" somehow to either live up to their own expectations or that the staff didn't respect the birth plan (and their wishes) enough and derailed the event from what it could have been.

"Just as a woman's heart knows how and when to pump, her lungs to inhale, and her hand to pull back from the fire, so she knows when and how to give birth."
~Virginia Di Orio

Chapter Fifteen

Shoulder Distocia!

I went with Makda to her clinic appointment. The midwives had referred her to an obstetrician because they were concerned that she still had two weeks to go until her guess date and her baby already felt rather large. Another concern was that her last baby had gotten stuck during delivery with a complication called shoulder dystocia. Shoulder dystocia is scary enough that the last midwife made sure to attach an alert to Makda's chart.

The doctor did an ultrasound and guessed that Makda's baby, a boy, was about eight and a half pounds, which was what the last baby weighed, though she was only at thirty-eight weeks now. She had two little girls at home, a five-year-old named Qwara and a three-year-old named Retta. They were used to me by now, though remained a bit skeptical, especially since I couldn't understand a word of their language, Amharic, though they tried to talk to me. The little girls settled on high fives as a greeting and went back to the toy box in the waiting room while Makda and I went into the exam room.

I was impressed that her doctor didn't rush into the early induction option, especially since the weekend was fast approaching (most C-sections in the U.S. occur before 10:00 p.m. and not on weekends). He explained that since this was Makda's third baby she should be able to push out another big baby, which she did, after all, the last time. However, he hoped she would go into labor on her own in the next week.

Her husband, Semere, would be staying home with the other children when she delivered, which wasn't unusual. As mentioned earlier, in traditional African cultures men are not usually in attendance at births, which is one reason our doula group has become so popular with immigrant women. They have aunts, sisters, sometimes their mothers, and girlfriends go with them when they have their babies, but the idea of a doula who can help them negotiate the often mind-boggling American medical system is a godsend to them. In turn, I tell them that I am deeply honored to be invited to be a part of their most intimate moments and made to feel so welcomed at their births.

Makda and I had talked about her wishes, what she liked or didn't like about her last two births, and together we had written a birth plan. She and I had spent some of our prenatal visits watching YouTube births, especially water births, home births, and natural births. I wanted her to understand her many options. She was especially intrigued by water birth, so we talked about that and included it in her plan.

I could tell the doctor's words were a bit discouraging to Makda so I suggested that before she left that day we should get the interpreter back and talk about it a bit. I come from what we call the "midwifery model of care," where we trust that our bodies know how to birth and that they also know how big to grow each baby. The other model of care is the "medical model" that has crept into our collective consciousness and the American way of life for over a hundred years now and, in the process, undermined much of our instinctual knowledge.

Doulas try to find a way to navigate between the two, letting women know their alternatives, encouraging them to find that power that we believe is in each of us, but also stepping back when our sister is on this journey of self-discovery and may not be ready to be as daring as we would be (or wish her to be). We have to respect her choices and hesitations and not show even the least disappointment if she doesn't choose what we would have chosen for her birth. A doula has to be there to unconditionally support whatever choices a couple feels is best for them.

I told Makda there were a few things that might help her avoid having to be induced, if her baby was indeed ready. I suggested walking a lot, or having sex. Then I told her about Jeannie, who had been told that she needed a C-section the next day and how I had told Jeannie that she could also talk to her baby and perhaps find a way through the problem together. It had worked and she had a vaginal birth without complications. I wished Makda a good night and hugged her goodbye.

Makda called at 6:00 a.m. sharp two days later. She was feeling sick and not sure what to do. She had chills, her stomach was upset, she couldn't eat, and was experiencing cramps but not contractions. She complained that her back hurt, too.

It sounded like either early labor or a urinary tract infection, though I didn't voice that. As a doula, it was my job to direct her back to her midwife or doctor and let them decide what to do. I told her to call the clinic and let me know what they thought she should do. She called back to say they wanted to see her at the hospital, but she didn't want to bring her children, too, and asked if I could call the taxi and meet her there so Semere could stay home and watch their girls. I did so, and soon met her at the hospital.

When I arrived, a monitor was tracking the baby's heartbeat and another monitor was picking up contractions. She didn't feel the contractions at all, and her water hadn't broken. They ruled out anything else that might be causing her discomfort and decided to watch for an hour to see if anything changed. She was one centimeter dilated at that point.

So I visited with her and figured we'd be sent home in the end. An hour later she was actually dilating and the contractions were picking up. We weren't going anywhere yet. I ordered lunch for her and snacked on what I had brought, though I didn't have my big doula carpetbag. I hadn't thought we'd be staying. I was wrong.

Hour by hour she continued to open. Though slow, it was definitely progress. At one point the contractions picked up a bit and she started to feel them, but then they stopped altogether. We walked for a while, glad to finally be able to move around. Her doctor came by later in the afternoon, mostly just to encourage her. He was not in a big hurry. I kept her drinking plenty of juices, which I think got rid of the chills or whatever fever was threatening to appear. Dehydration alone can cause symptoms like Makda was experiencing. By evening, things had pretty much stopped. The nurse called the doctor, who suggested Makda just sleep and we'd see where we were in the morning. I was very impressed with this doctor's level of restraint.

I went home but assured Makda that I would return quickly if she needed me. I made sure she had my number handy and tucked her in. She had a good night.

The next morning the doctor suggested a very low dose of Pitocin to get the occasional contractions a little closer together. They were still there, but not at all effective. That worked quite well. Finally we entered that point of no return called active labor. With my own five births, I remember this as the moment when you ask yourself each and every time, *What could I possibly have been thinking to want another baby and to be back here again?* It is the moment when you think, and some say it out loud, *Let's all just go home now and come back and do this tomorrow instead.*

One of the resident doctors came to introduce himself and asked permission to observe the birth. Makda didn't understand what he wanted so I explained that he would like to stand in the corner and just watch—he would not touch her—and learn from the birth, that he was a student doctor and that this is how they learn—and how we can contribute to their education, including natural birth. That is how I learned, I told her, by watching midwives and doctors when I was in school. I explained that she had every right to say no, that there were enough people already involved, but she said it was perfectly okay and even put her hand out to welcome him. He read her chart and asked the senior doctor if, in light of the last shoulder dystocia, he was considering using the Gaskin Maneuver. I was floored! This was the first time I had ever encountered a doctor who not only knew about Ina

May Gaskin and the successful management of shoulder dystocia that was named after her, but was actually hoping to see it in action.

Ina May first observed this maneuver by indigenous midwives while visiting the highlands of Guatemala in 1976. The problem of shoulder dystocia has received increasing attention in the medical literature in recent years, probably because of the tremendous potential for litigation that accompanies this disastrous complication. It has been estimated that at least eight percent of malpractice claims alleging fetal damage involve a birth complicated by shoulder dystocia. True shoulder dystocia has been defined as any birth in which maneuvers in addition to lateral traction and episiotomy are required to deliver the baby's shoulders. The reported incidence of shoulder dystocia is somewhere around one and a half percent of all births. The most common fetal complications include asphyxia, seizures, brachial plexus palsy, and fractures of the baby's humerus and clavicle.

The OB overseeing Makda's labor at this point said it might help and he was familiar with it, but then added that a small vacuum extractor might also help. I assumed he was more familiar with the latter intervention by the way he was explaining it. I couldn't resist putting in my own two cents at this point and said, just as an aside, "Ina May was at my twins' birth at The Farm in 1982."

The resident practically hopped up and down and said, "Really? I just saw that video! That was you?"

I said, "Yes." Later that night he came by with another young intern to meet me. When did medical school ever look like this? It was very encouraging.

Makda and I walked, and labored, and breathed, thought about giving up, walked some more, and took a long bath. The only sound was the water slowly trickling over her belly in a dark, quiet bathroom and our breathing in unison, and then blowing each rush away . . . forever. Finally fully dilated, we tried different positions for pushing. Hands and knees worked well, and the doctor was in agreement with staying there, especially if it would help with big shoulders, but Makda wasn't sure it was working. The nurse checked and the baby hadn't come down any further, even with some really good pushes. Then the doctor checked and became concerned that he couldn't feel the lines in the baby's head. He wondered if he had turned somehow and could even be breech, so they rolled in an ultrasound machine to check. The head was still down, but posterior. That explained the back labor but didn't explain why he wasn't budging the least little bit. The doctor was fine with Makda pushing when she had the urge, but it didn't look like she was getting her baby to move. At this point he ruptured the bag of water, hoping that would help with some progress. What happened next was a surprise. Until then the baby had sounded great, with nice variable heart tones. But the water was full of meconium. That meant Baby was not happy.

The heart tones continued to look good, but all the pushing wasn't doing much good. Finally, the doctor suggested trying the vacuum that might help the baby's head to move, which he was sure by now was acyclic, or turned to one side and aiming down the birth canal at an awkward angle. Makda agreed to it right away. We all just wanted to see this baby out at this point. So that was tried and after three attempts, the doctor gave up on that too. Baby didn't move. We had tried different positions and just about every trick in the book by then. All of a sudden I looked over at the monitor at the same moment that one of the nurses announced as calmly as possible, "Fetal heart tones fifty . . . sixty . . . fifty . . ." which meant that our baby was in trouble. Serious trouble.

Back to hands and knees and monitors. I was the only one on the side of the bed by the oxygen port in the wall so I took the liberty to unravel the tubing, plug it in and turn it up to ten liters as I passed the mask to the nurse who had Makda breathe the oxygen. We tried having her on her side, then the other side, then upright. Nothing helped for long. After every contraction the baby's heart rate fell dangerously low. The doctor wondered out loud if the cord was being pressed somewhere next to the baby's head, both preventing further descent and causing the low heart rates. He explained all of this to Makda and asked if she would be okay with an emergency C-section because the baby wasn't doing well and we didn't want to wait further. She agreed.

The moment she consented, the staff went into high gear. She was asked to sign a consent form. Compression bags were put on her legs and a sterile cap covered her hair. The IVs were all detached at the pole, tossed onto the bed and monitors were shut off. A fetal scalp monitor was threaded in through the cervix to listen to the baby directly. Every minute counted. He still sounded okay, which I was glad I could tell her. I helped Makda pant through the contractions and take deep breaths as they passed. I tried to sound calm and quiet, hoping to diffuse the sense of panic around us. As Makda was being wheeled out of the room the interpreter and I were each tossed a set of scrubs, hats, booties, and masks, which we caught mid-air. We wiggled out of our clothes and into the scrubs as fast as possible, then ran down the hall to catch up to Makda.

While she was prepped for surgery I was able to tell her what was happening. The IVs were all reattached, the epidural line was transferred to the operating room, her belly was scrubbed, and then covered with a sticky sterile sheet that would stay in place during the surgery. Within ten minutes the doctor started the first incision. I explained that she would feel pulling as they held back each layer of skin and muscle and then they'd be ready to lift out her baby. I told her he still sounded good, the best yet since we left the room. A few minutes later I told her to expect some tugging and pressure. Then I reported seeing lots of curly hair and before I could say more he let out a huge cry as they lifted him up. He looked pink and didn't even need to be suctioned. Because of the earlier meconium, the resuscitation team was on hand but he did better than anyone expected.

Soon he was in the warmer. I lifted Makda's sheet so she could see him as they cleaned him up and checked his breathing. He was doing great. I whispered in her ear that he was beautiful, and that we were all very proud of her. In a very few minutes Makda was holding . baby boy who was suddenly perfectly quiet, blinking and looking at her.

Finally she was wheeled back to her room—this little hospital didn't have a recovery room so we settled back in where we had started. The interpreter called Semere and explained that his son was finally here and he should come when he could find someone to watch the little girls. Makda instructed the interpreter not to tell him that she had a C-section because she was afraid that he would race to the hospital and get in an accident. She asked me to explain to him what happened and why when he arrived.

About an hour later he came with their two little girls. They were dressed alike and their daddy had even fixed their hair. One was holding a huge bunch of flowers and the other had two balloons on strings for their new baby brother. An aunt was also along to watch the girls so Semere would be free to visit with his wife. I explained to him briefly that the doctor was concerned about the baby and after trying several interventions, decided to do the C-section. I gave him a very brief outline and told him we would talk more when I came back the next day. I did say that I was very glad we got the doctor we did and that the whole staff had been great, exceptionally caring and competent. I told him we had been very lucky. I told him, too, that he had a very brave wife and he should be very proud of her. I hugged them both goodbye and went home.

When I returned the next day Makda was walking around the room, taking care of her baby. He was nursing well and she looked wonderfully well and happy. She had a few questions as she was trying to process the rushed chain of events before his birth. We talked about it all again, and I told her that we were all very grateful for how supported she was and the great medical team she had.

The midwife part of me still tries to analyze alternative possible scenarios and what we might have done differently. The doula part of me knows I was there to try to bring a calm and balance to her birth that she would always remember. I wanted her to feel that she had done a smashing job in spite of the problems and that she was an amazingly strong, beautiful woman who was on this incredible journey of motherhood.

We visited over lunch in her room, so very grateful that little Azmera was here. She marveled that he was so peaceful and nursed so well. I reminded her what a good mama she was and that the older we get, the more laid back we often are, which babies seem to reflect.

Penny Simkin. PT, CD(DONA), childbirth educator, birth doula trainer, author (see resource page).

"One is constantly having to balance the high expectations of modern healthcare with the need to repsect the human soul."
~Penny Simkin

Chapter Sixteen

Doulas and Nurses

A call from Belem was the beginning of a very busy few days. As the Amharic translator, she called to let me know one of "my" ladies was in labor. I rushed to the hospital and found out that not only had Keleme not called me, but she had been in labor for over twenty-four hours! All of her thinking flew out the window when labor started, totally confusing her as to who she should have called when the time came.

Keleme, her midwife, and I were trying to figure out how to help her rest for a bit. She was exhausted and hadn't eaten or had enough to drink during labor. Her midwife suggested some IV fluids along with a muscle relaxant so she could sleep for a bit. It worked. Three hours later, after the drug wore off, she had a beautiful little five-pound boy, her first baby, with only three pushes! He was tiny but nursed immediately.

By 2:00 a.m. I was on my way home. I showered and slithered into bed—it felt so good—and fell asleep, only to wake up to the phone ringing at 7:00 a.m. It was my lady from Laos. Her water broke an hour earlier. She timidly asked if she should go to the hospital yet. "Yes" I told her. "I will meet you there. Remind me which hospital. Good. Okay, honey. We're gonna have a birthday party today, aren't we?" She was also a first-time mama. I grabbed her file. Yes, I thought this was early, though only two weeks. Not bad. I got dressed and called a taxi.

As I rode up in the elevator to the birth center my phone rang. Another mom was letting me know she just lost her mucus plug. I congratulated her, hoping she would be a bit more excited about her second baby than she'd been in our meetings and told her to keep me informed, day or night, reminding her that it could still be several more days before labor started.

The rushes had started by the time I entered Der's room. I scrubbed up at the sink then went over to the bed to hug her. Der was as stiff as a board, obviously very nervous. The monitor was blaring away and something else was beeping in the room. I hit the nurse button and asked if someone could turn off all the noise. They did. I massaged Der's hands while we chatted about what to expect next.

Der insisted she could give birth to her baby without drugs. We walked around, she sat on a birth ball, drank juice, munched on snacks, and walked around some more.

Her husband was even more reserved than Der. He sat in a corner and didn't say a word.

The nurse checked her and announced "Five centimeters. Great!" and left us alone again. Less than ten minutes later, during a rush, Der suddenly held her breath and pushed for all she was worth.

I knew that, in spite of being told she was only five centimeters, she knew what she was doing, even though it was her first baby, so I hit the nurse button again and tried to calmly say, "We are feeling a bit pushy down here and I think you ought to come now!"

Nurses rushed around setting up the room. An instrument cart and baby warmer were wheeled in from the hallway where they had been on stand-by draped with sterile sheets. Chairs went out the door and the bottom half of the bed was removed. Stirrups popped up, though I showed Der how to sit up and hold behind her knees with her hands and we didn't use the stirrups at all (I avoid them if at all possible). Another push and we could see Baby's black, curly, long hair. Her husband still silently watched all of this from his corner. I helped her rest and slow her breathing after the rush and she appeared to instantly go to sleep. When she woke with the next rush she pushed the little head out. It was perfectly round, barely cone-shaped at all. The rest of the baby slid out and Der immediately reached for her baby and started talking to her little girl in Lao. I had never heard her speak it since her English was so good. I asked what she said to her little girl and she laughed and said, "Oh, I just said, 'Hi, I'm your mommy and this is your daddy.'" We were able to keep Baby on her mother's chest skin-to-skin for a couple of hours, both covered with pre-warmed blankets. It was a wonderful birth.

I got home, showered, warmed up some leftovers and caught up on paperwork. I won't remember when what baby was born or the dates or weights if I don't write them down. Finally I decided I needed a nap before my husband got home. I had hardly seen him that week and was looking forward to having supper together.

The lady who had called me while I was in the elevator going to Der's birth called back as we were getting ready for bed at midnight. She was having contractions but they weren't regular. They had been coming and going for two days and she was done. She wanted me to know she was going to the hospital right then and insisting on being induced and wanted me there, too. She would start week thirty-nine in two days.

She had already hired and fired two doulas before me. She had numerous issues with them but for some mysterious reason decided I was okay. I learned that it was close to the two-year anniversary of her mother's death and she was angry that her mom couldn't hang around long enough to help her with her kids. Just the week before, at one of her prenatal appointments, we met at a clinic I had never been to, in the north part of the city. The entire area reminded me of Harlem in the 1960s. This was Harlem before gentrification. It was a very scary place. I had no idea we even had such pockets of poverty in Minnesota.

She was in the waiting room with her partner and their three-year-old that day. The little boy was snarfing down a whole bag of mini Milky Way bars and the mom was munching on Cheetos. After ten minutes she said to the little guy, "Okay, baby, let's trade" and they exchanged bags and continued noshing. This was lunch. Really. I didn't go into my nutrition spiel because I was absolutely sure her doctor had already had that conversation with her, probably many times.

She calmed down while we talked on the phone. I reminded her that was still two—or could be even three—weeks early and I really didn't want to see her deliver prematurely and not be able to take her baby home from the hospital with her if he ended up in the NICU. She finally agreed and asked what she could do to hang on a little longer. I agreed that it is hard to wait when you are so uncomfortable but she'd be okay and would soon see her baby boy. I tried to encourage her and told her again to feel free to call me any time.

I slept like a log. I needed it. When I got up I called my single mom, Stacy, who was due the day before. She told me she had been contract-ing all night but the rushes weren't yet five minutes apart. Her water hadn't broken. I offered to go to her house or meet her when she de-cided to go to the hospital. She was doing well, she told me, had girl-friends over, and said she would stay in touch.

Within an hour Stacy called back to tell me she couldn't handle it at home anymore and asked me to meet her at the hospital. She got there before I did and let me know she was already three centimeters as I walked in with my pink "Happy Birthday" tiara on. It always makes people laugh, so I bring it when I think we need a bit of comic relief. Stacy put it on as she got in the tub. I turned on the jets—it was a real Jacuzzi!—and she sighed with pleasure as she relaxed into it. So cute!

I noticed when I got to Stacy's room that a friend was guiding Stacy through the rushes beautifully. I held back a bit and just watched how she was able to calm Stacy and saw that they were really a great team. I brought in a bath stool and put it by the tub and invited the friend to just be there for her. I learned that Becky, a mom herself, was studying infant massage. I left them alone and busied myself cleaning up the room a bit. Then I walked down to the nurses' station and asked our nurse if we could order breakfast, which she agreed to right away. The hos-pital had twenty-four-hour cafeteria service and would deliver a tray to the room a half-hour after getting the order.

As her doula, I could have just ordered her breakfast and not asked her nurse's permission. I could also have just turned off the beeping machines at the last birth. I don't have to get the official okay either just to unplug monitors to take my client to the bathroom. But I have discovered that by setting the tone with these completely benign protocols I can get an awful lot of mileage with the birth team. I often try to find one or two ways of deferring to them early on in labor. It is a kind of body language that almost suggests subliminally that we can work together just fine and that I am not there as a raving advocate for my lady, ready to do battle on her turf. Somewhere along the line doulas, and midwives too, for that matter, have been seen as radical militants, and many health care professionals are not happy to see us. I am trying to change that image by looking for ways to work together and earn some respect for our profession. So far it has worked very well. They can tell right away that I have a relationship with the mom that they don't have, especially when a nurse suggests something and the mom wants my opinion on it. That could set me up for becoming a referee, which is not who I am. I just know that the nurse would go right back to the nurses' station and inform all of the other nurses that they'd "Better look out for that doula back there, guys."

A few years ago I was at a birth with a first-time mom and the baby was definitely not tolerating labor well. His heart rate decelerated with each rush and took a whole two minutes to recover before the next rush. Finally, his heart rate stopped going back up all together. Her doctor was worried and asked her to consider a C-section since she wasn't even dilated to six centimeters yet. She did not want a C-section, she wanted a natural birth, which we had talked about for weeks. She turned to me, with the whole birth team looking on, and said, "Stephanie, tell me what to do!"

I told her, "Dear Felicity, I wish I knew what to do, but if this was my birth, my baby, I would go for it. I would have a Cesarean right now." She couldn't see the doctor's face from where she was but I could. He was visibly shocked that I would be on "their side." I had never considered sides; I just assumed we all wanted the very best for this sweet lady and her baby, though he had assumed otherwise.

In an article recently posted by the doula organization DONA International called "Commentary: Nurses, Doulas, and Childbirth Educators—Working Together for Common Goals," Amy L. Gilliland wrote, ". . .one of the biggest challenges our doulas have experienced is trying to build relationships with hospital staff and forge a place for ourselves in the case room and on the birth support team." The article went on to eloquently state, "Birth is an experience parents and especially mothers will remember forever. The behavior and acceptance of the hospital staff coupled with the interactions they have with birth doulas will make the difference for each woman and her childbirth experience. This can result in a safe, woman-centered and empowering birthing experience, or one filled with tension, resentment and disempowerment . . . the choice is yours."

Stacy got out of the tub and decided to walk around for a while. Finally, baby was ready to come. I let Becky stand by Stacy's head to coach the pushing stage. I helped by holding her leg and massaging it when it started cramping. After some serious pushing the perfect, beautiful little guy arrived. Then I pitched in to help the nurses clean her up and change the bedding, her little boy on her chest the whole time.

I went home and slept, ate, and napped again and tried to get back to feeling normal. I did the laundry, thinking no one else could go into labor until I had clean clothes hanging and ready to go.

The next morning the chocolate bars and Cheetos lady called to tell me that her water broke but there were no contractions yet. I shouted my congratulations into the phone and told her I would meet her soon. Her first birth was induced, heavily medicated, and basically a blur, so I knew that much of this birth process would be new to her.

We walked the halls, danced, and did circular exercises on the birth ball until she got discouraged and asked for an epidural. She agreed to try the tub first, which she really liked. Then she got back to bed and explored the range of available meds with her nurse. She was able to rest and continued to dilate. It was getting close. The meds were wearing off and she asked for more but before the next dose arrived she shrieked: "I gotta shit!"

I laughed and hugged her and said, "Honey, that's your baby coming!"

She insisted even louder, "No it ain't!" and started pushing really well. I helped her sit up so she could push more effectively and helped her rest between the rushes. After one rush she looked over at me and said, "Today is the day my momma died." I hugged her again and told her that I was sure her momma could see her and would always be watching over her.

She named her chubby baby girl after her mother. Her three-year-old slept through the entire thing, rolled up in a lounge chair in the corner of the room, his tiny teddy tucked under his chin. He had quite a surprise when he woke up.

The next day, I gathered up the diapers and baby clothes I'd been collecting for her. I would visit later that evening. It is kind of sad when I say goodbye to my moms. We have been through so much together. In a way we have bonded and they may have become closer to me than they have ever been able to be with another woman. I wonder if I miss them more than they miss me. I think so, mostly because they are now very busy sleep-deprived mamas, entertaining friends and family who come to visit the newest member of the tribe and many also shortly return to school or work.

I am sure they will never forget the memory of their births, though. And if they look back and think of those times as wonderful, powerful, sacred, holy, and blessed, even if I am just a fleeting shadow in that picture, I have done my job well.

"The two most important days in your life are the day you are born and the day you find out why."
~Mark Twain

Chapter Seventeen
An Arabian Night

Anushe's birth had been going particularly well. The room was full of women, old and young, all beneath their *burkas*, robes, skirts, and lacy slips. Sandals were piling up by the doorway. I didn't understand a word of what was going on. It was just a very jolly celebration of life: a baby was going to be born tonight. This could have been happening four hundred years ago, or a thousand; in this hospital or in a tent in a desert. The scene has always been the same: low lights, grandmas sitting on the floor on rugs retelling their own labors, younger women tending to the midnight snack, the smell of fresh hot *naan* bread, and warm sweet tea filling the room.

The only thing in the picture that didn't exactly fit was me. But Anushe was adamant that she would have a doula. I had gotten to know her over the past weeks and, though she didn't speak much English and I didn't know any Urdu or Farsi, we understood each other. Her husband, a taxi driver in the city, had translated at most of our meetings. I explained that my job was to ensure, as best I could, her wishes for the birth, which were mostly that she wanted to eat and drink during labor, that she didn't want to be checked a lot, and that she did not want drugs at all. This wasn't her first birth so she knew what she was asking. I assured her that, along with the nurses, we would honor her wishes and let her know if we became concerned about anything along the way. The hospital had interpreters in abundance. We had a birth plan.

She dilated about one centimeter per hour, which is average. I could tell by her breathing when things started getting stronger, though. The discussions also heated up at one point, though I didn't have a clue what had changed. It turned out that some of the younger women were telling her how much easier an epidural would make labor. The opinions flew back and forth for a while as I sipped my tea. Finally, Anushe turned to me and said she wanted to try it. I conveyed her message to the nurses and she got set up for her epidural. She was at six centimeters when the anesthesiologist came in. When it was all in place, she leaned back in bed, grateful for a break from the rushes.

At one point her husband made an appearance and she turned toward him and let out a long string of something. I assumed she had said something like, "I am doing just fine. You go home and keep the kids happy. And make sure they all bathe tonight . . ."

He nodded and left. I was surprised when he was back only fifteen minutes later with a huge, hot, dripping Italian meatball hoagie, which she proceeded to devour. She had perhaps two bites left when the nurse came back in the room, looked at the remaining morsel, frowned at me and said with obvious disgust, "You know that is going to come right back up!"

I just shrugged and said, "I am ready," pointing to an emesis basin on the nightstand.

A few minutes later it seemed the epidural simply wore off. We were back to square one again, breathing together, with Anushe singing a funny little "Whowhowhoooooooo" song after each rush. Then her breath caught and she pushed.

I hit the nurse button and said, "We are pushing in room 4245" but at the same moment I could see the little head crowning. I don't really remember a second push. He was just here—pink and squealing and grabbing at the air.

I started patting him off with a corner of the sheet as the nurses flooded into the room and took over. (The hoagie did not make a second appearance, by the way.) The same nurse scowled at me again as if this precipitous second stage was my fault.

When Baby and mom were cleaned up and tucked back in bed with fresh sheets I settled into a chair in the corner and started to fill in my statistics report. Anushe kept rubbing her head, retying her scarf, then taking it off, and then asked for a cool washcloth. She was getting a whopper of a headache, which I explained was a common side effect of the epidural.

The women in the room all joined the conversation and I didn't think much more of it, though we let the nurse know and asked for something to help with the headache. One of the grandmothers looked through the cupboards in the room and, finding a bath towel, wrapped it tightly around Anushe's head. Another grandmother took the sleeping baby from her and settled in a chair with him. Another woman pulled out a cell phone from the yards of skirt fabric and started a very lively conversation with someone at the other end.

Soon more people were coming into the room. There were older men and their wives and they all started chanting. It was obvious to me they were reciting *surahs* (chapters from the Quran) because every few words was "Allah." This went on for a couple of hours, growing louder and louder. I finally prepared to leave, promising to come back for a postpartum visit in the morning. On my way out I asked one of the younger women if this was what they did at all births. She said, "No, this isn't normal at all. She has a *jinn* who is giving her a migraine headache. He entered her after she gave birth. They have to ask Allah to send the *jinn* away. It is like a devil." Oh. Wow. *The Arabian Nights* flashed through my brain in that moment. They believed there was a genie loose in here. My heart skipped a beat and then started racing.

I didn't know what to think. Anushe was just resting with her eyes closed, not in any dire pain it seemed, but just resigned to whatever the elders were doing. She obviously was not overly anxious by this turn of events and seemed to know what was going on around her. I decided not to mention this latest event to the nurses, thinking they would just go ahead with the usual protocols anyway—blood pressures, temps, fundal massage, and so on, which is what they did.

When I returned in the morning Anushe was sound asleep, as were two other women who had spent the night with her. The baby was nowhere to be seen. Rather than wake them, I went out to the nurses' station and asked if the baby had gone to the nursery. The nurse told me that the dad had taken the baby home with some of the grandmothers, explaining that his wife should rest for the day and he would pick her up the next morning. I couldn't believe it. Didn't they know their baby needed to nurse, and that she needed him close? The nurse said that the family told her they had formula at home and went on to explain that the hospital couldn't refuse the family if the mom was in agreement, so that is what they did. It was so bizarre! No wonder she had a baby every year, if this was her version of breastfeeding. And it was no wonder she ovulated right after each birth, following the Muslim injunction to shun birth control, but also ignoring the Quran's recommendation that all babies be nursed for two years, which would have naturally spaced their children.

I visited with Anushe when she woke up. I didn't want to register my unhappiness but tried to tactfully ask if she would be nursing once she was back home, which she convinced me she would. She fully trusted that her aunts were taking great care of her baby for her until she had weathered this uninvited intrusion by whatever had visited the night before. I asked if she wanted me to visit her at home in a week, which she said would be great.

The following week I went to their apartment in the housing projects. One elevator serviced all twenty-eight floors. I played sardines with at least thirty other people crammed into it on the way up, trying in vain not to rub up against one of the Muslim men, thus causing him to have to immediately wash again before prayer.

I was relieved to see that Anushe was nursing Abdulahai (pronounced ab-DOO-luh-hi) and he was already filling out his little pudgy frame. I didn't bring up the demon possession again. She said she was happy with her little boy after having two girls. Then she told me that her first two children were also boys, by her first husband who had died back home. They were eleven and twelve years old, still babies in my book. I could instantly picture my own two boys at that age. How could she stand being away from them? She explained that their father's family was taking very good care of them and she was hopeful they could come to the U.S. in the next couple of years.

As we sat down to eat lunch I realized that I didn't have a clue what these people had been through.

"Waking up this morning, I smile. Twenty-four brand new hours are before me. I vow to live fully in each moment and to look at all beings with eyes of compassion."
~Thich Nhat Hanh

Chapter Eighteen

Rhoda

I received Rhoda's referral for a doula late in her thirty-seventh week. She had gone to a few childbirth classes but was not super prepared for this birth. As we talked at our first meeting, I realized she had other priorities. Addressing the abuse issues in her relationship was paramount. Getting the help she needed for her depression came next. At least she knew when to ask for help. We had work to do, though, to prepare for her baby, so I offered a plan: I could meet her at her prenatal appointments twice a week and spend time afterward covering the childbirth education series and talking over any questions she might have. She was easy to talk with and very open about her situation. I knew we would work well together.

Her baby had experienced a concerning amount of tachycardia, a racing heartbeat, in his seventh month. She had been admitted to the hospital at that time so they could figure out what might help her baby. When she was discharged, she was referred to a high-risk clinic that would closely monitor him. There was some talk of inducing her at thirty-eight or thirty-nine weeks. By going to her prenatal appointments I was able to meet her OB, a wonderful woman, and ask my own questions about their birth plan. I was glad I could tell her OB that I was looking forward to supporting her at this birth and working together. I get a lot of mileage out of using the word "support" with doctors. It tells them right away that I respect their role at the birth and that I do not have a natural-birth-only agenda.

With a "high risk" label already in place, Rhoda's options were a bit narrower than I would have hoped for. I knew I would be with

Rhoda 200% more of the time than any other single caregiver during this birth, and that number would go up with each additional hour of labor.

Rhoda had warmed up right away at our first meeting. I asked the clinic if I could use one of the rooms after her appointment to watch my doula video with her so she wouldn't have to figure out how to add one more appointment to her busy schedule. She was still in therapy, went to a support group, and the high-risk pregnancy meant extra OB visits, ultrasounds, and monitoring. They were very accommodating and we agreed to do it again with the breastfeeding videos at her next appointment at the clinic. I hoped to bring up the subject of induction, too, before it was scheduled, so she would be prepared.

We met again the following week and talked about her birth plan and what she expected from me as her doula. This gave me a chance to tune into her expectations and talk about what her labor might look like and how we could work together to help her to be comfortable without medication, which was her wish for this birth. The nurse gave her all the information for the following Monday's induction and answered all of her questions. We had our breastfeeding class, watching two of my favorite teaching videos, then she tried different nursing positions with my baby doll, Tofiq, before we packed up to wait for her taxi.

While we were waiting, she told me that she didn't feel right about being induced. Her baby looked great through all the last tests the clinic has ordered, so what would be wrong, she asked me, to wait another five days and see if she went into labor naturally? I explained that she had a valid point, but that she would need to ask her OB what her thinking was. The doctor may have just assumed that because Rhoda's pregnancy was considered high risk the baby would be better out so he could be treated if there was an issue, thus an induction was warranted. But did the doctor really have a valid reason for inducing at what might be two or even three weeks early? The last thing I wanted, which would reflect badly on all doulas, was to have Rhoda say her doula told her she might not have to be induced, so I was extremely careful how I worded my response.

I explained that there were a few sides to this puzzle. First, they wanted to do everything possible to ensure that her baby was okay, so they turned to all the available technology (interventions) to be sure they "are doing everything possible." That also would hold up in court and protect the hospital from "not doing enough" should a suit ever be filed. Second, their hospital was being watched, just like every other hospital, to see if they were attempting to limit or lower their C-section rates and thus attract more clients (money is the motive here). Were they perhaps thinking that her chances of having a C-section might go up with every week until her due date? I didn't know. Third, there might actually be data from studies that show that this kind of pediatric heart problem has a better outcome when they don't wait until term. Rhoda's doctor hadn't told us that—yet. So I proposed she ask and find out what was really going on, and she could ask for one more week to see if labor would start on its own. I could not, as a doula, encourage her to push for waiting for labor on its own.

I may have the experience and knowledge from my years working as a midwife, but the doctor doesn't know that, and it is not in my "scope of practice" as a doula. I also knew that this particular hospital keeps abreast of the very latest research and may have a very good reason based on "best practice" that I would not have even heard about yet.

Rhoda said she would call me that night. I was surprised and glad that she had come up with questions on her own. I somehow imagined she was of the school of thought that dictates, "Doctors know best, just do whatever they say." Again, all I could tell her was, "Welcome to parenthood, my dear. This is the beginning of many tests of your strength and courage." I assured her that I thought she would be a great mom.

After the conversation with her doctor, Rhoda felt that they truly were doing what was in her baby's best interest. I assured her during our phone conversation that we parents frequently doubt, after the fact, that we have made the right choices, but this is the new territory all parents find ourselves in. We have to make choices that are best for us and our family. Sure, we will make mistakes, but we have to work with what we know at that moment. I believe our kids know, or will know, that we did our best, always, for them.

We met at the hospital on B-day. We went over her options for pain meds and some of her wishes. She didn't want to be asked repeatedly about her pain level. She had done her homework and knew she could ask if she wanted something for pain. She wanted to try the tub, birth ball, and different positions first. She definitely did not want male providers during the birth, if at all possible, and no extra interns or students milling about. She absolutely didn't feel comfortable having to deal with crowds of people.

It was Sunday evening and the plan was to use a prostaglandin cervical "ripener" called Cervidil or dinoprostone, which is inserted into the cervix, sits there for twelve hours while the mother sleeps, hopefully, and prepares the uterus for further induction in the morning. Occasionally, the Cervadil alone will initiate labor. I had encouraged Rhoda to eat a good supper before going to the hospital because, I cautioned, she might not be able to eat much once in active labor. Each hospital I work in has a slightly different protocol for this.

Her partner took her out for supper and they arrived in a great mood, ready to welcome their baby into the world. I had brought two of my favorite movies, which we settled down to watch together after the Cervidil was in place. Rhoda had been concerned that the insertion of the Cervidil would hurt and was relieved that it didn't.

We watched *Birth Story*, which also helped set the mood in the room. The DVD has a "down-on-the-farm" feel—literally. It's about Ina May Gaskin and The Farm midwives in Tennessee. This initiated several questions about the use of imagery during labor and we talked about several aspects of that after the video. Then we watched *Everybody Loves . . . Babies*, which brought up lots of observations about parenting in other cultures and models of bonding.

Three hours later, Rhoda was ready to sleep. The nurse brought in some juice for her and a pile of bedding for her partner so he could fold out the lounge chair/cot next to the bed. I lived very close to the hospital so I suggested I go home and sleep, too, assuring them I could return within ten minutes should they want me to come back; otherwise, I would be there when they talked with the doctors in the morning about the next plan of action. They agreed and settled in for the night.

I didn't hear anything during the night and both of them were still sound asleep when I arrived the next morning. They were up, though, when the doctors came at 9:00 a.m. Rhoda's OB checked her cervix, which was three centimeters dilated. Great news! They suggested augmenting the labor with a small dose of Pitocin to encourage contractions that, in turn, would hopefully help her to fully dilate. The couple agreed and the nurse unplugged the monitors to let Rhoda shower and walk around for a while. Before the doctors left I asked if she could eat until she was in active labor. They readily agreed so we ordered a big breakfast. She told me she wasn't sure she could eat and was afraid that she would throw up later if she did, but I reminded her that it could be an all-day or even an all-day-and-all-night process and that she needed the calories and natural sugars on board to do it. I assured her we were prepared if she did feel her breakfast coming back up and showed her the drawer by the bed stocked with Chux pads and the little disposable "hats" for "returning" meals. I laughed and told her we were very used to it and that after you are a mother it doesn't bother you as much as before.

I opened the curtains to a beautiful sunny morning. Her breakfast tray was delivered and Rhoda tucked in. I encouraged her partner to get some breakfast in the cafeteria. He hesitated until I assured him that he had plenty of time and wouldn't miss the birth even if he was gone an hour.

The nurse started the Pitocin at the lowest possible dose. Baby's fetal heart tones sounded great on the monitors and Rhoda was quite rested and feeling well. The monitor picked up some contractions but not strong enough for Rhoda to feel. Throughout the morning the couple rested, walked, and she sat on the birth ball. She ordered lunch at noon.

The Pitocin was increased and by 2:00 p.m. Rhoda was having rushes every five minutes and had dilated to four centimeters. I asked the nurse for a dilation chart and went over it with the couple. We talked about imagining opening up and I told them how I had seen it help and knew it helped my own births. By evening we were working together to breathe through the rushes, which were coming every three minutes and getting stronger. Before her doctor left at the end of her shift, she checked Rhoda again. Four centimeters. This was discouraging for Rhoda but I explained that induction is not the same as natural labor and often takes longer.

I assured her that she was holding up well and her baby still sounded good, that there was no need to do anything differently. The doctors were not in any rush. I explained that it is far better to go slowly because it gives the baby's head plenty of time to mold and this slowly stretches the birth canal, rather than tearing it from going too fast. By just reminding the couple that their birth was going really well, they could relax and try to rest another night. Again I went home to sleep. The phone didn't ring all night.

By the time I returned in the morning, the nurse was checking her once again—four centimeters. She explained that they really didn't want to break her water until the baby was a little further down in her pelvis. It was still early. We took turns eating and walking with Rhoda.

Around noon, two doctors came in to say that although the baby still sounded good, they didn't feel that the Pitocin was doing much and they wanted to see her dilating better. They suggested that she rest a while and offered some fentanyl or morphine to take the edge off the pain and give her a break since she didn't sleep much during the night. Rhoda agreed and was sound asleep in no time.

She was almost six centimeters when she woke up. Her water had broken on its own. But by evening the doctors once again gathered to talk to the couple. First they explained that although the baby still sounded good, they were afraid that Rhoda's uterus would become tired, and if labor went on much longer it might be more prone to hemorrhage after birth.

They had checked her when they first entered the room and her cervix was back down to five centimeters and swollen. Even though the water bag was now out of the way, the baby had not budged at all, possibly because the cervix/uterus was tired or that the baby was still so far up that the cervix didn't have the baby's hard head to dilate against, which we expected it to be doing by then. They offered a Cesarean section, explaining that she could wait another two hours or ten hours, but she might still end up with a C-section. Rhoda and her partner asked for a couple of hours to think about it and the doctors left.

Rhoda tried to figure out what she was "doing wrong" and I explained that she was not doing anything at all wrong and that we don't always have control over our births. She wanted to know if she should try imagery, or walking more, or lunges, or "maybe we can just go home and come back next week?"

I offered to leave the room so they could talk but they both wanted me to stay. Then it occurred to me that perhaps they were totally in the dark about what happens during a C-section so I asked them if they wanted me to explain. They both nodded.

I told them that the operating room was not much bigger than the room they were in, but it also had a warmer for the baby and two NRP nurses waiting nearby to help their baby breathe if he needed it. I explained that only one in about 1,000 babies will actually need neonatal resuscitation and some just need suctioning and stimulation to get going. I explained that the OR would be bright and that she would get an epidural but would be awake the whole time, which surprised her very much. She just assumed she would be "knocked out" and the baby forced out somehow.

I assured them that her partner would be sitting by her head and be able to hold her hand, and that I would be on the same side of a big sterile drape and would tell her everything that was going on and what to expect. I described the "bikini" cut, that the incision would be low on her tummy in the fold of skin above her pubic bone.

She would have two doctors, one on each side of her stomach, two anesthesiologists, several nurses floating around the room, another one at the instrument table and possibly a resident doctor or two. (We actually managed to avoid having any men at this birth, which I had forgotten we had requested earlier. She would not have noticed by then, but I was touched that they had honored her wishes.)

I told her that it usually only takes about twenty-five minutes or less from when they start before they lift the baby out and get him right to the warmer. Often the dad can go over there with him and touch his baby and take pictures before bringing him over to mom. She could hold him and talk to him then if he was breathing well and didn't need any help and she could even try nursing. Then she would be sewn up, starting with the uterus, then the surrounding muscles, and lastly the outer skin would be stapled shut.

She and Baby would go to the recovery room together, probably in the same bed with her holding him. She would be there about two hours before going to her room on the postpartum floor, where dad could spend the night and their baby could room-in, and she could finally eat and celebrate his birth.

I went on to say she would be in the hospital three or four days and have time to rest and recuperate. I explained that it is a longer recovery than a vaginal birth and that she should ask her family and friends for help during the first three to four weeks at least.

I realized that by demystifying the entire surgery it had become a choice they were willing to make. She asked if she could first meet the doctor who would do the surgery. She wanted to be okay with the new doctor. The nurse arranged for the doctor to come in, who was also a woman, and they clicked immediately.

When it was over, Rhoda couldn't believe how fast it went or that she was already holding her baby. Rhoda was a very petite Latina señora, so I was not surprised that her *hijo muy guapo* (very handsome son) was just under six pounds. The moment the doctor lifted him up, head first, she said out loud, "Oh, so you were trying to come down forehead first!"

It is called a brow presentation, which explained why the cervix didn't have anything hard to dilate against and also why he remained too far up in her pelvis. He wasn't in a total face and flexed neck presentation, but it was obvious he was looking up, basically, at the start of his descent. His face and forehead were very swollen and the front of his head had tried to mold, but the back of his head had not even begun to. So we had our answers about what was going on.

I always marvel at how nature does and also does not do things according to any script. The last time I had seen anything like this birth was almost thirty years ago, when I was called late one night to translate in the labor and delivery department of a big public hospital in St. Paul. A Hmong family was having their first baby, who was presenting face first. The family did not like the idea of an operation at all. They had emigrated only a year earlier from Laos and had their own set of beliefs surrounding birth and death and bad spirits that might enter a body once it is cut open. And this was a pregnant body, besides. No, they would not okay a C-section, which the doctors were recommending and hoped I would talk them into. The mother-in-law was pacing around the room when I arrived. I listened for a minute and realized she was basically saying, "Let her die. No *uah-pi* (operation). We will get him another *too-paw-nia chia* (wife)."

The first thing I did was have Grandma removed. The poor girl was terrified that she was dying! And that they were going to let her. I assured her that she had some options and that she didn't need to worry. The dad was just as terrified as she was. I explained that the baby was coming down okay, though his face would look funny and swollen for a while but it should be fine after a few days.

They had two options: continue with a vaginal birth, though that might not be easy, or go with a C-section. I knew they couldn't go against their elders' wishes and had absolutely no recourse there, but I explained that they did have a say in our country and we would support them. They both said they wanted to try a vaginal birth, though the doctors had hoped I would simply talk them into surgery. I couldn't. I knew that the entire clan had been called together and consulted already and their answer had been "no." I also didn't believe that her life was in imminent danger so I didn't go into my "take charge" mode and try to scare them further. I didn't tell the doctors that I tried my best to talk them into a C-section but I simply said they were going for a vaginal birth and that they understood the implications. I told the couple that she wouldn't die, though she might have in the primitive conditions back in Laos. I tried to help them feel that the doctors really were on their side and wanted to help them. I don't believe the doctors had ever said she could die if she didn't have a C-section. They just strongly suggested that it was a better route with a first baby and the grandmother took off from there. She gave birth to their baby shortly after that and it went quite well.

That was decades earlier and this little guy had tried the same thing. I couldn't help but wonder if it would not have shown up on a late ultrasound in Rhoda's case, which she was having often anyway because of the earlier tachycardia episodes. It was also a bit curious that with all of the internal exams no one picked up on the different alignment of the baby's head sutures, or even feel the nose, but I could only wonder to myself.

I went back for a postpartum visit the next day and found Rhoda walking a bit stiffly around her room, but ecstatic. She was just happy that her baby boy was here and that she felt as well as she did. The C-section was definitely not as bad as she had imagined. I gave her a (very gentle) hug and told her how very proud we all were of her. I reminded her that she had done the very best she could and was an amazing and strong lady.

"You are assisting at someone else's birth. Do good without show or fuss. Facilitate what is happening rather than what you think ought to be happening. If you must take the lead, lead so that the mother is helped, yet still free and in charge. When the baby is born, the mother will rightly say, 'We did it ourselves!'"
~Lao Tzu, father of Chinese Taoism, from Tao Te Ching: The Way of All Life, written in the sixth century B.C.E.

Chapter Nineteen
Doula as Gatekeeper

Midwife: "I would like to check to see if you have dilated."
Vietnamese interpreter: "Tôi muốn xem tử cung bạn đã giãn chưa."
Midwife: "Is that okay?"
Interpreter: "Có được không?"

My client, Khou, only spoke Vietnamese. She was a beautiful first-time mom whose water broke two days earlier but had just called me.

Midwife: "Now, put your heels together and let your knees fall back."
Interpreter: "Bây giờ, đặt gót chân của bạn với nhau và để hãy thả lỏng đầu gối."
Midwife: "You can relax. That's better."
Interpreter: "Đừng lo, đúng rồi."
Midwife: "Now you will feel my touch."
Interpreter: "Bây giờ bạn sẽ cảm thấy tay tôi."

I could only guess that she was either expecting labor to start with contractions first, or a huge gush. A small tear high up in the bag of water can drip like a leaky faucet and was obviously not noteworthy to this mama. As soon as she called me I insisted on meeting her at the hospital and asked her to let her midwife know before she left the house.

Midwife: "Now I want to put this speculum inside to look." She held up the speculum.

Interpreter: "Bây giờ tôi muốn đặt mỏ vịt này bên trong để xem."
Midwife: "Sorry it's cold."
Interpreter: "Sẽ lạnh một chút."
Midwife: "I will first test and see if this is amniotic fluid; this won't hurt."
Interpreter: "Đầu tiên tôi sẽ xem đây có phải nước ối không; nó sẽ không đau đâu."

This little exchange would have been fine and dandy except for the fact that the agency sent a male interpreter that night. I couldn't believe what I was hearing.

Midwife: "All done."
Interpreter: "Xong rồi!"
Midwife: "But your water has broken. It seems that it started two days ago."
Interpreter: "Nhưng bạn đã vỡ nước ối. Có vẻ như nó bắt đầu từ 2 ngày trước."
Midwife: "There is some concern that labor hasn't started and we want to avoid an infection."
Interpreter: "Tôi lo rằng bạn chưa lâm bồn và chúng tôi muốn phòng ngừa nhiễm trùng . . ."

When he first walked into the room I had leaped off of my perch on a little exam stool by Khou's bed, looked straight at him and said, "You and I will go behind that curtain by the door and you can translate from there!" as I ushered him away from the bedside.

Midwife: "So would it be okay if we started labor with something that will soften the cervix tonight?"
Interpreter: "Chúng ta có thể bắt đầu chuẩn bị sinh với cái gì đó làm cho tử cung mềm hơn tối nay có được không?"

Midwife: "And hopefully get things going in the morning?"
Interpreter: "Và hy vọng có thể bắt đầu vào buổi sáng?"

There was no way I would have him gawking at Khou lying there. I couldn't believe they sent him!

Midwife: "Yes? Okay. I am going to put some medicine into your vagina and into the cervix."
Interpreter: "Có? Okay. Tôi sẽ đặt một số thuốc vào âm đạo của bạn và vào cổ tử cung."

I was about ready to stomp out to the nurses' station and demand a woman interpreter. How could they do this? I was furious!

Midwife: "You will need to stay flat for two hours now. Do you need to go to the bathroom first?"
Interpreter: "Bạn sẽ cần phải ở lại căn hộ cho 2 giờ sau đó. Bạn cần phải đi vào nhà vệ sinh trước không?"

Why should you come to a foreign country and have to put up with this? I thought. *I would feel so humiliated!*

Midwife: "Can you put your fists under your bottom so I can reach your cervix a little better?"
Interpreter: "Bạn có thể đặt nắm tay của bạn dưới mông của bạn để tôi có thể tiếp cận cổ tử cung của bạn tốt hơn một chút được không?"

It was awful! He acted as if he does this every day. He *does* do it every day. It's his job. She must have been feeling *so* embarrassed.

The last time I had to throw someone out during a birth was when I worked at a free-standing birthing clinic and found both sides of the family of the couple in the kitchen smoking up a storm and setting up a bar. They were going to party until their baby was born. I tried to nicely explain that we weren't set up like a hospital exactly, we didn't have a waiting room, and we would need the run of the whole floor so she could walk around during labor (not to mention any other clients who might show up that night to fill the remaining two birthing suites). I suggested a motel down the road—some of them had driven from more than an hour away—so they reluctantly packed up and camped out in our parking lot for a while, serving drinks from the car's trunk until it started raining around midnight. We assured them we would have the couple call them when the baby arrived. BYOB to a birth? Really?

Midwife: "Just breathe slowly. You will feel my touch now . . ."
Interprer: "Hãy thở chậm lại. Bây giờ bạn sẽ cảm thấy tay tôi . . ."

How humiliating! "You will feel my touch now . . ." said the smooth, deep voice coming from behind a flimsy curtain.

Midwife: "Just breathe slowly. Great. Thank you."
Interpreter: "Thở chậm lại. Tuyệt vời. Cảm ơn bạn."
Midwife: "I hope you can get some sleep now."
Interpreter: "Tôi hy vọng bạn có thể ngủ một lúc bây giờ."
Midwife: "I'll check back in the morning."
Interpreter: "Tôi sẽ kiểm tra lại vào buổi sáng."

One Friday night I brought my baby doll Tofiq when I met with Khou. We had been meeting for the past three months discussing her birth plan, seeing videos together on birth and the stages of labor, and breast-feeding, and going to classes about interventions and options. She asked if I had a camera and begged me to bring it to her birth. I promised I would.

Khou, though barely eighteen, had asked at our last appointment who was going to teach her how to bathe her baby when s/he was born, so I arranged for a translator and we all crammed into her tiny bathroom that evening: Khou; the interpreter; the shelter director, a young social worker who had never bathed a baby before, either, and had asked to come; and Tofiq and I. So I filled the tub, lined up the soap, shampoo, towel, and washcloth, and gave Tofiq a real bath, showing Khou how to first test the temperature of the water by dipping in an elbow and then how to support him in the water (he is even anatomically correct, which sent her into giggles). Then I had her do it all over again by herself. She did a great job until she laid him on the towel on the floor. I suggested at that point that her baby looked pretty cold to me. She quickly dried him off and wrapped him up in the towel and held him close, looking up at me for approval. I said he looked better but, "Look, his mouth is open and he is probably hungry."

A look of panic spread across her face. I didn't need the interpreter to repeat what she said then: "Oh, no!" as in, "What do I do now?" So we had a mini class there on the bathroom floor about how to get him in the best position for nursing: "Belly to belly, chest to chest . . . nose and chin should touch the breast."

She reminded me for the umpteenth time to be sure to bring a camera to the birth. I promised again that I would.

Midwife: "Well, you have dilated to five centimeters! That's great news!"
Interpreter, as he clipped his nails: "Ồ, bạn đã giãn ra đến 5 cm! Thật tuyệt!"

I rummaged through the cupboards in the room until I found a dilation chart. I got the interpreter to explain what dilation is and what "five" looked like. Finally, I said, "You can go now." I pointed to the door and thanked him. At last he was gone. It wasn't his fault. But couldn't he protest? She could have been his daughter, for heaven's sake!

Doulas sometimes need reminding to breathe slowly, too. I would explain myself in pantomime from now on if I had to and show Khou how she would open up the rest of the way until she could push her baby out.

The nurse wheeled in some kind of a reclining lounge chair and to my utter surprise made it up with clean sheets and pillows for me. Khou and I finished the last of the snacks I had brought and I went down to the nutrition room and got us hot drinks. Most hospitals will even give doulas the door combinations to the kitchen or linen closet so we can help ourselves and take care of our moms without having to get a nurse every time. Warm blankets? No problem. Just dial 1-5-3-2 on the door's lock pad.

The rushes continued for another two hours but eventually settled down and Khou was sound asleep by about 3:00 a.m. I slept too and didn't hear anything until she called my name at 8:00 a.m. In her limited English she sheepishly said, "Stephy-ah, me hungry." I stretched, got out of my little bed and fumbled around the bedside stand until I found the folder with the menu options and the extension to call to order meals. She knew the words for "bread," "eggs," "tea," and "meat," so I ordered it. While we waited for her breakfast, she again asked if I had the camera ready. I pointed to it sitting on the counter.

When the food tray arrived she dove into it. They had included a blueberry muffin, which instantly became her favorite American food. She tried to order just blueberry muffins for lunch but we were told they were only a breakfast option. Later that day I let the secretary at the ward's front desk know so she could make sure Khou got two blue-berry muffins on her tray every morning while she was in the hospital.

Soon after she finished eating, the rushes started again in full force (it is amazing what a little food and sleep will do) and breakfast suddenly made a surprise appearance once again. I told her not to worry about it and helped her clean up and rinse her mouth. I told her what Ina May Gaskin says about this: that you actually dilate one centimeter every time you vomit during labor. It works this way because a person can't totally relax their throat and mouth without also relaxing the sphincter muscles down below.

Before long Khou's labor was picking up speed beautifully. We stood, we walked, she sat on the birth ball. She asked for pain medicine at one point and asked about an epidural (and in the same breath asked if I still had the camera handy). The midwife said that she could get an epidural if she wanted it, but that she had other options too, and suggested some fentanyl, which would take the edge off the pain but still allow her to be up and moving around. She explained that it worked for an hour or two at the most. Khou said she wanted something and agreed to try it. She was very happy with the results and was able to rest. She asked again if I had the camera ready and I assured her I did as I pointed to it on the bedside stand. She closed her eyes and was able to manage the rushes better.

She asked the midwife the next time she was in the room if Mary, the midwife she had been seeing in clinic, was going to be at her birth. She was assured that Mary had been called. Khou again closed her eyes. We breathed through each rush and then rested. We were in a pattern now: "Breathe . . . slowly . . . blow it away . . . rest. Breathe . . . slowly . . . blow it away . . . good work!"

Suddenly Khou's eyes opened wide and she said, "I go toilet now!" I knew this was the urge to push without even knowing if she was at ten centimeters. The midwife with us did, too, and didn't even check her cervix. Then Khou asked, "Where is Mary? I want Mary!" just as Mary walked in.

She checked Khou and said, "Well, she's complete. Can we get the room ready?" The nurses spun into action. The warmer was turned on. They checked the equipment, unfolded baby blankets and stacked up towels as Mary robed up and I tied the strings on the back of her gown.

We helped Khou lean forward from her sitting position and put a squatting bar in place while I stacked pillows behind her with one hand, the camera ready in my other hand. The nurse lowered the end of the bed slightly before the next rush. Khou flashed Mary a panicked glance, which we recognized as the classic "Tell me what I am supposed to do next" look. Mary smiled and told Khou that she was doing just great. She waited for the next rush and, nodding her head, said quietly, "You can push a little now." It took a few more rushes for Khou to get the hang of it but very quickly the little head was crowning. Then Baby literally dropped out onto the end of the bed during the next push, completely surprising Khou. If looks could talk, hers would have said, "Where did that baby come from?" I did get pictures, lots of them.

I voiced my complaint about the male interpreter as civilly as I could manage as I passed the nurses' desk on my next trip for coffee and was able to get a woman interpreter for my postpartum visit the following day. As I waited at my bus stop earlier that morning in front of a florist shop, it occurred to me that no one would be bringing Khou flowers after all her hard work. I wished I had the money for a huge bouquet but I didn't just then.

As I walked into Khou's room, a young nurse was arranging a beautiful little arrangement of pink tea roses on Khou's bedside table. It was the nurse's birthday and someone (special, I could imagine) had sent flowers but she said she wanted Khou to have them. I had never seen an act of kindness such as that in a hospital before.

I asked Khou if anyone had explained how or what they had done to fix the tear after her birth. She shook her head. Her midwife had simply explained that she was going to repair a tear, though I doubt any of it registered with Khou then. I knew she had been quite mystified by everything and could not take in one more thing, so I postponed that discussion.

When we did talk about it I drew a picture of her anatomy at the time of birth, explaining how the baby's head had stretched her vagina as he crowned. Then I drew a picture of what it looked like after birth, with the tear along the vagina's back wall. I explained that Mary had used a small round needle to first pull together the underlying muscle, pushing everything back into place there, and then closed the tear with small stitches along both edges of the torn skin. I told her that the string was a self-dissolving material so the stitches wouldn't need to be removed later. Then I told her that her midwife was a real artist and she looked absolutely beautiful down there. She questioned the interpreter, wondering if she had heard that last comment right and I assured her that she had, and that I had seen lots of women so I should know.

At this point another nurse came into the room to do a blood pressure check and stopped to look at the diagrams. She glanced at Khou and then back at me, looking very puzzled. I told her that no one had explained to

Doula as gatekeeper.

Khou what had happened or why, so I was taking the time to show her what had gone on "down there." I added, "I think she should know what happened and understand what was done to her own body." This seemed to be a completely foreign concept to this particular nurse.

Epilogue

Khou had been married before moving to the U.S. She arrived pregnant, with her husband and his parents. The home situation deteriorated quickly as culture shock set in and the men in the family could not find work and had to attend English classes, both of which they found profoundly humiliating. Apparently, from the little I know, Khou's husband took out his frustrations on her, which landed him in jail. She was placed in the shelter by the courts. When her baby was three months old she relocated with him to another state and with the help of an aunt there has been able to return to school and was recently accepted into a college.

[Heartfelt thanks to Mr. Vu Nguyen of the University of Minnesota, for his excellent translations for this story.]

"Putting women in the position of coping with conflict when they should be concentrating on having their babies counts as an intervention in itself!"
~Anonymous

Chapter Twenty

A Doula for a Doula

When Jessica came to Everyday Miracles for our first meeting, I gave her a tour of the offices and visited with her. She was quite excited about her baby and she and her husband had both already read a lot of information about natural birth and knew what they wanted. She gave me a copy of her birth plan, which looked perfect. I didn't add a thing. Then she told me she was in training to be a doula. *Oh, wow*, I thought. *This will be fun!*

She had taken the DONA birth doula course already and sent for the certification package. At that point she had two years to meet all the requirements and submit her paperwork. She had attended a few births already and was gathering the rest of the information she would need. I invited Jessica to meet at my apartment for her next appointment and offered to lend her any books that I had used when I was being certified. Thus began our friendship.

Since I didn't need to educate her about labor or breastfeeding we used the times we got together to look at birth videos. I had several other teaching videos that Jessica had not seen, so we watched those together and talked about everything about birth and doulas and midwives and hospitals.

It was just after 5:00 a.m. several weeks later when Jessica's husband, Jim, called to let me know she was in labor with regular rushes. I asked if I could speak to Jessica (which would give me a clue if this was early labor or the real thing by how well she could talk to me during a rush). I encouraged her to labor at home a while longer if she was comfortable there. I called back about an hour later not having heard again, and spoke to Jim because Jessica could no longer speak through the rushes. I asked if they were thinking of heading to the hospital soon and he said they were still thinking about it. I offered to come to their house but they felt they were doing okay on their own. When I called back another hour later I asked if they wanted to have this baby at home or in the hospital and that got them out the door in no time.

I was very excited for Jessica and had been looking forward to this birth. She was so down-to-earth, so well prepared, and so healthy, I knew it would be a great experience. I quickly dressed, checked my doula bag, and called a taxi. I was at the hospital within fifteen minutes. I asked at the desk if Jessica had shown up yet and they assured me they had not come in. A half-hour later, I checked at the desk again and they said she had still not arrived. They asked again what her last name was, and they couldn't find her in their system. I called Jim and quickly realized I was at the wrong hospital!

I had never done that before. I hadn't opened her chart; I just assumed I knew which hospital they were going to. Apologizing profusely, I hung up and again called the cab company. I couldn't believe it. Was I getting senile? After this birth I put a pad of paper and a pen next to my alarm clock and I ask every single time what hospital we are meeting at, even if I think I know, and write it down . . . each time.

I arrived at the right hospital twenty-five minutes later, wearing my "Happy Birthday" tiara. Jessica was still in the triage area of labor and delivery. There were no free rooms in the regular section. It was early, but there was really no room to move around at all. We couldn't walk around the halls because family members of all of the emergency room patients were milling around. After monitoring the baby for a while the nurse said she would let us know when something opened up on the floor.

In Jessica's own words: "We were finally moved to a labor and delivery room, though not in the midwife section, and they brought in a portable tub right away but had issues filling it, so y'all were grabbing buckets of water from the sinks to fill it. I had to pee but just couldn't and spent some time on the toilet whilst the tub was being filled . . . oh, and the popsicles, those were life-savers!

"Once filled, I labored in the tub until I got too warm, then stood in the tub and swayed and slow danced with Jim while you and my friend rubbed my back and fed me popsicles and water. Things were moving rather quickly. I came in at six and my waters broke—a water balloon between my legs—and a couple of hours later I was eight centimeters. Then things slowed down and I labored on all fours in bed while y'all reminded me to breathe and gave me my elixirs—water and popsicles. Once I felt the urge to push the midwife checked my cervix and I still had a lip on one side, which I later learned is a sign of the malposition of a baby's head. I waited until I could push."

Her midwife assured her that the baby sounded very good when she listened using a Doppler. Jessica explains, "Once pushing, I didn't feel like any progress was being made and asked if this was really possible." It was hard to tell her she was doing everything right when she knew her baby wasn't moving down much.

"They made me change positions a few times, not delightful in high-pushing mode, and I finally ended on my back with my legs in the air, pulling on the sheet attached to the squatting bar. [Finally we could see a tiny circle of baby's head.] Then the little guy came out after two-plus hours of pushing. Bring on the waffles! This mama's hungry!"

Jessica pushed for what seemed like forever and finally her baby boy was born, all nine pounds, six ounces of him. And as he came out, out of the corner of my eye I saw a geyser of blood shoot straight up in the air. The midwife was at the bedside and saw the blood at the same time. We both reacted immediately. Somehow it registered in my mind that the cord must have broken at that moment, and in one move I spun around, grabbed a medium forceps clamp from behind us on the table and, opening it up, handed it to the midwife. She pinched the cord still at baby's end with one hand and, taking the forceps, grabbed the placenta end of the cord as it disappeared back up into the birth canal.

A bruise on the side of the baby's head confirmed that he had been in an acyclic position, meaning his head was turned sideways, his ear almost touching his shoulder on his journey down to being born, which made it difficult to mold and descend properly. And now we knew his cord was short, too. We were just very grateful it didn't break before he was out, which would have been catastrophic. It had taken all that time to stretch so he could be born. It never ceases to amaze me how nature accommodates such exceptions to the rules.

The combination of all of these factors caused Jessica to sustain a fourth-degree tear, which caused some complications later on, though she was able to find help for it. Tears are graded by the depth of the tear into skin and muscle. First-degree vaginal tears are the least severe, involving only the skin around the vaginal opening and the birth canal. Although there might be some mild burning or stinging with urination, first-degree tears aren't severely painful and heal on their own within a few weeks, often without stitching.

Second-degree vaginal tears involve vaginal tissue and the perineal muscles—the muscles between the vagina and anus that help support the uterus, bladder and rectum. Second-degree tears typically require stitches and heal within a few weeks.

Third-degree vaginal tears involve the vaginal tissues, perineal muscles, and the muscle that surrounds the anus (anal sphincter). These tears sometimes require repair in an operating room, rather than the delivery room, and might take months to heal. Complications such as fecal incontinence and painful intercourse are possible.

Fourth-degree vaginal tears are the most severe. They involve the perineal muscles and anal sphincter as well as the tissue lining the rectum. Those who experience complications from severe vaginal tears are often referred to a urogynecologist, colorectal surgeon, or other specialist.

I saw Jessica and Taran a few months later. He was so amazingly strong, self-assured and inquisitive—a real "in arms" baby. The difference is very obvious to me when a baby's needs have been met during his early weeks and months and he has not been forced to "learn" to put himself to sleep or not been picked up when he needs that, thus spending more time than not "in arms." And Jessica, having herself been on this bizarre, wonderful, outrageous, momentous journey of birth, is truly a doula, able to put herself into another mother's sandals, socks, or bare feet at their birth.

Taran, a real in-arms baby!

"We are the mothers, after all, the ones who speak the cultural narrative and teach it through, well, old wives' tales, which is to say, the ancient, subversive, and immediate mother tongue, the language of metaphor and myth."
~*Ellen McLaughlin*

Chapter Twenty-One
Four Memorable Births

Four births from a recent year stick out in my mind. All of the mothers had written birth plans and educated themselves about natural birth. None were easy. Interventions were used at three of the four births. I continue to wonder what I could have done differently as a doula. The most interesting factor, though, was the mothers' perceptions of their births. They were decidedly different. One felt utterly traumatized. One was deeply disappointed and felt she had "failed." The third mother felt good about her choices and grateful her babies were doing so well. The last mother was happy it was over and did not feel any of the negative emotions the first two did. All were first babies. So what was the difference?

Birth #1

Hadassah and her husband, Orthodox Jews, had long looked forward to having their first baby and absorbed all the information they could from the Internet, books, classes, and friends. Her labor at a freestanding clinic went very well until her water broke at around seven centimeters. There was meconium. Lots of it. Her midwife was not comfortable continuing the birth there and advised a transfer to a nearby hospital. As her doula, I rode in the car with Hadassah to the hospital, coaching her during the rushes, trying to maintain some of the same calm we had enjoyed working together until then.

The clinic had worked with this hospital before and we felt very welcomed when we arrived. The staff assessed that she was indeed progressing nicely and because the baby's heart tones still sounded good, the obstetrician suggested that going for a vaginal delivery still seemed fine to him. I stayed by her side throughout the birth and she delivered a beautiful little girl later that evening. I was glad she had not needed a C-section and that her baby did not have to go to the NICU. So why did she feel that this birth was the most traumatic event of her life and she needed to go through intense therapy for the next eight months? In her words she felt "humiliated, vulnerable, exposed, degraded, and in shock." Hadassah felt the nurses didn't respect her because they chatted about "insignificant things" during her labor. She was also upset that her midwife withdrew all of her support the moment they arrived at the hospital, after having built a relationship with her over the previous seven months, and that having a male obstetrician was an "unfeeling" choice the hospital dumped upon her.

Birth #2

Tessa, a yoga teacher, had eaten extremely well, exercised daily, and seemed to have an amazing attitude toward natural birth. Her labor was long—two days of prodromal labor, or early labor, had worn her out. Instead of sleeping when she could, she and her husband had hiked the neighborhood the whole first night, trying to encourage the real thing. They checked into the clinic in the morning but little progress had occurred in her labor. At that point her midwife suggested they hire a doula to work with them at home until she was in active, effective labor. That is when I was called.

I had not met this couple before but felt right at home when I went to their house. I explained that it seemed the contractions were petering out because, like a car that won't work unless it is refueled, her body was telling her it needed rest and food. I suggested she rest, which she didn't object to this time, while I cooked up a pile of whole grain pancakes and served them with yogurt and honey. She ate the entire plateful and then they both slept for six hours. A huge rush woke Tessa up. When they were five minutes apart we went back to the birth center.

She labored in the tub for several more hours but seemed to get stalled at eight centimeters. Her midwife tried having her climb stairs, squat, walk, and do lunges but nothing was helping her baby move down any further. By evening she was again exhausted and very discouraged. The last ultrasound had suggested her baby was about eight pounds. Tessa was six feet tall and seemed to have plenty of room.

The couple finally decided to transfer to the hospital. Tessa wanted something for pain at this point and asked me to come with them. The baby sounded great and the OB felt she just needed more time. Tessa opted for an epidural, which gave her much-welcomed relief. As she was able to relax, she became fully dilated. She started pushing but after an hour, the baby still felt very high up in the birth canal. The doctor tried massaging the posterior wall internally hoping to stretch it further and help the baby along. It seemed to help, so for the next hour he kept his hands where he could direct her pushing from inside. She pushed until the head was finally crowning but the doctor explained that what we were seeing was "caput," or the baby's swollen scalp, which had also stretched, but that the bones of the baby's head were still molding and had a ways to go yet.

I had never seen someone push so hard for so long. I wondered what we could have done differently or better. I would have my answers when he was finally born: he weighed eleven pounds, two ounces, almost three pounds bigger than anyone guessed. He also had the shortest umbilical cord I had ever seen. It took that long to stretch without detaching from the placenta, which would have proven fatal for this baby. So nature did know that what was needed was time, more than most births. Much more. Tessa felt afterward that she had not prepared herself fully for the rigors of childbirth. She felt keenly disappointed and robbed of what she thought should have been an ecstatic experience. She felt cheated and regretted having "failed" by asking for the epidural. It should have been different, in her mind at least, meaning better than it had been, and she asked me if she would regret these choices for the rest of her life. She wanted to know if she could have somehow been stronger or better prepared, still blaming herself. I did my best to tell her that this was the land of parenthood and that she had done what she needed to do to birth her baby, and that I was very proud of her. I think in her mind, though, she still thought she should have been stronger.

Birth #3

Amber couldn't believe it when the technician at her first ultrasound congratulated her for being pregnant with twins. But the euphoria completely wore off when, toward the end of the pregnancy, she was put on bedrest for three of the longest weeks of her life. She read books, talked on the phone for hours, watched TV, ate and slept, then did it over and over until she went into labor one morning at almost thirty-seven weeks. I met her at the hospital within an hour.

She spent the day walking, resting, sitting on a birth ball, in the tub, and munching on snacks. The hospital staff was amazingly open to intermittent rather than continuous monitoring and allowed her to eat and drink. They left us by ourselves for most of the day. Things were going really well until about seven centimeters, when Baby B's heart tones became a concern.

Twins are labeled A and B, with A engaged or lower in the pelvis and most likely to be born first. Surprisingly, the obstetrician didn't rush in to intervene but waited and watched for enough of a change that he could be reassured. Other factors, none critical by themselves but enough in combination to raise concerns, included the fact that all of a sudden the contractions were spacing themselves out from five minutes apart to ten or fifteen minutes apart. This, along with Amber's slowly rising blood pressure, led the doctor to call together the birth team and the parents to rethink their plan.

Although Amber had written a birth plan and had educated herself extensively about natural birth and the possible interventions, she was amazingly relaxed about having to switch gears. She asked me what I thought and if I had any suggestions. I told her once again (this had come up several times in our prenatal meetings) that I would not make any decisions for them, but I could give information to help them figure out what would be best for their family. I told her that she could again take a wait-and-see approach and ask for more time, or go with a Cesarean section right then, which is what they opted for. Dad and I were given bunny suits to put on over our clothes along with sterile hats, masks, and booties to cover our shoes. Amber had been given an epidural by the time we joined her in the operating room.

I stayed by her head, where I could narrate what was happening step by step. Dad held her hand and sat in his assigned place trying to take it all in. Within ten minutes I was explaining that she would feel quite a bit of pressure or pushing and tugging and that the first baby would soon be out. Within another minute, Baby A was crying and being rubbed down on a nearby warmer.

Within three minutes Baby B was also out and on his way to a second warmer. Two sets of nurses trained in neonatal resuscitation were standing by ready to assist either or both babies to breathe if needed, but they were both doing really well on their own and were given good Apgar scores. All of a sudden two very healthy babies were both crying while they were being wrapped up to make the trip over to meet their mom.

Dad was given a baby on each arm to hold where Amber could see and touch them. It was beautiful to watch this little family of two that had suddenly doubled. They asked me to take pictures so I tried to get lots of different angles without stepping on a nurse's toes or bumping into one of the anesthesiologists. Finally we were all transferred to the recovery room, where Amber could nurse their babies. Vincent and Victor were safely here!

Although she had a long recovery ahead of her, Amber was happy and grateful for the way things went with their birth. She told me simply, "It was what it was" and everyone was here and healthy. She knew she had done everything she could.

Birth #4

When I received the referral for a first-time mom newly arrived from Ethiopia, I was excited. I met with Eleni every week leading up to her birth. We covered all of the material in the childbirth education series during our prenatal visits, which we squeezed in between her busy work and school schedules. She couldn't go to a regular class offered at one of the local hospitals because she had to take the bus to get there and did not want to do that at night. Her husband worked the night shift so he couldn't accompany her. So we met and watched teaching videos and addressed all of her questions during our visits together.

She had a difficult pregnancy, complicated by an infection contracted before she arrived in the U.S. and then another rare event affecting her fluid retention. Her OB carefully monitored both her health and the baby's during this pregnancy and felt that a natural birth was still possible as she neared her fortieth week. Both conditions would be treated after she gave birth but could only be observed and followed until then. She was still not showing any signs of going into labor at forty-one weeks but everything looked okay, though her OB was guarded about waiting much longer. A few days later Eleni called me from her OB appointment to tell me that she was being advised to go in that same day and have her labor induced. We would meet at the hospital later that afternoon.

When I arrived the family was still waiting for an Amharic translator. The OB doctor wanted to explain their options for starting labor and wanted to be sure the couple understood everything. That done, we settled in for a long day. The prostaglandin, a cream that they used, worked quite well to ripen her cervix and within two hours we had contractions, light ones but increasing, and she began dilating. We kept waiting for active labor to begin—the point where she would be four centimeters and have good, regular contractions—but instead of the ideal one centimeter per hour, we were going along at about one centimeter every three or four hours. Eleni's OB seemed unconcerned and told us that as long as the baby sounded good, and he did, we didn't need to rush things at all. This was a far cry from the "old days" that I remember, where they simply kept adding intervention after intervention to make it "work" within some magical time frame, no matter what, and almost without realizing it slid into what we call "the domino effect." A mom would get Pitocin to ramp up labor, which caused more pain and a request for more drugs that in turn affected the baby so different drugs were tried. Then they would break the water to speed things up, and the baby would react badly at some point to everything that was now on board and before she knew it the mother was being wheeled into the OR for a C-section. That is the "domino effect."

Eleni ate and drank, rested, sat on a birth ball, walked the hall, and rested some more over the next fifteen hours. At one point the doctors suggested trying Pitocin if things slowed down any more, but put off that idea for a few hours. By morning, they asked if the couple was okay with that or what they would like to do. We talked about it and Eleni asked if she could get something to help her rest for a while and see if the rushes would pick up on their own if she was less exhausted. We had discussed some of these options during our prenatal appointments and as Eleni was still wishing for this birth to be as natural as possible, the doctor agreed. We turned off the lights, closed the door, and Mom, Dad, and I all got in a two- to three-hour nap, which felt great.

We woke up when her water broke on its own (called spontaneous rupture of membranes) toward the morning of the second day. The water was clear and her baby girl still had an amazingly good heart rate when they checked her. Still at a rate of about one centimeter every three or four hours, Eleni slowly progressed. It was enough progress, and no regression, that the doctors—there were now three female doctors checking in with us—didn't feel anything had to be done, but said that they could offer a few ideas if Eleni was interested in speeding things up. I assured her that this was up to her but that her baby sounded very good. She continued to eat and rested when she got tired of walking or being on the birth ball. She spent the next few hours in the candle-lit tub room, dozing as I slowly dribbled a steady trickle of warm water over her belly. She was at five centimeters, still considered progress.

When the rushes started getting stronger, Eleni told me she was scared. She didn't know what to do next. She didn't know if she would be too exhausted to push later. She didn't know how much more she could stand. I explained again that this was the longest and the hardest part of labor, that going into transition is the end of this stage and that she was doing wonderfully. I told her that her baby still sounded really great and that we would help her with each rush as it came. I reminded her that she only had to get through one rush at a time.

She closed her eyes and lay back down in the water. I was calcu-lating in my head that at this rate we could be doing this for eight or nine more hours.

I thought maybe imagery would help so I said, "Sweetheart, look up at the ceiling. See that big black circle (the exam lamp)? That is how big you need to be. You will open like a flower, petal by petal. You won't break. You have lots of room and your baby isn't huge. She is probably six or seven pounds, just right for you.

"Your body knew exactly how big to make her and your body knows just how to get her out. You don't have to really do anything. Just let the rushes open you up that big. You won't break. We were made to do this . . . " And so it went for the next fifteen minutes or so until suddenly she had some really big rushes and Eleni said she had to poop, like right now! I told the nurse that she hadn't been to the toilet in over an hour so we got there and convinced her she shouldn't try to push yet. Next she got up on the bed and the nurse checked her. Nine and a half centimeters!

I used imagery alone for all five of my babies' births, so I know that it is possible. I had not taken Lamaze or other classes, but put aside time before I fell asleep each night to visualize how each particular birth should look, how beautiful the room looked, how quiet, how calm, how the waves or rushes would rise over me and wane and how I could ride each one until the time came that I could push. I would continue to imagine my beautiful, wet, fat (they were all quite pudgy) baby quietly sliding out, and lifting her to myself, checking her cord for a pulse and reminding David to clamp and cut it. I trusted that nature had planned birth this way. I trusted that my body would and could know what to do. I knew I had cared for us well during the last nine months and I knew what I did not want interrupting such a sacred moment. The only problem was that for the last two births I had completely forgotten to fit the midwives' arrival into the plan as I had mapped it all out in my mind. Baby and Daddy and I greeted the surprised ladies as they walked in too late, twice, just three years apart.

While attending a birth a few years ago as the assistant midwife at a free-standing clinic, I puzzled how I could redirect some of the negative energy that the mom was exuding. She was determined to have an unmedicated birth, however with each contraction she would yell or scream through gritted teeth with her eyes tight shut, "Shit! Shit! Shit!" until the rush had passed. With the next one she yelled even louder, "Fuck! Fuck! Fuuuuuuck!" until that one subsided. This went on for quite a while.

Finally I very quietly knelt down next to her and whispered, "Sweetheart, on the next contraction, just try saying, 'Baby. . . Baby . . . Baaaaby,' or maybe, 'Open . . . Open . . . Oooopen.'" It worked.

She had invited her mother to the birth, who was vehemently opposed to birth outside of a hospital and sat bold upright in a chair in the corner of the room, arms crossed over her chest, lips tight shut, scowling at us the whole time. I had suggested to the mom that I could invite her mother to hang out in our little kitchen, but grandma-to-be had already staked out the birth room and would not budge. After the baby arrived, which was a very calm, very beautiful birth, this new grandma cornered me in the kitchen and thanked me for "such a professional job," adding, "I didn't know y'all knew so much!"

Eleni and her family were Muslim. We had written in her birth plan that she wanted only women at her birth, did not want any male residents or students observing, and that her husband might not stay for the actual birth, which was part of their tradition. Knowing this, I made sure to alert him every time a nurse wanted to do an exam and gave him the chance to leave the room if he wanted to. Even with only women present, she kept her headscarf on the whole time. I also made sure that she was covered with a sheet whenever she changed positions and had a robe over her nightgown whenever she was not in bed. I was careful about keeping the door curtain pulled so she couldn't be seen from the hall. During exams I made it my job to hold up the sheet enough to give the doctor or nurse access, but shielding her from the other women in the room. I had incorporated this into my doula job description early on when I began working with Somali women.

Finally, Eleni could push! Her two sisters helped with her legs while I wiped her face and neck and helped her breathe. Her husband had stayed but preferred to sit nearby and pray, too overwhelmed by everything to trust himself to be any closer. I gave him an update every few minutes as the baby's head and thick curly black hair came into view. I couldn't see what was going on down below. It was my job to be where I could encourage her and calmly whisper in her ear, "You're doing it, honey! You are so strong! That's it! Okay, rest now . . . That's it. Okay, another deep breath . . . slowly . . . you're doing it! Wonderful job!"

Suddenly, the three doctors moved into high gear. I wasn't sure what had happened, but I knew something wasn't right. I stayed where I knew I was needed as I watched one of the doctors get up onto the bed and begin fundal compressions. *Oh my God!* I thought, *shoulder dystocia*—every midwife's and doctor's worst nightmare. They had three minutes to get the baby out. If they waited too long, oxygen deprivation could cause cerebral palsy or permanent brain damage.

I knew the doctors and nurses had the drill down and could do it in their sleep, and Eleni was still holding her two sisters' hands, so I turned to her husband. He looked terrified. No wonder: it looked like the doctors were giving his wife CPR. I took his hand and told him the baby was stuck and that they were working to get her out, that they were trained to do this. Within three minutes, they were carrying Baby to the warmer where the NRP team was waiting. I then assured Dad that his baby was out and was getting the help she needed.

Eleni had her eyes closed but was still holding her sisters' hands. Within a few more seconds we could hear her baby cry, at first little whimpers and then huge yowls. I told Dad to go over and see his baby and be sure and take his camera. For the family's sake, I could go back into an "All is fine" voice and reassure them. I tried to sound like "This is all perfectly routine," though I knew we had just been in a very scary place. They would never perhaps fully understand the gravity of the situation.

Eleni tore quite a bit, possibly from the attempts to pull the baby's shoulder out. She needed the fourth-degree repair done in the OR afterward. She was happy that it was over and that her beautiful big girl—eight pounds—was now snuggling on her chest where they could get to know one another. We gave Baby to her daddy and I accompanied Eleni to the OR to have the repair done. She was positioned on the table and offered a shot for pain, which she agreed to as they hoisted her legs up into "candy cane" bars, which are even higher than regular stirrups, for the best position for the repair. I overheard that they were waiting for the OB to come to do the repair and asked if it was a "he" OB or a "she" OB. They said "He" just as he walked in, so I explained that it would be nice if she was draped except for the area he had to work on. Without hesitating a moment, they all flew into action looking for the sterile kit that actually has leg covers and other drapes. They had never used them but didn't hesitate for a second when I asked. Eleni was awake during the two-hour procedure. I stayed by the head of the table and told her how well she had done and how good her baby looked. I told her that she would look really nice when the swelling went down and they had fixed the tear.

When we returned to the room Abrihet's daddy was holding her, still looking completely bewildered. It was a lot to take in. He was happy, but his look of utter wonder stayed with him all evening. I told him he should be very proud of his amazing, brave wife. The sisters called relatives who fixed food and brought it in for all of us to eat. At one point we were all eating fragrant rice while Eleni, holding her baby, was being fed and given the proscribed spiced hot milk traditionally given to new Ethiopian mothers.

Dad looked over at me and asked, "What was all that about, anyway?" So I explained what had gone on, how when we see a baby's shoulders are stuck behind the pubic bone, and the baby's face has a distinct "turtling" or scrunched-up look, we know we don't have much time to get her out because if she doesn't get air in time, she could have brain damage. That is why they had to hurry and try different things to get her out. I explained I was glad they acted so quickly and told him they would X-ray the baby later because she might have a fractured clavicle bone (there was a strong suspicion she had because she wasn't lifting her right arm) but, if that was the case, babies heal very quickly and they would show him how to care for it before they went home.

Eleni was happy that she had not had a C-section. She was grateful to the doctors, whom she kept thanking whenever they came in her room. She was in love with her baby right away and was still holding her two days later when I did a home visit.

I continue to wonder if by respecting Eleni's wish for modesty, her requirement for satisfaction with the birth was met. I seriously wonder if we had made a concerted effort to use drapes throughout their labor and births, perhaps Hadassah's and Tessa's feelings of "being exposed" and "humiliated" might have changed, especially after they had been transported to hospitals.

As we are beginning to see more research into what constitutes traumatic birth and even the symptoms of PTSD after some births, I wonder if we could not somehow think more about honoring or respecting mothers' bodies differently. Many women are fine giving birth completely *au natural* but in the first two cases described here, I would like to think it might have made a difference.

"The source of love is deep in us and we can help others realize a lot of happiness. One word, one action, one thought can reduce another person's suffering and bring that person joy."
~Thich Nhat Hanh

Chapter Twenty-Two

"I Don't Want a Baby!"

I didn't have a clue. Becca and Stan were taking every childbirth education course we had to offer and we met monthly to connect and work on a birth plan. Educated, socially conscious, laid-back, unselfconscious, thoughtful—they seemed to have it all pretty well together.

I discovered during labor, though, that there were enough obstacles to sink a ship: past sexual abuse, a history of depression, substance abuse, gender issues, fear of being unable to birth, fear of not having whatever it takes—hormones or feminine qualities—to mother a child, fear of failure and being as horrible at raising a baby as her mother had been, fear of her body failing to know what to do to birth her baby, and somehow "failing" by needing drugs or a C-section. Between contractions I learned she was absolutely terrified of the little creature she was about to produce.

Becca's water broke around 10:30 a.m. Stan texted me to say they were going to hang out at home for as long as they could. They would call me if they wanted me to meet them at home or at the hospital should things really kick in. I agreed it was a good plan. We texted back and forth throughout the day. He also called the hospital and their midwife group and kept them abreast of their progress. Later that afternoon they went into the hospital to have the baby monitored and check in with the midwives. Contractions had started by then and everything looked great. Becca was one centimeter, but eighty percent effaced and the baby was head down with great fetal heart tones. All systems were go! I reminded them that first babies take time and we didn't want to rush this birth.

I wasn't too concerned that Becca was taking so very long to begin to dilate. Twenty-four hours is not unheard of for a first baby. We would like to see the cervix dilate about one centimeter per hour, but Becca was walking, eating, and drinking so there wasn't anything to change at that point. I suggested the birth tub when she got to about six centimeters. She said the tub felt better and she was content to hang out there for a couple of hours. There was no change in her cervix, however. She had stopped drinking, though I kept offering juice and water. Nausea had set in and then Becca's last meal made a surprise comeback. I told her that this was all perfectly normal and that her body knew exactly what was needed, but she was not at all happy. She was no longer the laid-back whatever-it-takes lady.

"This sucks!" was the next pronouncement, followed by, "Fucking awful!" and "I don't want to do this," which elicited the response by her partner, "You have no choice."

An hour went by. Everything was increasingly negative. Their birth plan explicitly said not to offer anything for pain and not to ask about her pain level during labor, but when I gently offered that she might get some relief from a short-term IV medication she said she was interested. I explained that it would not stop labor, and that she would still feel the contractions, but that it might take some of the edge off and let her rest for an hour or two. The midwives had not been doing internal checks since her water broke, and we didn't know where she was was at that point, so her midwife offered to check before giving her anything. We were very surprised to hear that she was at eight centimeters. I was elated, as was the midwife.

I explained to Becca that the meds might not be a good idea now that we knew she was so close to pushing, since they could affect the baby and we might not have the two hours we had originally thought we had for the drugs to get out of her system. I explained that we certainly did not want a sleepy baby who might have trouble breathing.

At this she surprised both her midwife and me, saying, "I am actually horrified of babies. I don't want a baby!"

Her partner countered, "We have been talking about this for nine months and you said you had let that go!"

Um, no, I thought. *You don't just let that go that easily.* What planet had I landed on? Then the rest all spewed out: she didn't want to repeat her mother's horrid mothering; she would ruin her baby's life; she didn't have enough feminine qualities to be a mother; and maybe the instincts had never been there at all.

Her midwife, Barb, took all this in and said, "Becca, you are safe here. Your baby is safe. Your body knows how to give birth. Your body does have what it takes to be a mother."

Becca silently listened. Two more hours passed. Becca was back in bed and Barb asked to check her cervix once more, which she agreed to. Ten centimeters. We were all ecstatic, though exhausted by this point.

All except Becca. I tried to get her to drink some juice but she refused. She definitely did not want to vomit again. I explained that it was okay and that she might not have the energy to push if it took awhile.

Barb tried again. "Tell me what you are thinking."

Becca was quiet, then said, "I'm afraid I will fail at this too, and need a C-section."

Barb replied, "You have lots of room. Your baby is not a ten-pounder. You can do this. We'll help you. You can try little nudges first and see if your body is ready to push."

So she sat up, legs stiffly stretched out in front of her, took a deep breath and—blew it back out. I let her try it her way a couple of times before moving in.

"Let's try this on the birth ball, okay? If it doesn't feel right, you can tell us," I said as I helped her up. Her knees had to relax and stay open and the birth ball was softer than the bed, so I hoped it would feel better to her. With the next rush I asked if I could touch her shoulders to help her relax, and breathe with her, which she said was fine. I reminded her to breathe in, hold it, put her chin down to her chest and . . . little nudges . . . at which she again blew out.

"I can't do it," she whispered.

I came around to her side and said, "Becca. You won't have to do this alone. You have Stan. I have seen tons of deadbeat dads in this business, and he is definitely not one of those. He is here for you. He is going to raise this baby with you. And you have us, and many other people will also help you."

Another contraction was building. I took her hand and said, "We will do this one with you. Let it build, okay . . . deep breath . . . hold it, push down into your bottom, there . . ." She gave a tiny grunt and blew out. Her legs were frozen in place and the push never got past her throat. I tried again. "You have lots of room for this baby. He sounds fantastic. Stan is going to hold him when he comes out. You don't have to do anything, honey. Just breathe, that's it . . . let it build . . . okay . . . now, deep breath in . . . hold it . . . hold it . . . and push straight down . . . yes! You are doing it, that's it! Sweetheart, you have got it! Again, deep breath, in . . . chin down . . . hold it . . ."

We could see the head crowning. Then he slipped back in. I explained that she was stretching beautifully. We didn't have to hurry this. He was doing fine. I whispered, "Just rest now. Good. You can sleep for a minute . . . that's it." I let her follow her body on the next one and didn't say anything. Barb silently knelt down on the other side of Becca, ready to catch their baby as Becca took in huge breath and pushed one final grand push, which did it. He popped out into Barb's hands.

"Open your eyes," I whispered to Becca. "He's here. You were brilliant, my dear!"

Barb let the cord stop pulsing and then clamped it, handing the scissors to Stan. Then she passed the baby forward to him while we let Becca recover and take it all in. We all told her how well she had done. I reminded her that she had done it without drugs, just as she had hoped, and told her she was really stronger than she had previously thought.

Stan and Becca spent the next couple of hours in bed getting to know their baby. He never cried. He was so peaceful and alert and kept looking back and forth, first at Stan and then Becca. He was beautiful. I told her how perfect he was and reminded her that she was actually really strong and had done a super job.

I met with Barb in the nurses' station before I left later that afternoon. We both agreed we were disturbed by Becca's reactions to labor. I said I was particularly worried about postpartum depression and was not comfortable leaving her alone with the baby, even in the hospital, much less when they went home. She agreed, so we discussed several options to refer them to, including a postpartum depression clinic and a social worker specialist who could follow them when we both signed off in the next few days.

The next day I returned for her postpartum visit. I needed to be straight with them and bring out some of my concerns. Postpartum depression and its related cousins have been taboo subjects in the past, but no more. It must be addressed. It is 100% curable and is now thought to be caused by the high levels of hormones during and after delivery that play havoc with the brain and amplify any preexisting depression or bipolar issues.

When I entered their room the next day, it was crammed with visitors and their baby was having a difficult time nursing. Becca was obviously nervous about baring her breasts in front of so many people. I sidled up to Stan and suggested there were too many visitors and that I thought they would understand if they were gently asked to go. So we cleared out the room, which was quite a relief to Becca. Stan's parents had hoped to hold their first grandchild during the visit but it was definitely too soon to be passing him around.

Becca needed time to bond first. He really was having a hard time latching on and was screaming when it didn't work. I finally asked if I could look in his mouth after we tried several different positions. It was a good guess. He, in fact, did possibly have a very tight frenula which meant his tongue was not able to fully protrude beyond his gums in order to wrap around the nipple and properly latch. I suggested they mention it when the hospital pediatrician came by later in the day and have it checked out.

We also put together a list of resources should they want extra support. I explained that postpartum depression could appear anytime during the first year, not just at the beginning. And then it was time to say goodbye. I hugged both of them and wished them the very best.

I worry about their journey, whether they will become stronger now that they actually accomplished birth, and whether Becca would realize she does indeed have what it takes to birth a baby and be a mother. They have a long road ahead of them.

What makes some first-time mothers confident that they can birth their babies naturally and others almost as confident that they will fail and everything will go wrong? When is confidence or a lack of it developed in the psyche? Is it inherited or acquired? Or both? When is the seed planted that will invade the totality of the human mind's consciousness and unconscious regions either positively or negatively? Can one choose or find the will to change direction? Do we get that choice?

"Speak tenderly to them. Let there be kindness in your face, in your eyes, in your smile, in the warmth of your greeting. Always have a cheerful smile. Don't only give your care, but give your heart as well."
~Mother Teresa

Chapter Twenty-Three

And Then There Was Rose

My phone rang early one Sunday morning. I often volunteer at a women's shelter run by Mother Teresa's nuns, the Missionaries of Charity Shelter. There are seven beds, ready at a moment's notice for any woman who is homeless and pregnant in Minneapolis. Sister Rosetta was calling to ask me if I could come and help decide what they should do for one of their guests who had recently given birth. They didn't know what they were seeing, but wondered about postpartum depression.

I visited later that morning and tapped on Rose's door. Her two-year-old, Hannah, was bouncing up and down in her playpen, grinning from ear to ear. Rose had Luke, only a week old, in her lap and was giving him a bottle. He looked clean and had on a cute little outfit. Rose was dressed and her hair looked nice, too. It wasn't quite what I was expecting.

I had met Rose before Luke was born when I worked at the shelter earlier that year. She was usually upbeat and friendly. Hannah was a handful, spunky and bright. I picked up Hannah and sat down on the end of the bed and asked Rose how things were going. She told me about the birth, how Luke was such a good baby, how she was looking into a permanent situation for her little family with her social worker, and so on. She mentioned that she didn't want to go back east to an abusive father and addicted boyfriend. She really wanted to go back to school and get her life back on track. I encouraged her and told her that she was still young and could do so much.

I finally said I wanted to talk about what we call "baby blues" or depression, because it is very real, especially after birth, with all the other stresses in her life. I knew she had a history of mental issues, though I didn't know specifics. She admitted that she felt frustrated trying to keep her kids quiet at bedtime and that she couldn't always let Hannah run loose when she had to feed the baby so she had to plop Hannah into the playpen where she would scream bloody murder while everyone else was trying to go to sleep. Then she mentioned in passing that they had not given back her meds after the birth, even though she had asked for them at her postpartum appointment. I asked what they were and it turned out she had been treated for bipolar disorder.

I could not believe she had fallen through the cracks in the system just like that. Of course she had agreed to try to hang on without meds during the pregnancy, if at all possible, and she had been okay, but as soon as she delivered Luke, she knew she should go back on the program she had been on, which had worked well for her. Yes, she was depressed now, but felt it could all be sorted out. She was also prepared not to breastfeed her baby, though she would have liked to, knowing the medications were not good for him. She was willing to forgo nursing in order to be a more-together mom who needed to take care of both her kids and also happened to need meds.

Sometimes women only exhibit symptoms of bipolar disease for the first time after having a baby. If they are referred early they can work with a doctor and have it under control quickly. Too often women fear sharing their feelings when they don't seem to be in line with what is "expected." They've just had a beautiful, healthy baby. Shouldn't they be happy? Grateful? Cheerful? They shouldn't be crying all the time, or having scary thoughts or flipping out, should they? They often fear their baby will be taken away—some fear the baby *won't* be taken away.

Again: postpartum depression is 100% curable. Research has now found that the flood of hormones released immediately during and after birth account for many of the mood swings and problems women run into. The sooner they get help, the shorter the time it will take to over-come this period. If we don't talk about it, it will remain a taboo subject and each woman will continue to believe that she is the only person on earth to have ever felt this way. The fact is that it is far more common than we thought before. And there is more help than ever.

Postpartum depression can occur anywhere from the first days or weeks after birth up to anytime during the first year after having a baby. If not treated, the symptoms can get worse and postpartum psy-chosis can become an issue. What is crucial to remember is that:

1. It is 100% curable;
2. Help must be sought early; and
3. No one will fault the mother for not being cheerful and happy or having it all together.

I think it has become even more prevalent in our Western society because we don't have an intact extended family system for support any longer. In other cultures, women are cared for after they've had a baby and are never left alone. They are free to rest as much as they need and don't have to cook, clean, tend other children, do laundry, or lose sleep, much less go back to work within weeks of delivering. We are doing a disservice to our mothers in the U.S. by ignoring this im-portant aspect of care. Many countries—France, England, Denmark, Sweden, and Holland, to name a few—offer all mothers a helper in the home for up to a year, paid for by the government, to take the workload off new mothers so they have the time needed to bond with their babies and recover. These governments understand that this investment will pay off in the long run with healthier, happier families.

I suggested a plan for Rose. I asked her to call her neighborhood church lady friends and find someone who could watch her children for a few hours later that evening. Then I told her I would go with her to the hospital and we'd ask for her meds. I suggested she try to "keep it together" because I told her if they decided to admit her and I had to refer her babies to foster care then I would be depressed, too. I was hoping they would believe me that I would be in contact every day with Rose and she wouldn't be alone at the shelter at any time, either. Supervision is important for someone using strong medications but I reasoned that she had been on the meds before and tolerated them well. Rose readily agreed and started calling. I went home and took care of what I needed to finish up there (including doula backup for the night for my other clients) and then later that day I picked up Rose and we went to the hospital. I had packed some snacks, thinking we would be in the emergency room for hours. This was one of the biggest medical centers in the city and was known for its waiting room marathons.

Rose had given birth to Luke at the same hospital earlier that month, so I knew her records were there. When we got to the emergency department we settled in on a couch by the TV for the long haul and I went up to the desk to register. I couldn't believe it when the receptionist told me they would call the resident doctor on the psych ward and had a room we could wait in all ready. Wow, talk about service! So we picked up our coats, snacks, and bags with magazines and followed her to a little room.

We chatted about some of the original things Hannah had come up with since Luke was born. Then Rose asked me if I noticed anything funny about the room. I looked around and said, first, there weren't any cupboards with meds or equipment.

"Right. What else?" she asked me. I noticed the two chairs were bolted to the floor.

"Oh, I see. What else?"

"Well, there's a window in the door."

"That's right," she agreed, you couldn't hurt yourself in this place.

"Oh, I get it," I said. She explained that she was a veteran of the psych wards and could spot the program a mile away.

I told her that I was glad she wanted to get her life back on track and that I really admired her for setting goals like school for herself. We agreed that Minnesota had more programs than most states for scholarships and other possibilities. We talked about some of her ideas about different colleges and how to find out more information.

Before long a nurse from "upstairs" came and introduced herself. I was immediately impressed by how respectful yet straightforward she was. Rose talked about not being able to get a new prescription even though she had asked for one and said she was more than willing to be compliant, take her meds, and attend therapy or whatever else they recommended. Therapy could address many of her problems and give her the help and support she needed during the time ahead. Then I told the nurse about Rose's living situation and that I thought it was an ideal arrangement for her to start back on her medications while staying there. Soon a doctor came in and introduced himself. The nurse filled him in and he readily agreed that our plan sounded fine to him, too.

We both thanked them profusely. They were really concerned, respectful, and listened. I don't know what I expected, but I was amazed. We were a really great team, all rooting for Rose to do well, all doing what we did best, coming together to support her. I was so grateful. It changed my perception of the big, impersonal medical center.

Rose returned to the shelter and I checked in with her by phone daily. A few days later, I met her and took her, along with Hannah and Luke, out to lunch. It was scattered, like any meal with two little guys vying for attention always is, but we did manage a nice visit.

Rose still has her ups and downs (don't we all?), but I don't know if I have ever been so proud of a young mom before. I know I haven't met many with as many obstacles in front of them and yet could overcome so much. We are still in touch. She has her own apartment now. She is truly another amazing woman who I have been honored to know.

Steps to take if you have symptoms of depression or anxiety during or after pregnancy:

1. If you are having thoughts of harming yourself or your baby, it is very important to get support immediately. Call 911 or go to the nearest emergency room. Though it can be scary to ask for support the first time, they can help keep you and your baby safe and help you take the first steps toward getting better.
2. Tell someone you trust how you are feeling. It is important that you feel safe with the person and that they support you in a nonjudgmental way. Ask them to help you find support. Examples of someone you can tell:
   - Your partner
   - A family member
   - A friend
   - A healthcare professional like your doula, midwife, or doctor
   - A pastor or someone at your church

Other Resources:
- Jenny's Light: http://www.jennyslight.org
- http://www.mayoclinic.com/health/postpartum-depression/DS00546
- http://www.babycenter.com/o_postpartum-depression-and-anxiety_227.bc
- http://hcmcmn.org/index.php?content=mother-baby-day-hospital&clinicid=393
- Hennepin Women's Mental Health Program, Minneapolis, MN: Dr. Helen Kim, MD
- http://www.maternaloutcomesmatter.org/
- http://everymothercounts.org/film

"A wizard is never late, Frodo Baggins. Nor is he early. He arrives precisely when he means to."
~Gandalf in J.R.R. Tolkien's The Lord of the Rings

Chapter Twenty-Four

There's a Placenta in Our Freezer

My husband didn't know there was a placenta in our freezer. He would have freaked out and then insisted I bleach the whole refrigerator and freezer and I would never have heard the end of it.

One of my clients had a scheduled C-section. There were multiple medical problems on board, not the least being that she had had bariatric surgery earlier that year, lost over 150 pounds and then got pregnant. She had one complication after another after that. She was very nauseated during the entire pregnancy, had been bleeding on and off into her eighth month, remained anemic, and had dizziness throughout, causing her to fall several times a week.

Bariatric surgery essentially reduces the size of the stomach, making it almost impossible to eat large quantities of food. In her case Megan could barely eat at all, which served the purpose of losing weight, but in the process her body became depleted of much-needed nutrients. She tried liquid diet supplements like Ensure, which didn't help much, even when she could keep it down.

Her hair started falling out, she couldn't maintain enough red blood cells, and she became dangerously anemic. By the seventh month, her baby's growth had all but stopped.

The doctors considered inducing labor so the baby could be born six weeks early and begin to get nutrients pumped into him via IV after his birth. There were tests to see if her hormone levels were mimicking labor, which would let them know that preterm labor was a possibility.

This was baby number four so it wasn't possible for her to rest much during the day. At night, joint pain became unbearable, probably caused by the extreme anemia and vitamin deficiencies. A chiropractor was able to help a bit and had some good suggestions as far as nutrition. Megan tried yoga and meditation, too.

The day before she hit the thirty-nine-week mark, her water broke about 3:00 a.m. She had never been allowed to let the bag of water break spontaneously with the other three births. When she called me she was sure she couldn't give birth without medical interventions. I congratulated her and for the hundredth time told her that her body really could do it and she was stronger than she thought.

I had sent her this quote the week before:

Promise me you'll always remember:
You are braver than you believe,
Stronger than you seem,
And smarter than you think!
~Christopher Robin to Winnie the Pooh

I told her to let her doctor know, who in turn wanted her to go to the hospital immediately. I met her in the hospital triage wing of the labor and delivery floor. Like a mini-emergency room, the nurses there could decide if a mom was in early labor and could be sent home without setting up a whole birthing suite, or if she was active labor and they could transfer her to a proper labor room that at that hospital included a large tub, birth ball, and all the works.

They first confirmed with a test strip that the water bag had broken. Then they Velcroed the monitors onto her stomach to watch the baby's heartbeat, which was great, and the rushes, or contractions, though there weren't any yet. We hung out and visited while her husband snored away on a lounge chair. Breakfast was served, then later lunch while we continued to flip the channels on the television suspended in a corner of the room. Later that afternoon the official neonatal team of doctors descended on the room. They explained that they had hoped contractions would start on their own but since they had not and we were at about twelve hours out, they were hoping to talk about some options for birth. She could get Pitocin through an IV or in conjunction with a cervix softener like prostaglandin or Cervidil. Or they could do a C-section, which was their suggestion since she had one previously.

As a doula it wasn't my place to suggest either direction. I had done my best at our prenatal visits to extol the obvious benefits of vaginal delivery and enumerated the very real risks of surgery, but at this point Megan was so sick, so undernourished and anemic, she could not imagine summoning the strength to endure labor.

She had thought the stomach surgery would solve all of her weight issues, not understanding the havoc it could wreck on a body, much less a pregnant one. She chose the Cesarean route.

She woke up her sleeping husband, Joe, and asked him if he wanted to go into the OR with her. He had not planned on it. It had never even occurred to him. It sounded overwhelming. What if he fainted? There'd be a lot of blood, right? What if he had to leave? He was working himself into a panic attack. So I got out my phone and found some photos of C-sections. I pointed out that there is a huge drape that separates us from the actual operation, that it is bright in there but relatively quiet. I also told him it takes only about half an hour and that he could go over to the warmer and be with his baby and then bring him over to Megan and get to know him after he was wrapped up. He studied the pictures and finally said he could do that.

Megan walked down to the operating room with the nurses while Dad and I donned our bunny suits and waited in the room until they called us. Dad quickly fell back to sleep. He had been doing nights for months with their other three children to let Megan rest and regain her health, so I didn't begrudge him his naps.

Finally we went back and were given our posts on two little swivel chairs that had been placed on either side of Megan's head. She had already been given the epidural and was excited about finally seeing this baby. They were already starting the surgery when we entered the OR and Baby was born fifteen minutes later. He came out with a loud cry—

a good sign, since he was so little. He weighed in at six pounds, ten ounces, a miracle, really, considering all of the problems with the pregnancy.

Joe did really well, too. I checked in with him several times during the surgery and told him he was doing great. Then I went with him over to the warmer where he reached out to his little boy, who promptly grabbed his finger. Joe started sobbing, overwhelmed with it all. The nurse wrapped up his baby and Joe proudly carried his son back to his wife.

In the recovery room, baby Abel latched on immediately, another miracle since I had assumed he would act more like a sleepy preemie. He nursed at both breasts before falling into a peaceful sleep on Megan's chest.

Her recovery went well. I did a final postpartum visit with her two days later. I had suggested she ask for a belly band, or pregnancy belt, which would both hold in her sagging tummy (which was profoundly out of shape after the weight loss) and help put her muscles back in place while she healed from the C-section. They had already delivered it from the hospital pharmacy before she left the hospital and she was again able to eat, though only miniscule portions. I also referred her to a nutritionist. Nutritionists have a wealth of information and can suggest numerous options for regaining health.

Megan wanted to take her placenta home but Joe balked at the idea. Megan patiently explained the value of encapsulating it and the benefits it could afford her. He got more grossed out by the minute and then flatly refused to carry "that thing" home on the bus in a red hazardous materials bag. She begged. She pleaded. Finally from across the recovery room on my little swivel chair perch, I offered. I knew how much it meant to her. She could collect it from my house a couple of weeks later and I would get to see her baby again. We were all happy.

"There is no way out of the experience except through it, because it is not really your experience but the baby's. Your body is the child's instrument of birth."
~Penelope Leach

Chapter Twenty-Five

Tiger Mama

How do you help a mom prepare for labor when you know the baby is no longer living or when doctors have said the baby will live only hours or days? Is it any less intense than the birth of a healthy baby? More intense? Is there any way to celebrate this short life? Is that what the mom and dad want? How do I begin to talk about it?

I received a call from my midwife friend, Molly, late one afternoon. Years ago we had worked together and remained friends. I was in awe of her years of experience and intellect. Nothing was too small for her to research and understand in order to help one of her moms. She was constantly learning, reading, and stretching her knowledge, and it made me want to be around her and soak up some of her enthusiasm and curiosity.

She knew I had received a grant a couple of years earlier to learn from an infant hospice in Missouri how they were able to help over 500 families with babies who had lethal or fatal anomalies. At the time I applied for the grant I had two moms who were expecting babies with serious problems. An ultrasound had revealed one baby had only half a heart. Another client was expecting twins and had just been told that one of them had an omphalocele (where the intestine forms outside of the stomach wall, sometimes including other organs), which could indicate more serious problems. I wanted to know how I could best support them. What should I say? What shouldn't I say?

I had seen close to a dozen babies who had died before birth, at birth, or shortly after during the years my family lived in Pennsylvania and New York. These families were surrounded by love and support the entire time, day and night, while they agonized about the best way to care for their babies. Sometimes surgery helped, but more often it didn't. Most of the families felt that these special babies were sent to earth for a specific purpose that may not need a long lifetime to fulfill. We would all miss them terribly, but we had faith that each precious soul was not a mistake, no matter how disabled they appeared. I learned in Missouri that "each of these babies is a masterpiece from the Creator."

Some families thought of them as angel babies who were not destined for earth. Others felt that nature deals us both good and sometimes cruel decks, that it is part of an imperfect world that isn't always fair, but we will learn something from it. We must.

Aaron and Channah's baby's problems first showed up at a routine twenty-week ultrasound. There was an abnormality in the baby's brain. Subsequent ultrasounds revealed problems with her heart as well. She continued to grow, though her head remained small. Her arms appeared too short, too.

The parents decided to forgo further testing other than ultrasounds. Though they knew there were serious problems, they decided they would wait until her birth to see what was really going on. They knew she might not make it to term, that babies with multiple problems can die before birth (called stillborn). Some are born alive but cannot function once they no longer have the support of their mother's heart, kidneys, and other systems. Others are too weak to survive labor and birth.

Overwhelmed with all the possibilities, Channah slowly began addressing each problem, asking doctors questions and reading about each anomaly. She needed to take each step one at a time.

She had many questions. How do you birth a still baby? How will the hospital treat us? Can we keep her with us long enough to say goodbye? Can or should she be born at home? Will the hospital whisk her off to the NICU and attempt to perform heroic procedures that we all know would probably not help the baby? Would having her at home avoid that kind of drama? Would the doctors understand their wishes?

It was all foreign territory for them but we were impressed with Channah's courage and her questions. She wasn't willing to talk about saying goodbye to her baby or planning a funeral, but she was not in denial and was allowing others near her to provide the support she knew she needed. Channah understood the importance of remaining connected to her baby regardless of her condition.

Channah and Molly worked on a birth plan. She could not plan for every eventuality, but hoped it would convey a sense of peace and acceptance to her birth team that she was finding in her own heart. She knew they were doing as much as they could for their baby without holding out false hope. No one could know the extent of their baby's problems until she was born, and at that time she and Aaron would decide what to do next. If there was the possibility that she could be helped and that it might support her quality of life, then that option was open. If it was not a reasonable hope, then they would not want her to suffer longer only to grow worse in the end. Only a parent can make those decisions. She would have to find the right way for her.

With humility and honor I agreed to be part of their birth team. I wouldn't have all the right words, but I wouldn't say a bunch of wrong things either, like "You can always have more children," or "She would not have been normal" or "Time will heal this." It won't. I know the devastation, but I also know parents can survive and come out the other side able to understand others as never before, and that there would come a time when tears wouldn't fall each and every day.

That Monday in May was a beautiful spring day. How could we be meeting that morning to discuss death? My mind found it all surreal. Channah and Aaron were very friendly, and just . . . well, open. Molly read through the last ultrasound report and answered questions like, "What is IUGR (intrauterine growth restriction)?" Molly explained it meant the baby was growing much slower than normal and the concerns continued: short arms, small head compared to stomach circumference, enlarged heart, and brain abnormalities. But we could not say we had a true picture of intrauterine growth restriction. The neonatologists had scheduled an echocardiogram for the baby in four weeks. It is done much like an ultrasound before birth and would give us a much better idea whether the heart could be repaired after birth or if that was not a possibility.

The couple could decide what they wanted the birth to look like once they knew this piece of information. If their baby had a chance of benefiting from heart surgery we wanted to be at a hospital with neonatal cardiologists available at all times. Many hospitals cannot offer that. If their baby did not appear to have a condition that could be fixed, they said they didn't want to be at a high-powered, state-of-the-arts maternity unit but would lean more toward a quiet, natural birth, possibly at home.

On July 1, Molly picked me up. We were now visiting Channah once a week. We mostly talked about the discovery that an ultrasound had shown the baby was in a breech position (not head down). Even though her baby was most likely under three pounds and due in less than three weeks, and it was not her first baby, the neonatologist she saw wouldn't deliver a breech baby vaginally. He was insisting on a C-section. He even went so far as to tell her at the last appointment that her baby would die if delivered vaginally because her head would become entrapped inside the cervix, that her stomach was not big enough to keep the cervix dilated. Really? The stomach should not and would not be dictating the size of dilation. The cervix does that on its own and then the baby can begin to descend through the birth canal. If at that point the baby is allowed to come out slowly, the head will come down to the hairline, which will become visible and then the midwife or doctor can assist the head by lifting the baby up, releasing the head. It will not become entrapped if the cervix is allowed to dilate naturally and the woman is helped to stay calm. This was shown in Ina May Gaskin's 2013 movie, *Birth Story*.

Channah said that she had almost asked the doctor why he was trying to scare her into a C-section. He was obviously terrified of natural birth and untrained in breech birth.

She switched to plan B, which was to find a practitioner with hospital privileges who would agree to attend a vaginal breech birth. I called two former home-birth doctors I have known for decades and Molly called several of her contacts.

I offered to do a belly cast for Channah as a way to remember this baby that I was convinced could not live long after birth, given the list of problems we had heard about. It was a beautiful belly cast. She was in her ninth month and as big and round as all of my other mamas, though we were told this baby was still only around three pounds. Was there too much water? What could account for her size, then? I could only wonder.

About ten days before her due date I got the call. Channah's water had broken and some contractions confirmed that it would be the day. Molly had thought that perhaps this baby could become overdue, citing statistics suggesting that babies with multiple anomalies often bring with them a deficit of labor hormones and frequently require induction around forty-two weeks, a full two weeks past the due date. Molly was out of town. I called her and she offered to fly back but Channah said that she was happy with me being there and to tell Molly not to feel like she had to rush back.

I met them at the hospital. Soon a friend of Channah's who was also a doula arrived. She had attended the birth of Channah's first baby. I was glad for her help and loving energy. She radiated love with her caring presence. She was so good at what she did, including massaging Channah's legs and back, I told myself that I was going to step back and just learn from her, and I did. She was more than good; she was brilliant.

The hospital staff, however, wasn't too good at relaying information to Channah, who had expected to be informed about her progress throughout her labor. Her baby's fetal heart tones were exhibiting some "hiccups" that concerned them a bit, and then Channah developed a slight fever, which elicited more concerns. When she got to nine centimeters an obstetrician was called. He explained why they wanted to do a C-section at that point, but Channah said she didn't feel it was really necessary.

She wanted to understand their rationale and was trying to explain her need to understand when one of the nurses asked if she could check her dilation once more since it had been awhile. When she did, while keeping her fingers inside of Channah's cervix, she told the other nurse to hit the emergency button on the wall as she jumped onto the bed. She knelt between Channah's legs and whispered to the closest nurse, "Prolapse." My heart froze.

The umbilical cord had either washed down the birth canal or fell forward and was protruding out the vagina, ahead of the baby. Should the baby come down further, either butt first or head first, it could pinch off its oxygen supply. The room instantly filled with people. The nurse was still on the bed with her whole hand inside Channah now.

We all knew the drill: cup the cord into your palm and extend your fingers forward at the same time, find the baby's head (or butt in this case) and push the baby's body back up into the uterus. Then hold him there, off of the cord. The nurse was preparing to hold this baby back from descending at all until Channah could be prepped for an emergency C-section.

Nurses were racing to unplug the IV and anything else attached to the bed and were soon racing it down the hall to the OR with Channah and the nurse on it. No one explained to Channah why she was suddenly being taken out this way.

I knew Aaron nor I would not be allowed into the OR, that there would most likely not be time for an epidural, and Channah would be given general anesthesia instead.

Channah later told us what happened next. She insisted on being told what (the bleep) was going on before they could operate. As they were explaining, much too fast for anyone to take in, the surgeon came in, stood at the end of the bed and sized up the situation. The nurse confirmed that Channah was complete at ten centimeters, so this doc-tor, who had experience with breech births, and knew how opposed to a C-section Channah had been all along, simply said, "Well, just push your baby out." He grasped the baby's feet when they appeared and, while flat on her back, arms strapped down on a very cold operating table, Channah pushed her baby out.

A nurse ran back to the room and told us the good news, which we didn't believe at first. But we knew Channah was capable of just about anything, knew what she wanted and what was best for her baby and never wavered on that.

I wondered to myself whether the OB thought the baby wasn't going to make it through delivery in whatever form, or if he simply un-derstood that this baby was so tiny, at three pounds, that we weren't in the same danger with a prolapsed cord that we would have been with a bigger baby. Channah's baby was brought to the warmer and intubated, whisked past her to touch briefly, and then on to the NICU, followed by her daddy.

Channah was brought back to the room and promptly washed and dressed herself and ordered some breakfast. Then she headed down to the NICU, walking on her own steam.

Her baby was hooked up to numerous tubes and lines by then, but Channah looked past all that, wriggled her hand under the wires and onto her baby's tummy and began singing to her. The baby was bigger than anyone had guessed—four pounds, two ounces—and her arms were not too short. Unfortunately, though, multiple anomalies involv-ing her liver, brain, heart, and eyes soon became apparent.

Over the next few days the baby continued to astound us. First her IV was removed and then shortly after that, her respirator. She was breathing on her own with a tiny bit of oxygen coming in through a nose cannula. A few days after that her feeding tube was removed when she proved she could breastfeed. In the meantime, the neonatol-ogists, pediatric cardiologists, and pediatricians continued to be completely stumped. Genetic tests failed to point to any syndrome or known anomaly. The genome DNA test results were negative. There was no infection, bacterial or viral, that could be attributed to her problems. No one understood the whys, but Channah didn't care. Once her baby's oxygen tube was discontinued, she took her home. The power of love is mightier than all of us. Just a few know how to use such power, though, and Channah was one of them.

It is these mamas and babies that put doulas and midwives in our place. We don't know nothin' when it comes to miracles. I had the honor of meeting a true Tiger Mama.

"Women today not only possess genetic memory of birth from a thousand generations of women, but they are also assailed from every direction by information and misinformation about birth."
~Valerie El Halta

Chapter Twenty-Six

Two More Amazing Births

Two of my other moms gave birth during May that year. The first was a Latina *madre* giving birth to her fourth *niño*. She had medications with the other three, so when she went from three to six centimeters in one hour and started asking for some IV pain relief, her midwife hesitated. She ordered it from the hospital pharmacy but by the time it came fifteen minutes later, she insisted on checking Carmen just once more. Sure enough, she was between eight and nine centimeters. Fentanyl, morphine, or another short-term drug would affect the baby, though it usually only lasts between one to two hours. But the downside is that it can, and often does, make the baby sleepy or dopey, too. It can make him so drowsy that he might forget to breathe at birth, in which case we have to switch to a full-blown neonatal resuscitation, which is not without risks. We knew Carmen's first stage, getting to ten centimeters dilation, could be over within minutes at the rate she was going. And it was.

She leaped out of bed, not an easy feat for a 215-pound mama, and announced she had to poop, our signal that a major push was imminent. She came back to the bed but didn't want to lie down so as I raised the head of the bed I maneuvered Carmen into a kneeling position with her arms over the top of the head of the bed. Two pushes and her baby was out, being passed forward between her legs so that she could pick up her squalling *niño*. She looked at me then, completely overwhelmed.

I said, "Honey, you did it!"

She replied, "I never tried that before."

As she lay back down with her baby he raised his head and threw himself toward her nipple and within minutes latched on. She looked at all of us and said, "I've never seen anything like this!" Well, right. He didn't have any drugs on board. No wonder he was so alert. She was delighted with her unexpected natural birth.

The second mom was a Native American lady, Aponi, whom I had become very fond of while we got to know each other. It was also her fourth baby. She was over forty and diabetic. For several days before her prenatal appointment she had been experiencing headaches but didn't tell anyone. Not a good idea. When she went to the appointment and they took her blood pressure they realized she was in deep trouble. She was experiencing preeclampsia. She could have gone into a seizure at any time. She and her baby were at serious risk. She was rushed to the hospital by ambulance for an emergency Cesarean section. She didn't have time to go home and fetch her hospital bag and didn't have my number in her cell phone. It was on top of the suitcase by the door in her kitchen.

Her baby was safely delivered, a ten-pounder looking more like a two-month old baby. His sugars were tested at birth and were dangerously low, so he was whisked off to the NICU where an IV was started to stabilize his sugars until his mama's milk came in and could replace it. Her blood pressure remained high during the next twelve hours, which worried the doctors very much.

With all this drama going on, Aponi had not really taken in any of the explanations about what was happening, either with her or her baby. Her partner did not speak English, so he also had not been able to grasp what was going on. Halfway through the morning he called me while she started texting that the wanted me to come right away. Of course I had no way of knowing what had transpired during the night. Her texts kept coming and made little sense. I assured Aponi I was on my way.

When I got there she was rather hysterical. I would have been, too! She had not seen her baby again since her blood pressure was still not stabilized. She was receiving IV meds for that and had been told that it was slowly improving but she didn't really understand that either, being more worried about her baby. It seemed to me to be one of those "take charge" moments, as we doulas call it, so I thought for a moment and proposed a plan. I told her I would stay with her for the day and we would sort out each concern, one at a time. I said we would go over the events leading up to the C-section and why the interventions were necessary. She said that would be a good idea.

I ordered her a breakfast tray and got her to eat a bit. I wanted to get her feeling better first. I reassured her that I would stay all day and we'd straighten everything out. We talked about the headaches and preeclampsia. I explained what the doctor's fears were and why they had acted so fast, though she didn't understand half of it at the time. I left the room to get coffee and give her time to translate what I had said to Pedro. Next she wanted to know what was going on with her baby and how soon he would be brought to her room. Was he in danger? What was wrong? Why weren't they breastfeeding yet or bonding?

The nurse had brought in a breast pump during the night but Aponi had not known how to use it or that her colostrum would be fed to her baby, so we talked about that next. I helped her pump and realized her milk was already coming in. We gave a whole ounce to the nurse when she came in, who was delighted, labeled it, and took it down to the nursery right away. I suggested that I go down to the nursery with Pedro and see what I could find out about the baby. Being so frightened had not helped to lower Aponi's blood pressure.

Pedro proudly led the way to the NICU, where their baby lay sleeping. He was attached to an IV and several monitors. Pedro had briefly held him earlier in the day. The nurse asked his permission to talk to me about their baby, which he immediately agreed to, so she went over everything that we wanted to know. Then I translated what she said back into my "pidgin *Española*" for him. It turned out that the baby's blood sugars had been so low that they started a glucose IV immediately at birth. They were also giving him a concentrated formula in a bottle every hour to keep his sugars up and would slowly wean him from that as his mama's milk came in. He was doing well but seemed very sleepy to me. The nurse explained that he was also under bilirubin lights to help a mild case of jaundice and that sometimes that makes babies sleepy. I took in the whole picture there by the incubator and wondered if he wouldn't be happier skin-to-skin with his mama or even his dad. He was not connected to a respirator and did not appear to have any other problems, so I asked the nurse if Pedro could hold him for a while. She readily agreed and began untangling all the wires so she could give him to his daddy. I didn't know how receptive Pedro would be to the idea but decided to give it a try: I asked if he would please take off his shirt.

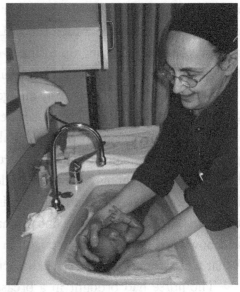

Giving a newborn a bath.

"Now?" he asked.

"Yes, now, so that your baby doesn't get cold out here. It will keep him warm." This was a new idea, but I guess my grandma status won out and he obediently removed his shirt. I noticed he was blushing. He sat down and held his baby. This was a first. It was his first child, by the way. Then his baby woke up, opened his eyes and mouth and looked up into Pedro's face. It was priceless.

By suppertime the nursery decided the baby was doing well enough to room-in with his mommy. Her blood pressure was finally staying in an acceptable range. I helped her order supper and reviewed her choices for pain meds for the night. Aponi told me that she was so glad I had come and she felt she could now manage the days ahead.

"Three hundred thousand women will be giving birth with you today. Relax and breathe and do nothing else. Labor is hard work; it hurts and you can do it."
~Anonymous

Chapter Twenty-Seven

Doulas and Dads

One night I watched the British PBS TV series *Call The Midwife!* which is set in the 1950s and '60s. In the episode the drama being played out was between one young couple as the mother went into labor while the Korean War veteran dad-to-be was suffering symptoms of what was referred to back then as "shellshock," which we now recognize as PTSD. As soon as their baby girl was born, the wise midwife hands the baby to the father. He sees blood, one of the "triggers" that has been setting him off since the war, but this time it is "good blood," as the midwife tells him. He is healed as he holds his tiny miracle. His wife has been through the worst with him and now he is no longer the victim and not only supports her but shares this amazing gift of life with her. It was a very moving moment.

As I watched, I was struck by the coincidence since I had been thinking very much about two recent births I had attended. Under two very different circumstances neither mother was able to hold their newborns immediately after birth and in both cases their babies had been left alone on warmers at the other end of the room.

Only a month earlier I was privileged to spend time with Dr. Nils Bergman, a researcher from South Africa. Dr. Bergman speaks all over the world about his findings about skin-to-skin contact, or "kangaroo care," especially the benefits to premature infants. He goes so far as to say that preemies will actually do better if kangaroo care is introduced immediately at birth and we do away with incubators all together. My own research into bonding, or maternal-infant-maternal attachment, also points to zero separation at all births and is now being scientifically confirmed by Dr. Bergman's and others' studies.

Conchita and Enriké had come from Spain to study at the University of Minnesota. Toward the end of Conchita's pregnancy, they asked me to be their doula. It was their first birth and Conchita had been dealing with multiple chronic health issues that she was quite successful in controlling with natural methods. They had really done their homework and were determined to have a natural birth. We were able to squeeze in two visits before her labor began. We had put together a birth plan, listing all of their wishes and all of the things they hoped to avoid, though they were very realistic about the possibility of interventions in their case.

A week later they called in the middle of a snowstorm. I met them at the hospital as the nurse was hooking up a monitor on Conchita's belly. Baby sounded fine. Her midwife was called and luckily she was in the hospital. She walked right over to check Conchita's dilation. We were breathing through each contraction, which were very regular. I thought Conchita was handling this stage very well and expected to hear she was two, or maybe four centimeters along at that point, since it was a first baby. When the midwife announced she was eight already I was surprised.

With a flock of nurses now setting up the room and the midwife gowning up, I continued to breathe with Conchita. With the next contraction she instinctively pushed for all she was worth. I knew she didn't need to be checked again, but the midwife wanted to be sure she was fully dilated, which of course she was. Two more mega pushes and the head was out. Another contraction and their beautiful baby girl slid out, followed by a rather impressive river of blood. It looked like a lot to me, so I waited to see how I should back up the midwife's next move. The nurses also saw that there would be something other than the regular plop-baby-on-mom's-tummy program happening next and carried the baby to the warmer after hastily clamping the mother's end of the cord and cutting the baby loose.

Dad Enriké had never seen a birth so he thought all of this was routine and very normal. The midwife was talking to Conchita while the nurses were hooking up an IV with Pitocin and fluids. She was in good hands so I turned my attention to the baby, concerned that she not be left alone. I went over to the warmer and learned the baby was doing beautifully with a Apgar score of ten.

Especially after my own work on bonding and then hearing Dr. Bergman talk, I was, and am, completely convinced that babies are born fully expecting a continuum of contact: there should be zero separation from the first moment. Not only are human babies fully hard-wired with this expectation, they will not fully thrive unless it is provided. Some researchers are now suggesting that the multitude of developmental disorders that are mysteriously proliferating in this century—in spite of all of our advanced science and medical knowledge—may very well be due to unnecessary separation and lack of attention in some cases.

No one was paying much attention to the baby at this point. All of the drama was across the room while everyone was trying to figure out where the hemorrhage was coming from. So I loosely wrapped up the baby and replaced her soggy little hat with a dry one while I talked to her. I held her close and walked to Dad, who was still standing at the head of the bed by his wife. The midwife was trying to sound calm and reassuring as she explained to them that she was poking around down there trying to find the source of the bleeding.

I walked Dad back to the other side of the room and motioned for him to sit down in the rocking chair by the warmer. I suggested he take his shirt off and keep his baby nice and warm and skin-to-skin until Conchita could take her. He did what I asked immediately. I find that dads are especially compliant at this stage and will do absolutely anything I ask them to. I could have just said, "Strip," and he would have.

His baby girl had already started blowing bubbles and was rooting around when I picked her up. I told him she already knew him and his voice and was smelling him as she got to know him. The look on his face said it all. He was smitten. As she cuddled into his chest I could tell he had probably never held an infant. Then she started throwing her head back and wiggling. I told him just to hold her close as I wrapped them both in blankets. When she reached the point where her head was cradled in the crook of his arm and her cheek was touching his furry chest, she stuck out her tongue and started licking his nipple! Dad looked up at me with tears in his eyes. He completely melted. I just repeated to him that she knew him and needed to stay with her parents.

In the meantime, the room had now filled with a couple of doctors and additional nurses. They had found the source of the bleed. Its apex was behind the cervix in the posterior or back vaginal wall that rides above the rectum. One of the medical issues that Conchita had been dealing with was a problem with the clotting factor in her blood. Because her baby had descended down the birth canal so very quickly, where most women would have stretched slowly as the baby's head molded, her tissue had simply parted and broke open. It was about the worst fourth-degree tear I had ever seen but they were tying off the bleeding veins and soon had the situation under control.

Enriké was somewhat oblivious about what was going on. I was glad I could reassure him and get him and the baby away from the electric vibes on the other side of the room and create a safe, sacred space for his baby during this time. Within an hour we were able to get the baby girl onto her mother's chest where she immediately raised her head and latched on the first try without any direction from us.

I visited them the next day in the hospital and the day after that at their home and both times found Enriké still holding his baby with his shirt off. I marveled at this continuum bonding as I had rarely seen it.

I wondered how I could do this more. How could this affect father-baby bonding especially? I did not have long to wait to find out.

A week later I was at a birth at a different hospital with a couple who were living in one of the most crime-ridden neighborhoods in the city. You can automatically add social and economic poverty to the list of things this family was dealing with. It was this mom's third baby, though it was his first. He was clueless. But it was his baby and he was going to be there.

Unfortunately, one out of every three children in America (thirty-three percent) live in homes without a father. The African American community continues to struggle with the highest rate of absentee fathers in the nation, with nearly two in three African American children (sixty-four percent) living in father-absent homes.

I knew all this but wondered if bonding could lead to a reversal of those statistics. While I was busy pondering this, I was referred to Sh'neice.

I was able to meet with Sh'neice four times in the weeks before her guess date. She was taking very good care of herself and her other children and we had enjoyed getting to know each other.

At her request, I went with her to her last prenatal clinic visit. She had hoped to have a VBAC (vaginal birth after Caesarian) but her OB wasn't budging. The doctor convinced her that after two C-sections already, another was the best choice for her. As a doula it wasn't my call. As much as I would love to have supported her having a VBAC, it would have only undermined her relationship with her physician, so I bit my tongue. Hard.

I met her at 7:00 a.m. at the hospital on the appointed day. When she was finally wheeled down to the OR at 11:00 a.m. her boyfriend and I put on the scrubs the nurse had handed us. He looked at himself in the mirror and I could just barely hear him say under his breath, "I will not faint . . . I will not faint . . ." I realized then that this was his first-ever birth. Was there any way I could involve him and have him feel intimately a part of this birth? I wondered. It was easy when a dad is at an all-night birth and I can have him rubbing Mom's back, fetching juices, wiping her face with cold cloths and walking the halls for hours on end, but this was all going according to hospital protocol and I didn't know what I could do to fit him into this picture.

I did all the usual things I do at C-sections. He took pictures as his baby was taken to the warmer and he held his baby's hand as the baby was assessed. I usually also direct the dad to hand the baby back to Mom, but Sh'neice was still quite uncomfortable and the doctors had a lot to do to repair, not only the incision but also the extensive scar tissue from the two previous Cesareans, so she was not ready to hold her baby when he did return.

Dad was happy to just sit and hold his fat bundle where she could see him. I checked in with him periodically to make sure he was okay. He did really well, and I told him so.

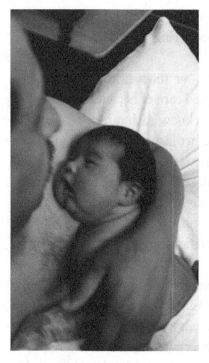

When it was finally time to move into the recovery room we all followed the bed out of the OR and down the hall, Dad proudly carrying his very own baby. As soon as we got there Sh'neice began vomiting, which is not all that unusual after surgery. She needed a little more time to recover. She still was not ready to hold her baby.

I looked over at Dad standing nearby, rocking from side to side with his little bundle in his arms. He was in his own world with his baby girl. *Good*, I thought. I pushed over a glider-rocker and, offering to take Baby, suggested he take off his shirt and hold her skin-to-skin to keep her warm. Of course I had him under my spell by now, and he would have gladly done whatever I requested. As he sat down I handed him his baby and helped him unwrap her. I wrapped them both back up then with a warm flannel blanket.

The next time Sh'neice looked over to see where they were, she saw him talking to his baby, who was now looking up into his eyes. She had not tried to open them in the OR with all the bright lights.

I thought, *This is right. Only this baby can change this big dude with his huge, tight abs and fly swagger. Only this baby can turn him into a real dad.*

"The truth for women living in a modern world is that they must take increasing re-sponsibility for the skills they bring into birth if they want their birth to be natural. Making choices of where and with whom to birth is not the same as bringing knowl-edge and skills into your birth regardless of where and with whom you birth."
~Common Knowledge Trust

Chapter Twenty-Eight

A Different Dad . . .
and Forgiveness

I kept bumping into dear Suzanne in the Somali neighborhood where I often work. She had a little store on one of the side streets. A forty-something quintissentially Irish woman with flaming red hair, she was raising two boys and a daughter within a very unhappy marriage.

We got along as if we had been kindred spirits in a past life. We were both very moved by the recent influx of African refugees to Minneapolis, both of us finding little ways to make them feel welcomed and helping to make their move halfway around the world a little easier. Suzanne was able to employ some of the teenagers in her store and begged donations of warm coats to give out during their first winter in America. For most, it was their first experience of snow.

We soon realized we could do twice as much if the two of us teamed up, so we did. With her car and my referrals for expectant moms in the nearby neighborhoods, we started doing what we could, finding church and Salvation Army food pantries to help families; we even found shelters for homeless moms. We took one mom on a shopping spree when it looked like she would burst her non-maternity clothes.

I figured the bad-marriage stuff was none of my business but when she and I became such close friends, she decided to tell me her story. I listened. She had been praying for her husband for most of their nineteen years together. Many years earlier a priest had counseled that if she fasted and prayed enough, she could fix their marriage and somehow "cure" her husband's alcoholism. Year after year of abuse continued and the advice she got was to pray harder. At one point she did pray harder: that she would die and the whole nightmare would be

over. She fantasized about a car accident that would be swift and virtually painless. She fasted until she became anorexic.

Her father had also been abusive, so when she married and things began to go downhill she figured it was just the "new normal." She blamed herself and her lack of faith. Maybe if she was able to become "good enough" he wouldn't treat her so badly or drink so much. She went to church, sometimes daily. They drifted into two molds: one good, attempting to be a martyr perhaps; the other, an unrepentant sinner.

I couldn't believe that in this day and age people would put up with so much hurt for so very long. I told Suzanne that I only wanted to support her and be a friend, but that I could not have withstood what she had endured for so long. I told her I would kick him out and only then pray for him. I did not believe any God or higher power would demand this suffering of her. There was no way that that was right. End of sermon.

So she did. She kicked him out. It was liberating. Freeing. But it was hard raising teenagers alone and trying to work and keep the business afloat. The business did go under, but at that point it was the least of her worries.

Over soup in my apartment one day she told me she was three months pregnant. She was convinced her kids would hate her, her church would judge her, and her family would be furious with her. She admitted that she had thought about an abortion for a fleeting moment, but that was all. She could not do it.

I told her that I still loved her and would do anything at all to help her in the coming months and that this baby must have a very special task here on earth. And of course I would be her doula.

Over the next weeks we continued to talk about how this baby must have a very special mission here on earth, though we could not imagine what that might be. We would find out soon enough.

I had not pried into the circumstances of this baby's appearance but one day Suzanne offered to tell me about it. While she was working in the neighborhood she had met someone tall, dark, and handsome. He was Irish and nice, the nicest man she had ever met. He knew how to treat a woman. It was totally new to Suzanne. No one had ever not hurt her. She fell in love.

Eventually she did tell her kids. The older ones were shocked and one stopped talking to her. The youngest was still confused by the separation, and now was trying to deal with another shock. She assured them all that they would make it, that things would get better and that she was excited there would be a baby in the house. They were still a family and they still had the house and each other. It would be okay.

Then the tall, handsome love of her life vanished as if into thin air, simply disappeared. No one has heard from him since.

Suzanne and I continued to do what we could at the women's shelters and in the refugee community. Before we knew it, her midwife was talking about induction and a C-section for a whole host of reasons, though her age was not one of them. Her care was transferred to the clinic's obstetrician. Suzanne was ready to be un-pregnant by this time. Pregnancy in one's forties is not fun. The date was set and we tried to get psyched up. It wasn't what we had hoped for this birth, but it was okay.

The week before B-Day, who should appear but Suzanne's ex-husband, asking if they could go for a walk and talk. They met and walked every night that week. He had started therapy to address his issues— the drinking, the abuse, all of it. He also wanted her to know he had started going to church. He didn't want to lose his family or her. He asked her forgiveness and said he would agree to counseling or anything else she wanted. He knew she had no reason to take him back.

He also pointed out that the baby she was carrying would need a daddy to bring her up. Suzanne was floored, to say the least. She couldn't imagine why he would want her back, especially with a baby that was not his. At this point they both realized neither was a lost soul nor a saint. She asked his forgiveness. They were both on the same bench for the very first time in their nineteen-year relationship. They both felt somehow unworthy and needing forgiveness. He wanted to step up and be there for her, be a better dad to his kids, and stop throwing everything dear to him out the window.

I continued to be wary of his sincerity but Suzanne agreed to take him back on a trial basis, with absolute agreement on his part to her list of requirements.

Then he told her he wanted to be at the delivery to support her. He had been there for the last three and didn't see that this one was any different. I doubted this guy was for real. I had turned into a skeptic, but she was determined to give him yet another chance.

And he was there. He asked to hold the baby as soon as she was born and proudly danced around the operating room with her. One of the nurses commented, "Oh, look! She has your eyes!" to him, at which Suzanne and I rolled ours at each other.

As this is being written, he has turned out to be for real. It hasn't always been easy, but when Suzanne told me one day that she found it sad that her baby would never know her real dad, I told her in no uncertain terms that her husband was her baby's real daddy, that the Creator had brought the perfect daddy for her back and she should never again doubt that. This baby does have a mission: she is a real peacemaker, as much as Gandhi or Mother Teresa. I had never seen anything like it before.

"Ask me for strength and I will lend not only my hand, but also my heart."
~Anonymous

Chapter Twenty-Nine
Waiting for Radiya

It was a Thursday night. My bag was packed and sitting by our front door. Two whole outfits were clean and hanging in the closet. The sticky note was still on the door by the lock so I couldn't miss it, reminding me to bring my phone, phone cord, keys, snacks, etc.

Radiya was due yesterday. She worked nights at the St. Paul-Minneapolis Airport assembling the little meals offered for sale on airplanes. She stood at an assembly line with hundreds of other immigrant men and women from 3:00 a.m. until 11:00 a.m. every morning, as her swollen ankles told me.

We had met the previous week at the clinic where I could avail myself of the Amharic translator. Many of the 70,000 African immigrants live in ethnic clusters throughout Minneapolis and St. Paul. A large group of Ethiopians in Radiya's neighborhood have their own clinic with culture-specific assets: women translators, women nurses, and women midwives only, since few Muslim women would be allowed—or even wish—to see a male practitioner.

After Radiya's appointment she was given a portable crib, still new in its box, and another box with baby clothes, diapers, and blankets. I knew she shouldn't lift the crib box and would be taking a taxi home after her appointment. I had taken a bus to the clinic so I offered to go home with her in the taxi and do the lifting.

When we got there the taxi driver unloaded the boxes from the trunk onto the sidewalk and drove off, so I wrestled with the boxes while Radiya held open the doors to her building. I unpacked the crib and found the assembly instructions. They were not as simple as I had hoped. While I worked on it in the living room she fixed us lunch. I finally got the crib together and standing, but when we each took an end and tried to walk it into the bedroom, we couldn't get it through the doorway. I tipped it up on a side and then on its end and it still wouldn't fit. I didn't know that doulas need a certificate in carpentry. So we took it back out to the living room and disassembled it. We carried all the pieces into the bedroom and set it up once again, from scratch, and faster that time.

It barely fit between the wall and the bed but we got it in the room. The bed took up more than three quarters of the tiny bedroom. I suggested she leave the crib in the living room so she had a place for the baby while she cooked and just keep her baby in bed with her during the night. She had been well drilled at the clinic about the dangers of sleeping with her baby and seemed shocked that I would even suggest it. I asked if they had cribs back in Ethiopia and she laughed and said, "Of course not!" So I asked her what she thought her baby would prefer, being with her where he could nurse and see and smell his mama or off alone in a crib? I went over the basics of safe co-sleeping and told her how we had done it with our five children, even with our twins, reminding her that all pillows and blankets should be clear of the baby and he could have his own small blanket or go to bed in a warm bunting or suit.

When all the plastic wrap and boxes were cleaned up she invited me to the table to have lunch with her. She made her own bread, a round white loaf fragrant with spices and black pepper. A mug of hot, sweet, milky cardamom tea added to the warmth of the apartment.

Radya's husband was still in Ethiopia. She explained that when she becomes a citizen she could sponsor him, though she might have to wait up to five years for the whole process. As a U.S. resident with a green card, she could go back to visit him and still return to the U.S. So she came to Minnesota to work and to make her little apartment a home for when they can be together again.

The following evening my husband and I drove to the same housing project for a postpartum follow-up visit with another Ethiopian family. We were surprised when we got there to see Radiya in Belem's kitchen. We learned they were best friends and Radiya cooked for her friend every day since she got home from the hospital with her new baby. I had called ahead and explained to the new daddy that we wouldn't stay long, but that I wanted to drop off some baby clothes and have them fill out the survey for the doula program that I was required to turn in, but I knew when we got there that there was no way we were going to be leaving within the next hour.

It was an interesting visit. I looked at the baby in his crib and asked when he had last nursed. He was tiny at birth, just five pounds. She said it had been at least three hours, maybe more. I asked how long he had been sleeping during the night and they both agreed it was four hours or more. It was sweltering in the apartment, though it was winter, so I suggested they unwrap him a bit. As they did so I realized he had on two blankets, a fuzzy sleeper, a little dress under that, and a onesie under that. And socks.

When he stretched and yawned I noticed his mouth and lips were quite dry, but there was no evidence of jaundice. I switched gears and we talked about breastfeeding him more often and I laid out some ideas for that. His mom changed his diaper while we were talking and I was very surprised to see that he had not been circumcised. I looked at his dad and he explained that the insurance company just cut off (pun not intended) all non-emergency services and they couldn't have it done in the hospital because of that. They had shopped around and the going price at all of the clinics that performed circumcisions charged a flat $600.

I explained that circumcision is no longer deemed a necessary medical procedure by all of the American doctors' and pediatricians' organizations. I also explained that numerous studies had shown that not having it done does not increase the child's chances of getting infections,

HIV, or AIDS later in life. I explained that all little boys need to be taught correct washing and that it is even considered by many today as genital mutilation and an offense against boys who have no say in what is happening to them.

Half of the people at the apartment were Muslim and the other half Ethiopian Orthodox Christians, all educated, some with graduate degrees. None of the people present that night felt that circumcision was part of some rite of initiation. None subscribed to the idea that it was exclusively cultural, either. For both the Christians and Muslims, it was ordained by their religions. The Ethiopian Orthodox Christians cited the Old Testament injunction and the Muslims the Quran.

I told them that my own sons, Abraham and Isaac, were not circumcised and when they grew up both had said that they were glad it had not been done to them as babies. One of the women said that beyond the religious reasons, women prefer men who have been circumcised. I asked why.

I couldn't believe we were having such a frank discussion in mixed company. This was a first for me. Either we visited as women only and talked about labor and birth, or I visit a couple and the conversation usually stays on a somewhat formal level.

She explained that it is just nicer, cleaner, not as ugly, and she could not imagine sex with a man who had not had it done. I laughed and discreetly pointed to my husband who was still enjoying his *ingera* and *dahl* and didn't see my message at all. They got quite a laugh out of that!

I understood what the symbol represents for them within both religions and I realized that I had just wandered into quite a minefield. One of the dads even suggested that they could take their sons back to Ethiopia when they were five. They could be circumcised and see the relatives at the same time. The two mothers present protested, saying that it would hurt so much more when their precious little sons were older.

My fear was that an immigrant in Minnesota who had seen it done back in the old country would start doing it himself, "underground," so to speak.

Over the next several days, I called a few clinics and found out that very few insurance companies were still covering the cost of circumcisions. The lowest fee I could find was $377, which would still be quite a lot for an immigrant family. Then I found out that one hospital had their residents do them for free for patients who gave birth to their babies there. Next I called the hospital that most of the Ethiopians used and asked if they knew that the other hospital was offering circumcisions free and that they were at risk of losing an entire customer base because they were not. They knew it was an issue but did not know the full extent of the problem.

Then I called a reformed, or liberal, Jewish synagogue. I knew they had what are called *mohels* or non-medical people who perform the religious or ritual circumcisions in temples and in homes. The rabbi agreed to email me a list of *mohels* in the Twin Cities. She could not tell me if they would be willing to do it for non-Jews, or if their rabbis would allow it.

I called one other name on the list who turned out to be an elderly, retired Orthodox Jewish rabbi who was also trained as a *mohel*. When he started talking he sounded just like my own *zaide* (grandfather), who had died at ninety in 1981, and I melted. He suggested that I learn how to do it. He suggested I should find a nice (Jewish) doctor who would let me watch him a dozen times or more and then certify me. Yikes! That wasn't where I wanted to go. I would be excommunicated from the birth community.

I found one *mohel* who was both a physician and Jewish. She was very intrigued with the idea of performing circumcisions for the African communities here. She was employed by one of the big health networks and explained that she would have to look into the legal issues that might prevent her doing it outside of her own hospital. In the meantime, I was getting calls daily asking if I had found anyone to help them.

The following Monday the phone rang at 3:00 a.m. Radiya thought her water had broken and she was having a few random rushes about fifteen minutes apart. I suggested she call the midwife at the hospital and let me know what she said. This was a first baby. I knew we could easily be looking at a twenty-four-hour labor. I went back to bed until the phone rang at 4:00 a.m. It was a nurse at the hospital asking if I was on my way. The contractions were now four minutes apart. They had told Radiya to get to the hospital right away, so she had called 911. She and a girlfriend, who also didn't drive, were already at the hospital.

By 5:00 a.m. she was three centimeters dilated and seenty-five per-cent effaced. Radiya was asking for meds. I suggested that she get out of bed. Once up, Radiya said she felt so much better to be up rather than lying down with monitors strapped on. We walked the halls and tried the rocking chair in the room. I insisted that she drink a whole cup of juice and visit the bathroom, both once an hour. The midwife came in and offered some options for meds, which Radiya agreed to, so she was brought back to bed and an IV was started. She asked if it would help her labor. I pointed out that she would be more relaxed, which might help her dilate, or she could become sleepy and slow it down. I knew just being back in bed would slow things down.

Once she was on the IV the nurse asked her to switch to juices only, no food, and explained that they would need to do continuous electronic monitoring of the baby to be sure he didn't react to the drugs, which is exactly what happened in the next few minutes. His heart rate dropped with each contraction. The nurses and the midwife watched the numbers for a while and considered their next options.

In the meantime, it appeared that though the meds affected the baby, they didn't do much of anything for Radiya. She was still having some big rushes every four minutes and not getting much relief from the IV. They added another bag of IV fluids when she vomited all the juice she'd had so far. We dealt with each rush together and got into a rhythm.

"Breathe in through your nose, hold it . . . slowly blow it out . . . breathe in, slowly . . ..now breathe out . . . and rest." Her midwife encouraged her as did the nurses. They checked her again: four centimeters. The meds had worn off completely and she was asking for an epidural. I pointed out how well she was doing and talked her through more rushes using visualization, riding over each "wave" and then watching it go away. "There, you did it. Blow that one away now. You never have to do that one again. It is gone. It has done its work. Let each one open you up . . . that's it. You are sooo strong! Think of all of your grandmothers and great-grandmothers . . . all the women all over the world that are birthing their babies tonight. You can do this . . . breathe . . . Good job. You are brilliant."

At 7:00 a.m. the epidural was ordered though the nurses told her the anesthesiologist was in surgery and would come soon. The nurses all left the room and I suggested Radiya get up to go to the bathroom before the procedure. She agreed and then was again surprised how much better she felt standing rather than lying on her back in bed. We got through the next rushes while she was on the toilet. Radiya closed her eyes and leaned against the wall and rested.

The rushes seemed to be gaining strength, to me at least, so when the midwife came back to check on her I asked if she wanted to see what her dilation was before getting the epidural. The midwife said no because she was only four centimeters at the last check. While we were talking, the next contraction started and with it we both heard Radiya first breathe in and then push with everything she had. I was not surprised but the midwife seemed completely flustered. It had only been six hours since Radiya's water broke but it became quite apparent that her body knew exactly what to do and she was following along perfectly.

The midwife ran out to get the nurses to set up the room as I continued to support Radiya, who now had both my arms locked in her grip, resting her head on my shoulder. I was sort of half kneeling, half standing, leaning on the side of the toilet. I asked the nurse to get some pillows. Radiya leaned back on them before the next rush. The midwife came back with a flashlight and checked for the baby's head. She was indeed ten centimeters and bringing Baby down beautifully.

After the next rush, without opening her eyes, she asked if the epidural was ready. The flustered midwife tried to explain that it was too late to give it to her now and she is awfully sorry about that but her baby seems to be ready to be born. Then Radiya said in that case, they could do a C-section, now! I helped her with the next rush, telling her that she was pushing perfectly and would see her baby soon. She leaned her head against my shoulder again and rested, almost slept for a few minutes before the next one started. Behind us in the bathroom doorway one of the nurses was arranging a low wooden birthing stool and covering the floor with a clean Chux. I was impressed. She and the nurse helped Radiya up and we pivoted over to the birthing stool and helped lower her onto it.

Less than ten minutes later we could all see the baby crowning. As Radiya gripped my arms even harder, her baby's head slipped out. The midwife asked if she could keep pushing, but Radiya was asleep already. The next rush started and the midwife asked her to "push . . . longer . . . push . . . yes! Do it again . . . good! . . . push . . ." but she couldn't seem to help the shoulders out. I instinctively moved further back at least two feet toward the wall, still attached to Radiya, hoping that it might help with the shoulder instead of leaning forward like we had been doing. It worked.

The midwife helped Radiya lift up a very pudgy baby girl and I helped hold her there while the midwife busily assessed what looked like a lot of blood from my vantage point. I helped rub the baby's back until the nurses took her to the warmer, where she cried right away. The midwife said we had to get Radiya up on the bed and as I helped I watched a steady stream of blood dripping across the floor. We got her positioned on the bed and the midwife rubbing her stomach at the fundus (the top of the uterus) to get the bleeding stopped. She explained that it looked like she tore when the shoulders came through but that the bleeding was under control now. We could relax.

The nurse brought her baby back but Radiya insisted she needed a clean nightie before she could hold her baby. The midwife explained that the baby needed to be skin-to-skin but Radiya refused, saying she had to wash up first, so the nurse put the baby back on the warmer where she started to cry. I asked if I could hold her, which the nurse agreed to right away. I put a dry hat on the baby, wrapped her in warm blankets and hugged her close.

This birth occurred soon after I attended the all-day summit on skin-to-skin contact held by Dr. Nils Bergman, who had been research-ing maternal-infant-maternal attachment (your baby attaches to you, too, not just you bonding with your baby).

Dr. Bergman has made it his life's mission to provide the scientific ev-idence for the neuroscience of optimal birth, the role of skin-to-skin contact, breastfeeding, parenting for secure attachment, and to conduct the research as needed. He further seeks to disseminate this knowledge on mother-infant togetherness by educating all health professionals both here and abroad and by empowering parents. His work promotes practical changes in health systems and facilities that enhance mother-infant togetherness.

I was determined to get Radiya's baby onto her mom's chest, as were the midwife and nurses, but Radiya told us she wasn't ready, so I continued to hold the baby close while talking to her. She started root-ing and salivating, both signs telling us it was time to eat, and I believed her, so rather than letting her cry, I let her suck on my little finger while she gazed into my eyes.

The midwife asked the lead obstetrician to assess Radiya's tear. He was the only OB on that day, though I had assured Radiya that we'd keep her draped and not have any men in the room. She agreed to have him come in if he had to and promptly covered her head with a blanket and stayed like that until he left. He did not need to do the actual repair but made some suggestions to the midwife, who set up a tray to stitch the tear when he left.

I was still holding the baby, who was still staring into my eyes and nursing on my pinkie. I tried again to get her to her mama but the repair was still uncomfortable enough that Radiya said I should hold her until it was over. I certainly was not going to put her back on the warmer, so I hung out with the baby until Radiya was finally cleaned up and ready. She tied up her new clean nightie. I tried to convince her to untie it because her baby wanted to nurse. She didn't believe me until I gently unwrapped the baby and plopped her down in Radiya's arms, where she promptly latched on and vigorously nursed.

Dr. Bergman had also talked about alternative caregivers filling the place of the mother in certain cases, like adoption, but stressed the fact that it should be the same caregiver for at least the first two years, not numerous people coming and going. I hoped we did the best we could in Radiya's situation, so I contacted Dr. Bergman and asked. He assured me that we did.

Dr. Nils Bergman with his "kangaroula" wife,
Jill Bergman.

"Mothers don't breastfeed, babies breastfeed. Babies know how if we let them."
~*Dr. Nils Bergman*

Chapter Thirty

A Commune Couple

How would I describe them? Not shiftless, just idealists. Anarchist? Perhaps. Communists? No. But maybe Socialists. Hippies ... that could fit, too. They were living in a community of sorts: four houses on one street, with vegetable gardens and chicken coops in between the houses—in the city. Faded jeans and unbleached diapers always hung on the lines above the chicken coops. There were usually kids playing a game of tag, running past us at the speed of lightning.

My husband and I had gone to a few of their neighborhood cook-outs and once to a potluck wedding. The dozens of bicycle parts that had formerly littered the drive were miraculously all put away before the wedding. I can't crack on that wedding. It sure was better than taking out a loan to get married in a dress she'd only wear once and paying for a caterer when the food they cooked was much tastier.

There is something to be said for living simply: no debt, no car or car repairs, no phone bills. They could and did go dumpster diving behind all the co-ops and bakeries and grocery chains and harvested all the food they needed for a week. Sure, the luxuries of life were absent, but they found hidden treasures in nature and other people. They made some good points in our conversations.

But when it came to babies, I drew sharp lines through some of their judgmental beliefs. To boycott all hospitals under all circumstances because they are part of a "materialistic, consumer-based conglomerate and perpetuate our capitalistic policies that only enable the rich and don't serve the poor equally" was something I couldn't agree with. But it was exactly what Juliette and Pierre had decided: they would do without "the system" entirely and live on the fringes at the edge of the rest of the population.

My first baby was born in a hospital but the other four were not. However, if something had gone wrong we would not have hesitated to transfer to a hospital. That's what they are there for. There are countries all over the world where babies and mothers die every day because they don't have the facilities we have. We had several conversations about our different views but they were not swayed by my arguments.

So when Juliette got pregnant, they looked for and found an unlicensed home-birth midwife who shared their worldview.

Then they asked me to be their doula. I hesitated. Did they have a plan B should they need to employ one? No. Did the midwife have any backup? No. If she needed it, what would she do? "Nothing" was the answer; they'd be on their own. They could show up at a hospital, according to her, but she would not come along. Oh, boy. I wasn't sure I wanted to be part of this scenario.

We continued to talk and they grew on me slowly. They rented a birthing tub for their tiny room. They ate well enough and Juliette was gaining steadily. But then she told me that she had high blood pressure and a congenital kidney problem. Holy bleep!

I told them that I couldn't be their doula unless they had a doctor backing them up. And she would have to find one before her eighth month. For me to be their doula and be her primary care provider at her home until we called her midwife, I would need to know that she had been screened and approved for a home birth. My scope of practice as a doula does not allow me to do blood pressure checks. I also required a plan B, a doctor who already knew her and who had hospital privileges should we need to transfer.

I didn't hear from them for over a week. It was clear that they were battling between themselves over priorities versus idealism. Their relationship was not a committed until-death-do-us-part arrangement. She understood my concerns. He did not. He dug in his heels and did not want to budge.

I was worried. I was afraid they would "drop out," even disappear, perhaps with Juliette having a possible fatal complication. It was not entirely farfetched on my part, knowing some of the medical issues and the personalities involved.

I had received a call a week earlier from a birthing clinic asking if I could consult on a breastfeeding problem they were seeing. The couple was from the same communal group as Pierre and Juliette. The issue was that he thought she should be able to skip drinking altogether until they could find a 100% pure reverse-osmosis water source and that they could get along just fine with just raw foods they "harvested" from around the city. It quickly became obvious that he was dictating or controlling everything she put into her mouth. It turned out she had not eaten that day and possibly not the day before. She was very thin and very pale, had not taken vitamins and as soon as I started prying a little further, she simply looked to him to answer. He then tried to assure me that he had studied nutrition and that we should respect their choices.

Their midwife, who had called me, felt that the baby was getting dehydrated and losing precious ounces that he should have been gaining by now. The father would not let us visit with her unless he was in the room. Both the midwife and I spoke to them rather firmly, hoping to wake him up a bit. Mom had already given up any autonomy she may have once possessed, though I doubt she ever had any, at least not since meeting him.

When I called the next day to see how they were, the phone had been disconnected. The midwife went out to their house and was told by their landlady that they had moved out that morning. They were gone. Vanished. We never heard from them again.

Juliette finally called me. She had been to a regular "establishment" doctor who, she said, cleared her for a home birth. Great! Her blood pressure and sugars were within normal range. The couple was delighted and wanted to proceed with their original plan, but as another week unfolded, things changed drastically. Juliette was sick, feeling horrible, and vomiting. She went back to the doctor and, as she edged near her eighth month, was put on several medications and a restricted diet in the hope of stabilizing both her kidney function and blood pressure. In spite of the ominous recent chain of events, her midwife told them it was still the better choice to have their baby at home.

They had scraped together the midwife's fee by begging and borrowing from family and friends and selling an old car Pierre had fixed up. The midwife was officially hired. I knew they didn't have any savings and offered to barter. Pierre, an accomplished carpenter, could suggest something he could build for my family in exchange for my doula services. Everyone was happy.

About six weeks before her guess date, Juliette called saying she was having horrible headaches and feeling really crummy. I insisted she return to the doctor and get checked out before it got any worse. She had been under a lot of stress, she admitted. Pierre was nowhere near ready for a baby. He wouldn't pack up his tools or the mountains of junk that covered the floor of their tiny room. And though she had expressed the wish that they move their mattress onto the floor from its location on a platform built on stilts, which was too difficult to climb up and down in her eighth month, not to mention how she couldn't do it after the baby was born, he was not doing any of it.

Juliette blamed herself for being so picky and cranky, but they weren't really as "together" as she had hoped they would be, especially with their baby about to be born. I could only encourage her to keep the lines of communication open with him. In the end, I told her, she had to do what was right for her and her little one, even if Pierre didn't agree.

The report from the doctor was not good. Her overall numbers were alarming. Her kidneys were being taxed and her blood pressure was too high. He strongly recommended that she check into the hospital that same day and be induced. He felt that her health could still recover after the delivery, though she was getting into a danger zone, and if she waited she might not come out of it without some permanent damage. He also emphasized that the baby's health would be compromised, even at risk if she didn't deliver soon, given the new developments.

Negotiations with their midwife went back and forth all that day. She was willing to help them should they choose to stay at home, but I made it very clear that I could no longer be part of the team then. She countered that her job description didn't include being with them throughout the whole labor, which was why she had recommended they find a doula, even though they had paid her several thousand dollars. I told them again that hospitals are there precisely for their kind of situation and that I felt the doctor was on their side, committed to having a healthy baby and a healthy mother in the end. The battle had begun.

The cards were blatantly stacked against them. Her health might not recover if she didn't deliver the baby soon, putting her at grave risk. I pointed out that her baby needed a mom and that although we would like to have control over our health and our births, it was not always possible. Welcome to parenthood.

I could not tell her what to do, but I could encourage her to think on her own, without Pierre going on and on about corporate greed and disregard for the poor and multi-billion-dollar facilities. He simply did not understand that her life was creeping closer and closer to a point of no return; her numbers were now that bad. I had never had a mother so ill in my thirty years of midwifery practice.

I told them to call me if I could do anything for them and tried to let go. I had not been so frustrated in a very long time. I said a prayer and made supper. Later that evening Juliette called to tell me that she had decided to go to the hospital and asked if I would be able to meet them there. I said I would be glad to.

I explained what induction meant and how that might be attempted five weeks before a due date. She had written a birth plan and we had talked about the numerous options she had for a home birth; now we tailored it for a hospital birth, including induction.

She wanted to have her baby as naturally as she could with as few interventions as possible. I outlined the various options the doctor had for induction, explained that some interventions were more invasive than others, and that she would have time to ask questions and could ask for privacy to decide what she wanted to do. Once she was settled in her room, the doctor suggested using a ripening agent placed at the cervix that would help get things started. Then they could start a small amount of Pitocin by morning and get her into active labor. The couple asked for some time to discuss it privately. While they talked, I went down to the coffee shop.

They called me on my cell phone a short time later to tell me that they had called their midwife for advice and she had warned them about what not to let the hospital do to Juliette under any circumstance and suggested some alternatives to try. I did not realize she was still influencing them and found it rather bold of her to be making decisions from some undisclosed location.

Pierre and Juliette decided to try a non-medicated approach instead of the ripening agent and opted for a balloon catheter to be placed so it would stretch the cervix open and hopefully trigger labor. By morning it had succeeded in getting the cervix to dilate slightly but not appreciably. The next suggestion was to try Pitocin and then perhaps break her water if the baby's head came down further. Again the couple asked us to leave and talked it over, and as I suspected, again called the midwife who told them not to let them break the water under any circumstance. I had never seen anything like it. I did not understand their trust or devotion toward this woman. Even though I was a friend, somehow by being a licensed midwife and certified doula, they seemed to consider me as having gone over to the "other side" and I was deemed too medical or too swayed by "the system" to be consulted on how to stay on the natural side of things.

The nurses soon got the hang of how to approach this couple. Each step would require consultation, then consideration in private, then double-checking what I thought (but only after the midwife was called). Only then could the nurses and/or doctor come back in and negotiations would resume. I was beginning to feel like an international conflict-mediation envoy deliberating the politics of civil unrest. Many of the suggestions met with rejection as being too invasive or they simply felt that things were being unjustly and routinely rushed and asked for a few more hours of walking or sitting on the birth ball to let things work. I took to listing options for them from least to most invasive, knowing they would veto any and all suggestions unless their invisible midwife approved. I felt their midwife was calling the shots in a realm that was now outside her sphere of skill or experience.

The nurses started asking me to ask them thus and such, hoping I had more "say" because they realized they did not have any at all.

I do not go to any birth, at home or in a hospital, ready to do battle. I sincerely feel honored to be welcomed onto a birth team and readily defer first to Mom and her wishes and then follow her midwife's lead. But this tug-of-war went on all night and all the next day. By evening I was called out to the nurses' station and given an overview of the bigger picture. Baby was still doing remarkably well. Mom was okay—blood pressure and other numbers not off the charts yet. But it was time for the baby to be born. I asked what options they would propose next. Breaking her water was the least "medical" in their eyes and might speed labor up appreciably. I went back in and while slowly rubbing Juliette's feet I told them what I had learned. I told them that they were doing great, that Baby was sounding really good and that she was actually making progress, which is not the same during an induction as it is in a term birth. They were not agreed between themselves what to do next.

Juliette was able to eat and drink and was doing okay. She had refused all IVs and meds up until that point. I knew they would continue to call their midwife whether I was there or not, and I was frankly at my wits' end after forty-eight hours. I proposed I go home and sleep and that they try to rest, even if it was only dozing between the rushes. I hugged them each goodbye, assuring them I would be back within fifteen minutes if they wanted me.

I walked the short six blocks home from the hospital. I was so tired and drained that I just showered and cried until I got into bed.

I slept in and called the hospital once I was awake. The nurse told me that Juliette had just given birth to a healthy eight-pound girl. Their midwife had come in once she heard I had left, though they were instructed to say she was just a supportive friend. She helped them try different positions that helped the baby along and they were grateful.

Later that evening I called the couple and asked if I could visit. I congratulated them and told them how happy I was that they had been able to have the natural birth they wanted. She was nursing, which her baby took to right away. She was still five weeks early but was doing really well and did not have to go to the NICU. I was so glad all the drama was over.

Two days later I got a call from another woman who was living in their communal house. She reported that a public health nurse had come by to make sure the baby was doing well. She looked at the baby and voiced some concern about her color, that she seemed to look jaundiced and also appeared dehydrated.

Juliette and Pierre had read books on natural birth and said they had chosen to nurse on demand, meaning only when the baby awoke or fussed and asked for it. They had thrown out the doctor's instructions for preemies in which he insisted they needed to wake the baby to eat every two to three hours until she reached her original due date. He had explained that their baby might act very sleepy and needed to be fed to catch up, whether she appeared interested or not. But they thought the doctor was just spewing routine medical jargon and that "nursing on demand" sounded more natural.

The baby came five weeks early. She was sleeping up to six hours at a time. She did not cry. The baby was in trouble.

The public health nurse took a blood sample and told them she would call back later that same day after she got the results of the tests. They dismissed the nurse as just another member of the "establishment," turned off their cell phones, and went back to sleep.

Their baby did have seriously high readings for jaundice and she was in the danger zone for being dehydrated. When the nurse called both cell phone numbers over and over and no one answered she did what she felt she needed to do. She called Child Protection and explained her concerns, which were bordering on dire at that point. The baby had to be rehydrated immediately and under bilirubin lights right away.

A police car and an ambulance pulled up in front of the commune and I got another call. Later that night I went to the hospital and sat with Juliette for a while. She was nursing her baby in the NICU. The hospital gave her a room with a real bed so she could stay right there. She told me that she and Pierre just assumed newborns slept a lot and thought she would let them know when she was hungry. I explained again that preemies need an extra level of special care. She said, sounding surprised, "Oh. That is what the doctor kept telling us, too." She was still pretty shaken by the whole experience and totally exhausted. She was going on day four without sleep. She also told me she had decided to stay in the hospital this time until everything was taken care of and they understood what they needed to do, even if Pierre didn't agree.

I still see them from time to time. Luna looks too big for her tiny mama to be carrying her around anymore. She is very sturdy and has gained beautifully. Juliette is feeling well and taking care of herself. It was another example I could chock up to education. I still don't know what I could have done differently. I wanted to respect them even when our values differed and I wanted to advocate as much as possible for her wishes. I did not feel at any time that it was my place to act as marriage counselor, either. They were two adults whose ideas were different from mine, which did not make mine better or more valid. I come away from experiences like these convinced we must, above all, respect each woman we work with and allow that their points of view may not be our own. But I have also learned that I must set my own boundaries and equally respect those. I am just very, very grateful everyone is okay.

"Giving birth should be your greatest achievement, not your greatest fear."
~Jane Fraser Weideman

Chapter Thirty-One

Cherish and Jewel

I met Babette when I was given her referral by our agency for prenatal education, support, and doula care. Babette, a nurse, and her husband, who had a master's degree in economics, had recently come to Minnesota from Ghana, Africa. They had been in the U.S. less than six months when she became pregnant with twins.

An amniocentesis test had been conducted because an omphalocele was viewed on one baby during an ultrasound just before Babette's sixth month of pregnancy. The baby's omphalocele could be seen protruding next to the umbilical cord at the navel during the ultrasound.

The results from the amnio had not come back yet, but the hospital testing unit's doctor advised Babette that her baby had a serious problem that might also involve the chromosomal abnormality Trisomy 18 and other genetic disorders, and she was told (all this through an interpreter) that because the babies were possibly identical twins, the baby's twin most likely had genetic anomalies, too. During the same discussion—remember, the test results were not back yet—Babette and her husband were offered early interruption or termination of the pregnancy.

After that first devastating news, Babette had gone home and Googled the list of horrors the doctor mentioned as merely possibilities. She was alone that afternoon as she watched photo after gruesome photo of babies with all the terrible complications the doctor had named. An educated woman, Babette had read everything about each lethal or fatal anomaly, the expected life span of a child with each disorder, and the complications and probability of incidence of each syndrome.

Babette was understandably seriously depressed when we met for the first time and asked me if "the hospital would be mad at us if we don't abort." I told her no, that she had every right to carry her babies to term if that was her wish and that even no action was an option. She could simply let nature take its course.

I told Babette and her husband that they could also change doctors, or even hospitals, that those were their rights in our country, and I would help them do that if they wished. I also apologized for the hospital's actions. I told them that I strongly disagreed with the way it was presented to them, especially since the studies had not yet confirmed anything other than a small omphalocele on the ultrasound on one baby.

They were both greatly relieved and asked me to accompany her to all prenatal visits after that, which I did. I often explained the medical reports as they came in and did home visits in between to address other concerns, like finding cribs and so on.

Their four-year-old son was perfectly okay. He was a delightful little guy who climbed onto my lap without any invitation, sang to me in Dagbani, his parents' native language, and thought I was his grandma, even though I was (still am) seriously pigment-challenged compared to the rest of his family. I wondered why the geneticist said that the babies could have a hereditary syndrome. I am not a geneticist, nor a doctor, but the way this case was being handled seemed particularly cruel and uncaring to me.

When the test results came back, they didn't tell us much more than we already knew, except that no form of Trisomy was indicated, nor Down syndrome, but other concerns continued. They told us that there was an eighty percent chance the girls were identical, though they could not be 100% sure, so they may or may not mirror the same problems, but they persisted in their theory that both babies might be similarly affected. Babette refused all further tests from that point on except for regular ultrasounds.

In the circles of higher academia I recently noticed a startling new trend: People in the field are questioning, some for the first time, the connections between the rocket-science levels of medical technology, where tests can tell us if our as-yet-unborn child might have a gene that could elevate his or her probability of seeing symptoms of a disease by the time he or she turned five, twenty, or forty years old and the findings by these scientists and doctors that conclude that once a parent has been warned that a disease of some sort might exist, their parenting style actually changes. No longer is this baby a much-anticipated addition to their family, but is too often seen as a problematic addition to their family. Sometimes their lives stop at this unforeseen juncture and they delve into their own extensive research on the "intruder." They no longer attend the local mothers' groups to compare baby teeth and diapers but rather join support groups with other parents dealing with the same disabilities. I would wager that prenatal bonding, too, looks very different, even before the baby is born. Their babies are no longer treated as lovable, huggable, adorable little clones of themselves but as research subjects as parents become experts on every congenital or hereditary anomaly affecting the human race. I think pity takes the place of the funny faces and absurd sounds new parents and relatives make at their newborns. This is hardly the stuff conducive to continuum bonding.

In her book, *Testing Baby: The Transformation of Newborn Screening, Parenting, and Policymaking*, Rachel Grob pleads this case on behalf of our children. Another equally brilliant work is called *Saving Babies?* by Stefan Timmermans and Mara Buchbinder, in which the authors question whether the benefits of these screenings outweigh the stress and pain they sometimes produce, especially given the high number of false positives. Inaccurate results can take a brutal emotional toll on parents before they are corrected, if they ever are. Finally, the American Academy of Pediatrics, together with the American College of Medical Genetics, has put in place a statement to curb the testing of children to identify genetically inherited childhood diseases and those that can occur when they become adults. They further recommend that doctors should discourage testing in children for adult-onset genetic diseases, especially if there is no preventative treatment to give during childhood, stating that the screening tests often don't provide definitive answers, but whether they do or not, the test results may only lead to anxiety and more questions.

Babette expressed her desire for a VBAC but she was scheduled for a C-section four weeks before her due date. The baby with the omphalocele had dropped lower than her twin and would be born first. The doctors were concerned that one of the babies didn't appear to be practicing her breathing in utero, which could signal immaturity and the possibility that she might be better off outside of the womb where she could get their help, though they also could not tell if she never practiced breathing, especially if she had been sleeping during the ultrasound that particular day.

To get a definitive answer as to the maturity question, the doctor now proposed another amniocentesis to assess the overall lung function of the babies. Babette was understandably worried by so much speculation. She asked me what I thought, and I told her that this one wasn't up to me. Perhaps the doctors were right in trying to avoid additional problems, or maybe doing nothing would be right for her. I assured her I would support her in whatever she chose to do.

She decided to have the amniocentesis, which told everyone that the babies' lungs were, thankfully, mature so they didn't need to be born early.

That evening, however, Babette called to tell me she was "leaking." The amniocenteses had ruptured the bag of water and it was not going to reseal itself. So much for letting the babies go to term. A C-section was again deemed safest at that point by the powers-that-be, though when nailed down, one of her doctors did admit to us that there really was no reason not to try a VBAC.

I asked Babette if she still wanted a VBAC but she told me, simply, that she was tired—tired of being pregnant, tired of the questions, and tired of false hopes. She was also tired of imagining the future, the possibility of her being a prisoner in her dusty housing project, stuck at home year after year with two very sick babies and no hope of ever having a career again or of living the life they had dreamed of having in America. She wanted it over. She didn't care what they did at this point. She had no more energy.

I attended her birth in November that year. Both babies had acceptable Apgars and did exceptionally well after birth. The "well" baby, the one without the omphalocele, latched and nursed well in recovery. She was named Cherish.

At her parents' request, I accompanied the other baby, now called Jewel, first to the NICU and then to another children's hospital the next day where I stayed for the surgery at twenty-four hours to correct the omphalocele and the first few days in the NICU there. Babette stayed in the first hospital with Cherish. The father stayed with their four-year-old son.

At the children's hospital and also later in her hospital's neonatal unit, I asked the neonatologist if he had noticed some of the same markers I had observed in Jewel. He had and had already sent more blood work to the genetics lab but hadn't told the parents of his concern.

The tests came back confirming a diagnosis of a very rare chromosomal imbalnce, which occurs in about 1 in 15,000 births. I had done some research, too, and the next time I visited Babette and Cherish I noted similar visual markers in Cherish, which again I didn't mention to Babette. I called the doctor, who assured me that Cherish was fine, that twins rarely both carry this rare syndrome, and that he did not feel further testing was warranted.

About two months later, Babette asked me to go with them to a follow-up visit at a pediatric clinic, not one of the hospitals they had already been to. A pediatrician saw us and was very happy with both babies' weight gains, feedings, etc. I asked this doctor to refer Cherish for a genetic workup, listing the anomalies I thought I was seeing. Upon further examination he also saw them and agreed to refer Cherish for further testing.

I told the parents I wanted to be sure so that any early interventions that might help her would be in place. I tried not to convey any deeper concerns. They agreed. The parents were called a few weeks later and told that Cherish did indeed have the same syndrome as her sister Jewel, though her chances were also only about 1 in 15,000.

What is known today about the syndrome is that the body's chromosome 11 gets messages to reproduce at accelerated speeds, thus causing over-growth or a form of giantism. One leg might grow faster than the other. One kidney could grow beyond the expected proportions for age and maturity. The child will have to be monitored several times a year to try to detect any abnormal growth before it becomes a major problem. Growth that is faster than normal also puts a child at a higher risk for certain types of cancers.

Even before the birth, Babette confided to me that she felt she was doomed to spend the rest of her life in the housing project with two severely handicapped babies. She had hoped to go back to work after this pregnancy. She had planned to first become proficient in English and then apply to graduate school for any credits she might still need to transfer her degree from Ghana to the U.S.

I applied for a grant and got an English independent study course for her to do at home, which she and her husband have both completed. I explained that she could find daycare for her babies, she would be able to go back to school, and that in the U.S. her babies will go to school even if it is an adapted program.

When I last visited the family they seemed happy, but I felt that Babette had not bonded as well with Jewel, who was having some additional problems (further surgery had been recommended). Babette was very unsure about agreeing to the surgery. At one point she and I were alone in the kitchen and she said, "I just want to go back to Africa and leave the babies with him. He can put them in daycare." I asked if she just needed a vacation or whether she wanted to run away. She said, "Both."

I spoke with a clinic that addresses postpartum depression because of my concerns about Babette. Months earlier, when we went to the OB testing unit at the hospital week after week, she was routinely asked at each visit, "Are you depressed?" This became a running joke between us. She didn't think she was depressed. She should know—she is, after all, a professional, a nurse with a degree. She told me that the babies were in God's hands and that she was happy she had been blessed with two. She said God would take care of them, even if they were handicapped. However, I realized as the reality of caring for these two sweet, beautiful little babies day after day began sinking in, I thought it might be time to ask for extra help for her too. I am grateful this family is living in a country where multiple resources are available to help them in the years ahead.

"Attending births is like growing roses. You have to marvel at the ones that just open up and bloom at the first kiss of the sun but you wouldn't dream of pulling open the petals of the tightly closed buds and forcing them to blossom to your timeline."
~Gloria Lemay

Chapter Thirty-Two

Filsen

Through the years I've gotten to know the staff at many hospitals throughout the Twin Cities' healthcare system, but I hadn't had any clients deliver at one particular county hospital for quite awhile. I assumed they kept informed of "best practices" and were interested, if not actively invested, in being known as a "baby friendly" birth facility.

I was wrong. There were no midwives in this hospital. Although my client had a birth plan, it was generally ignored. Even some of the information the doctor gave her as labor progressed simply was not true. As a doula, it is certainly not my place to challenge a nurse, much less a doctor, on their own turf, but this was crazy. Still, I could not say anything.

Filsen's water broke at noon. She was admitted into the hospital where she was promptly popped into bed and monitored. She was experiencing slight contractions but nothing appreciable. Throughout the afternoon, Filsen was told that they hoped she would get into active labor with good contractions on her own but if she didn't, they would start Pitocin. They assured her it would be started at the lowest level. By 4:00 p.m. they were saying that there was a risk of infection if she didn't get the Pitocin and hurry up having her baby. I told her that I understood that twelve hours was closer to the time to start considering hours and risks. She was GBS (group B strep) positive and was already on a penicillin IV drip, so what was the rush? One clinic I worked at gave most moms forty-eight hours after their water broke, and I know of another where they have waited as long as seventy-two.

When the IV was put in, Filsen was told not to eat anything. Really? When she asked why, she was told because of the IV. Huh? She said she was thirsty, so they said she could have milk, but just little sips. I had told her when she first called me that she should eat before she went to the hospital because she would need the calories for the upcoming marathon. I was glad she did.

By 6:00 p.m. the doctor announced that it had been "close to ten hours since" since her water broke (it had in fact been only six) and "we are very worried about infection, so we'd like to start the Pitocin because that might take awhile to start working." Filsen managed to put them off until 9:00 p.m. Then the Pitocin was started. She was still not allowed to eat. I suggested she ask for juice or popsicles, but they didn't bring any when she asked.

The Pitocin was cranked up every half hour. The nurses did not tell Filsen what they were doing. They just appeared to be checking the monitors and pushed a few buttons here and there. Filsen's first baby had been delivered by C-section, then she had VBACs. I wondered if the Pitocin wasn't being ratcheted up a bit too fast and furiously for a mom who'd had a C-section. They had kept her in bed the entire time, though I reminded her to go to the bathroom every hour and finally got a birth ball for her to sit on, reminding her that gravity would help both with establishing contractions and dilation.

The Pitocin starting working so well that Filsen was soon having a contraction every two minutes and sometimes two at a time (called coupling). I helped her breathe through them and held the bag when she began vomiting. Finally the nurse turned the Pitocin down.

The doctor ordered another round of penicillin, explaining that they were still afraid of infection. She was four centimeters dilated in spite of the whopper contractions. She was finally brought ice chips. *What era are we in, anyway?* I wondered. I did not tell Filsen what I was thinking. I didn't think it would help but would instead undermine her faith in the doctor she had chosen.

So we visited, and breathed, and chatted and rested. It was obvious around 3:00 a.m. that things were changing. I had Filsen sit up first. I got pillows and made sure she was comfortable. I just knew she'd be delivering flat on her back with stirrups if that was how they found her when they all arrived. We didn't call the nurse until she started feeling pushy. I asked about a squatting bar and was told they didn't have any. At some point one appeared. It was put aside, but at least one nurse knew what Filsen wanted.

Filsen was hanging on until she got to ten centimeters and she could push. The doctor explained that they needed to see exactly how strong the contractions really were, so they placed an intrauterine pressure catheter inside, between the baby's head and the uterus. This is not an easy procedure when a woman is near the end of her first stage of labor. The contractions looked just fine. Duh.

When Filsen took a deep breath and we all knew she was going to give it all she had on that first push, the nurse told her to wait and proceeded to break down the bed and help the doctor to gown up. There were actually three doctors in the room at that point. I was a bit confused by this, but didn't ask. The baby's head crowned on the first push and popped out on the second. The shoulders were slow coming and the doctor didn't want to wait, or didn't know she could wait for another contraction, but started pulling on the baby. The cord was over one of the baby's shoulders, which didn't help, but instead of rolling it over the shoulder and arm, she kept pulling the baby, who did come out then.

The doctor went to put the baby onto Filsen's stomach while asking her, "Do you want the baby up here now?" but at the same time a nurse stepped in and said, "She should be crying more" and whisked the baby over to the warmer where she cried right away, without suctioning, and remained there.

Filsen had only briefly seen the back of her baby's head before she was taken away. I encouraged Dad to head over there and touch his baby. When I looked over there again, he was taking pictures of her while the nurse set up the vitamin K shot, eye ointments, and footprints. No one had held the baby yet.

I wedged myself into the last remaining space near the warmer, hoping to help Dad hold her soon. I asked the nurse what the Apgars were and while I was noting it on my chart she raised her voice and said to me in no uncertain terms, "You know, you are in my way and I have to finish up doing things over here."

The three doctors were busy repairing two tears. As I listened, I realized that the doctor actually doing the stitching was being coached step-by-step by one of the other physicians. I started to wonder if she had ever sewn up a repair before, based on the fact that her mentor was repeating each step and pointing out landmarks down there as they went along. It was a teaching moment.

Finally the stitching was finished and Filsen was cleaned up a bit. The doctors left the room, leaving Filsen completely naked on the bed. I found a gown in a cupboard and covered her the best I could. Throughout the birth I had tried to keep a sheet handy, knowing that modesty is pretty important to most women.

Baby was given her vitamin K shot, eye ointment, footprinted, and heart-monitored briefly, before being wiped down with a dry cloth. She had been fussing during all of this, understandingly so, but started howling her protests against the washcloth. She still had not been cuddled by anyone.

When the nurse finally gave the baby to Dad, he took her to Filsen's mom, who was waiting patiently. Grandma held her for a bit, though Filsen had not even seen her baby's face yet. It was about forty-five minutes after the birth. All of this was unacceptable in my book.

Then one of the nurses took the baby to Filsen and, without unwrapping her, positioned her for breastfeeding. I stepped up at this point ready to help, but the nurse pushed baby up to the nipple and started giving Filsen pointers about how to get her to latch. I quietly told Filsen, "She can just get used to your smell first or just lick for a bit," but the nurse was determined to get the baby latched on immediately. I knew it could take awhile, and babies will actually lead breastfeeding themselves and latch on in their own time it we stay out of it.

The poor baby had been kept away from the breast during her crucial first hour but now she was being encouraged to "perform" immediately. So wrong. I didn't volunteer the information that I was also a certified lactation consultant and educator because I was already on the wrong side of this nurse. The nurse had other things to do and was already miffed with me, so she busied herself elsewhere.

When I returned the next day, the baby was sleeping in a little cot next to Filsen's bed. A bottle was propped in the corner of it. I asked why it was there since all during her pregnancy Filsen had said she was going to breastfeed. She said the nurses had told her she should give the bottle of formula to the baby after every breastfeeding since she didn't have any milk yet.

The baby was getting colostrum, I explained, and her milk would come in. Her baby wouldn't go hungry. I went on to say that using the bottle would cause the baby to suck less on her breasts, which would cause the breasts to make less milk.

Babies can experience nipple confusion from being offered a plastic nipple after their little brains have already imprinted their first experiences at the breast. Breast, bottle, bottle, breast. *What is all this supposed to feel like, anyway?* they may wonder. Many babies go on strike at this point. Others find that the formula flows faster and they don't have to work at it as hard, so they opt out and prefer the bottle, causing their moms to offer the breast less and less until their milk starts drying up, having gotten the message that the demand is not there to make more of a supply.

Baby-friendly hospital? Uh, no . . . in so many ways.

"We've put birth in the same category with illness and disease and it's never belonged there. Birth is naturally safe, but we've allowed it to be taken over by the medical community."
~Carla Hartley, Ancient Art Midwifery Institute

Chapter Thirty-Three

El Doula Diario

I had been waiting for Alegra to call for many days. I was very glad that her midwife wasn't anxious about her approaching week forty-one. I had seen far too many inductions that year, though there is very little evidence that we are preventing post-dates complications by doing so, and there is even less proof that we aren't actually introducing more possible side effects by inducing at what only might be a post-date baby. Unless a mom is charting basal temperatures and knows exactly the date of conception (the only other reliable predictor would be artificial insemination or in vitro conception), we could very well be inducing a premature baby. Too many times I have seen induced babies who still have all the signs of prematurity: ears flat against their head, lots of the creamy vernix skin coating, furry little bodies, and so on. True post-term infants have long fingernails and often peeling skin. The placenta may have patches of calcification. We are still waiting for some direction, called "best practice" on this one about when, if ever, it is truly warranted to induce a so-called "late" baby. Opinions still vary widely among obstetricians. The whole topic is being revisited at this time, with good reason.

For ten days I had not ventured too far from home in case Alegra's call came, either before the guess date or like now, after. I had planned suppers around what my family could easily assemble should I be gone when they got home. I learned that one the hard way: One year when turkeys were super-cheap after Thanksgiving I bought one, thawed it for two days in the fridge and stuffed it with homemade dressing. I got it into the oven, set the timer, and went to start a load of laundry. One hour into baking the phone rang. A baby had decided it was a good day to be born. I turned off the oven, made room in the fridge for the giant roaster and quickly scribbled directions on how to continue cooking it once someone came home. Since then, I keep a steady supply of salads in the house, often homemade tabouli, cous cous, a freekah or quinoa dish that can be eaten cold, hummus or pesto, and washed raw veggies.

I checked my doula bag for the umpteenth time: Massage tools, olive oil, lavender and pine scents, a can of champagne to set in ice water for counter pressure for back labor (it works really well and we can open it to celebrate later!), mint gum, toothbrush, toothpaste, snacks—for me: dates, raw almonds, apples, trail mix, and honey sticks for mom, paperwork and two pens, a sweater—hospitals can be really cold at night—my rubber kneeler from a discount garden store for me to use by the tub or birth ball and for mom to use in the tub if she wants to stay on hands and knees for any length of time.

I also carry a book, should she fall asleep; my I.D. badge; a purse with money and I.D., and my "hospital shoes." I don't like the idea of street shoes bringing in all their germs so I change into my comfy canvas shoe/slippers. I try to have some handmade baby hats along too, since a group of grandmas are constantly donating them to our office. Also in the bag are a nail clipper, battery-operated "candles," umbrella, phone and charger, socks, and my headache medication. I also have my hair-band-type party tiara that says "Happy Birthday" in big pink letters. I have been known to tell a partner, "I don't need to wear this the whole time, but you do," and they usually put it on!

I got a call at 6:00 p.m., sure it was Alegra, but it wasn't. It was a desperate doula. Could I be with one of her ladies for a couple of hours until she got out of her college English exam? Sure. She was grateful.

A first-time mom, nervous about not having any support, Mary Smith was sleeping when I arrived. So were about nine other bodies camped all over the floor, each rolled up in sheets or blankets. It looked like she had support: sisters, brothers, girlfriends, and girlfriends' boyfriends were all sacked out.

Mary was not yet in early labor but the medical personnel were keeping her because of some concerns with her high blood pressure. They were talking about using Pitocin in the morning. When the nurse came in to check her blood pressure and temp she woke up and I introduced myself. I assured her I would stay until Julie, her doula, could come. When the nurse left, Mary told me that the pile of blankets on the floor closest to the bed was her partner and she wanted him at the birth. The FOB (father of the baby) would not be coming. I told her that was fine and that she was doing really well. Her contractions were weak but they could pick up. I also said it would be great if she could rest. I got her some juice and a straw and encouraged her to drink most of it. She did and went back to sleep. I pulled a chair up to the bathroom door and opened it just enough to read by the light. Less than two hours later Julie came to relieve me.

As I opened the door to my apartment the phone rang. I hoped it might be Alegra, but it was a mom who wasn't due for another month, asking what she should do: she had pelvic pain, fever, chills, and felt really crummy. I asked Carmen to call her midwife and let me know if they wanted to see her at the hospital. It might be a urinary tract infection, but as a doula I was not about to diagnose what it might be. She called back to tell me she was going to be seen in the emergency room and asked if I could come. I told her I would meet her there.

At 7:30 p.m. they were just hooking up Carmen to the monitors and had her in the maternity triage area. A woman was screaming in the next room and nurses were running every which way. It looked like they weren't going to get her up to the labor and delivery unit in time. Our nurse's pager went off and she left. Carmen and I visited until she came back, but not before we heard a very lusty cry from the baby in the next room. The nurse explained that they would monitor Carmen for about half an hour and then call the doctor to come and assess what was going on. Blood was drawn and they had her give a urine specimen. We hadn't had time to visit for two weeks, so it was nice to catch up. I just wished she felt better.

All the tests came back as normal but there were indications that she was quite dehydrated. They suggested she stay long enough to have an IV and she agreed. She felt 100% better after that and promised to drink lots more water than she had been drinking. I was glad that it wasn't early labor. Her baby needed to gain more weight before he arrived. I waited for her taxi home and hugged her goodbye when it came.

Back home I climbed into bed after checking that I had set a clean set of clothes on a chair should The Call come. It did at 10:00 p.m. At last, it was Alegra! Contractions were five minutes apart and she had called her midwife, who agreed it was time to go to the hospital.

I had not had a mom so well prepared for a long time. She had done her homework. She had even presented me with her birth plan at our first appointment.

We were settled into a large room and the midwife met us there. I suggested hanging out in the tub in the bathroom while the birth tub was set up and filled, which would take awhile. The room didn't have a built-in tub but the midwife and nurse hauled in a huge assemble-your-own-tub kit which was rather nifty, with a disposable liner. I brought in my battery-operated "candles," placed them around the edges of the tub, turned off the overhead light, got Alegra's jug of juice, and settled in for however long we'd be here. Her partner, Fernando, wasn't here yet. He would get off of work in an hour and Alegra assured him she would wait at least that long.

When the tub was ready we moved back into the room. Alegra was so relaxed that I was surprised when her midwife checked her and said she was already eight centimeters. Fernando arrived and was more than excited. Alegra was very quiet at that point, slowly breathing and not answering his questions. After one contraction she tried to tell him that it was getting too intense to talk. He didn't exactly "get it" and tried to bring up the subject of the baby's name, which they still had not agreed upon. He playfully tried to smooth back some of her hair and she smacked him square in the chest. He got the message that time. I suggested he take my place by the edge of the pool and just hold her hands. We switched places and they got into an easy rhythm, breathing, resting, breathing, resting . . .

He moved over at one point and Alegra grabbed his belt with both hands. He tried to pry her fingers off the belt and hold her hands but she had decided that that was what she needed at that moment. His jeans were creeping earthward, but he was the only one who was at all concerned.

I was telling her how well she was doing, that it wouldn't get harder than this, that she was really doing an awesome job when, with the next rush, I heard the universal "Grrrrrrrrr!"

Midwives and doulas the world over recognize the sound, at least wherever women are allowed to birth naturally, instinctually, and are not rushed into the second stage and pushing.

I whispered, "Uh huh" to confirm that this was it, that she was doing it right. After the next couple of rushes I thought I saw the head crowning, though with Alegra in a squatting position, I was not positive. I silently slid over and whispered to her midwife, "I think you want to be here." She took the cue as the baby's head became visible and told Alegra to pick up her baby.

That moment, at that time, was the most magical span of time in the entire universe. I watched in slow motion as Alegra reached for her baby as the rest of him slid out, face down. She brought him out of the water to her chest, dripping water the only sound.

Fernando was totally blown away. It was the most amazing thing happening in the whole world at that very moment and we were allowed to witness it.

Little Xavier started to cry on his own and then his daddy did, too. Alegra was still in shock. She told me later that she kept waiting for it to get worse, to hurt more. She was prepared for labor to be harder to navigate, but perhaps because she expected it to be harder, she was able to integrate each stage as well as she did.

We congratulated her and helped her to the bed when she was ready. We didn't have to do anything for Xavier. He was pink and breathing and thinking about rooting already, lifting his head to look around. She thanked her midwife and me, though I told her it was she who did all the work. We didn't do anything, really. She was brilliant.

In Alegra's words:

"The story of Xavier's birth began on a Saturday morning almost a week after his due date. At 5:00 a.m. I woke up with some spotting. Nothing happened after that, except that I couldn't really get back to sleep again. Mom and I went out shopping all afternoon. Around 3:45 p.m. I noticed that it seemed like I had some pressure that came and went; nothing serious.

"When we got home, dinner was spaghetti—our family Saturday night tradition. We must have gotten home a bit later, because we didn't eat until almost 8:00 p.m. Around 9:25 p.m. I called the midwives through my nurse helpline to leave a message. After a midwife called me back, I called my doula and told her what the midwife had said. I told her I'd take a bath and then let her know how I was doing. So I made a warm bath and hopped in, and it was so relaxing and wonderful, the contractions (which by now I had figured out that's what they were, even though there still was no 'whole-belly-squeeze') dissipated and I figured my labor was slowing down again. *It'll be another day*, I thought.

"But, when I got out of the bath around 10:45 p.m., wham! The contractions started up again and came quickly—every three to four minutes. Actually that was with the minute-long contractions, so it felt like every two to three minutes. After awhile I called my doula and she said it sounded like it was about time that I went in and that she would meet me there on the maternity floor. My mom was driving and by this time, though, I had to pause so frequently that it took us awhile to get out of the house with my hospital bags.

"'What department?' the security guard asked. I would have laughed if I hadn't been in the middle of a contraction.

"'Maternity!'

"'Oh, do you want transportation?' (Did I look like I needed a bus? Then it registered—a wheelchair.) Of course I chose to walk, which took more time. We had to buzz in through the secured doors of the maternity unit, and as they slowly opened, I saw my doula at the end of the hall in front of the check-in desk, waiting for me. Relief! She had gotten there first because it took me so long to get out of the house and then through the hospital once the contractions were coming more frequently. Heather, my midwife, checked my dilation and said, 'Good news. You're already a six.' They filled a warm bathtub for me to sit in until the big water-birth tub was ready.

"I kept waiting for Fernando to arrive, but he was at work and didn't come until after 2:00 a.m. When he did, I relaxed more and with a couple of heaves, revisited my spaghetti dinner. Actually, even though things were getting more intense, I remember almost laughing that the first thing I did was practically vomit all over him. I said something like, 'You came just at the right time,' but Stephanie was encouraging.

"'You know what Ina May says, "Every time you throw up, you dilate another centimeter!"' And even though I hadn't been nauseous, throwing up actually helped me feel a lot better.

"Not long after Fernando arrived (later I learned it was between 2:30 and 3:00 a.m.), the birth tub was ready and it was time to move in there. By then the midwife told me I was at ten centimeters, but the water bag was still intact.

"She asked if she could break it. I said yes, and after that, the pressure got a lot stronger. The lights were still low, except for a light over the bed by the monitor where the nurse was charting. The best part was that I was so grateful for everyone's help, yet even though I had no emotional energy to tell them, or even to say thank you, they were very present and continued pouring it out.

"After it seemed like the pushing contractions were slowing down, finally with a change of position, the intensity of the pressure got heavier and heavier. At some point I remember thinking, *This is why women ask for epidurals*, but it was a passing thought, especially with Stephanie and Heather's encouragement. I didn't realize I was tensing up instead of relaxing. Then I started making real progress (or rather, the baby did) and with each contraction, I felt a strong and repeated urge to push. Along with the pushing, I was grunting from deep down, primal sounds. I had a fleeting thought—*My vocal cords are gonna hurt* (and later they did), but in the moment I didn't feel anything except the pressure down under.

"Then Heather reached down and said, 'You can feel the baby's head. Reach down and feel it.' And I did—it was unbelievable. It was at that point that labor actually began to feel like pain—I felt the 'ring of fire,' the stretching around the baby's head, and I started panicking and felt myself closing up and was afraid that his head was going to go back up inside. Stephanie and Heather kept pouring out encouraging words for me to relax and not panic. Later I realized it hurt so much at that very end because I had both first- and second-degree tears. But I also reflected on the fact that I didn't register actual pain until the last fifteen minutes or so. Everything before that was increasingly intense, but not painful.

"I felt so desperate and to the point of no return that I just pushed as hard as I could. I started to feel his head push past the intense pain, then on a second push, his body. Heather's hands were there to help adjust his body as he came out, and then she held his head down in the water as he slid out. She kept him there for a second, then without thinking I reached down and drew him up out of the water and immediately he turned bright red and started screaming. His lungs were clearly working. I was in shock. I had expected to cry. Once again, I was surprised by my own reaction. I had no urge to cry at all. I just stared, gaping at the screaming creature in my hands. Later I learned he got an Apgar score of ten both at one and at five minutes. Yay for Xavier!

"The nurses and Stephanie and maybe Fernando (I was so not focused on them at that moment) helped me out of the birthing tub onto the hospital bed. The baby was still attached by the umbilical cord. I was holding my baby; they were holding me. We didn't cut the cord for at least ten minutes, and then Fernando cut the cord after it turned white—'like cutting chicken,' the nurse said, as she clamped it. The nurse and Stephanie encouraged me to place him on my chest and allow him to spontaneously breastfeed, which he did. From the middle of my chest he wiggled to the right spot and started to latch on. Amazing!

"Heather and Stephanie both examined the placenta and Heather explained what she was looking for to gauge its age, the attachment of the cord to the placenta, and how to know it was all there. She even remarked that it was asymmetrical and that the cord was bifurcated, meaning that it split at the base as it connected to the placenta. The fact that I remember that is incredible, since I had been up since 5:00 a.m. Saturday morning and it was by then at least 5:00 a.m. Sunday morning, but I was wide awake. Tired for sure, but on an adrenaline high. It was still dark outside and the room was peaceful.

"A little while after I was stitched up, Stephanie told me it was time for her to go. She had only been up all night. I was so grateful for her calming presence the entire time. My mom came back in from the waiting room, and she got to meet her grandson for the first time. I rested as they weighed and measured him, and my mom took the first pictures of him in my arms. Then a nurse came in and, as the first rays of morning light came up, I signed my admittance papers. Heather was going off-shift, but I was so grateful to her, my doula, the nurse, and Fernando for an amazing birth experience. Most of all, I was so thankful that I had had a natural birth in which I was free to move about freely and comfortably. I loved the calming and warming feeling of the water. I am sure this helped me to not have pain and to really appreciate and embrace Xavier's peaceful entrance into the world."

Two weeks later I got a call early one morning from Fernando. He wanted to pick me up at noon to go to a Salvadorian restaurant. I have never had their food and I told him I would be delighted. Lunch was amazing, but it was just as much fun to see how big Xavier had grown. Alegra was a pro at breastfeeding. Then Fernando's ulterior motive was revealed: he wanted my opinion about whether I thought Alegra had enough milk and if their baby was growing fast enough.

I assured him that she was doing better than ninety-nine percent of the moms I see and that his baby was perfect. Their doctor had told them as much, but he just wanted another opinion and wanted to be sure. I told him that he was such a good daddy for being concerned, and that he should continue to have skin-to-skin time with his son.

I added Xavier's picture to my collection of baby photos when they sent one. I now had one more baby. I stopped counting years ago after baby number 200. He may have been my first Salvadorian baby. There have been Mexican babies, Hmong, Thai, Kenyan, Somali, Ethiopian, Nigerian, a native of the Cameroons (Cameroonian?), Vietnamese, Lao, Togolese, Native American, African American, Liberian, Cambodian, Asian, and a melting pot of American babies.

I love each one. I worry about some. I pray for all of them. Each one has blessed me. Each is a perfectly unique little soul.

Xavier at ten months old.

"The traditional midwife believes that birth proceeds in a spiral fashion: labor starts, stops and starts, while the baby goes down, up and down, and the cervix opens, closes and opens. Nature has no design for failure; she holds her own meaning for success."
~Sher Willis

Doula
A Poem

~For Wyatt, November 4, 2012

We dance when all the world is asleep
Down long corridors,
Hallways lit by moonlight.
The full moon our only witness
To this soundless dance.
The waves the metronome we dance to,
Calling him to come
To be with us here.
We love you so
Come dance with us little one.
Come see moon and stars
Waiting, too
Silently waiting
For this Night of nights
This Night chosen from all eternity for your birth.

~sss

Ina May Gaskin

How would I describe Ina May? Fearless, discerning, intuitive, wise, and honest to a fault. By stepping outside of the mold of modern medicine and being free to ask the hard questions, like, "Why have we been doing birth this way, when it is clear it isn't working as well as we know it could?" she has led a brilliant movement of women (and men) toward the truth that the Creator has given us, a power to know and act as we were meant to, from birth onward.

What follows are some of my favorite quotes by Ina May Gaskin, many from the 2013 movie, *Birth Story: Ina May Gaskin and The Farm Midwives*. The movie spotlights a spirited group of women who taught themselves to deliver babies in the 1970s while living on what some would call a hippie commune. Through research and trying different approaches to birthing, they learned and have been teaching others to respect the natural ability of women to birth without drugs that can harm the mother and the baby and other interventions. Today, even though C-section rates continue to be too high, Ina May and midwives everywhere are slowly getting through to the medical community.

- "Remember this, for it is as true and true gets: Your body is not a lemon. You are not a machine. The Creator is not a careless mechanic. Human female bodies have the same potential to give birth as well as aardvarks, lions, rhinoceri, elephants, moose, and water buffalo. Even if it has not been your habit throughout your life so far, I recommend that you learn to think positively about your body."
- "It is important to keep in mind that our bodies must work pretty well, or there wouldn't be so many humans on the planet."

- "Many of our problems in U.S. maternity care stem from the fact that we leave no room for recognizing when nature is smarter than we are."
- "Whenever and however you give birth, your experience will impact your emotions, your mind, your body, and your spirit for the rest of your life."
- "If a woman doesn't look like a goddess during labor, then someone isn't treating her right."
- "Good beginnings make a positive difference in the world, so it is worth our while to provide the best possible care for mothers and babies throughout this extraordinarily influential part of life."
- "Asking a woman to give birth while hooked up to a bunch of machines is like asking a man to have an erection on command while strapped to a hospital gurney."

Release
By Liz Abbene

From the moment you see that first positive pregnancy test, the release begins. Every moment, every joy, and every challenge of parenthood, from beginning to end, it's all about releasing and letting go. Pregnancy begins, and seemingly in an instant, you begin to let go of your former life. Things that were once savored, like sushi and red wine, now are off-limits, replaced with soda crackers and ginger ale. Naps are favored over late nights. As the months go by, you release your body to the incredible process, your belly grows, your breasts change, your skin and hair take on lives of their own (for better or worse) and you release your body image to that of the amazing work of pregnancy. For some, this process is awe-inspiring, for others it's frustrating. Either way, it's preparation for the next release: birth.

The journey of birth begins with the last days of pregnancy and the final release of your current, pre-baby, life. The entire labor and birth process is the most incredible release a woman will ever experience in her life. Everything about birth is out and down, which means every sensation, every sound and every emotion is centered around letting go and succumbing to the power of the body. The release that is felt when a baby exits the body is like none other. The exhilarating feeling is the culmination of months—maybe years, days, hours, hormones, stretching, opening, laughter, tears, highs, and lows. Regardless of how the baby emerges, vaginally or surgically, intervention-free or intervention-full, the process of birth is amazing preparation for the next release: parenthood.

No matter how many books you read, how ready you think you are, or how long you've been pining for a child, there is nothing that can truly prepare you for parenthood. Many people are the "best" parents before they have children, vowing that their children will never do this, eat that, or be allowed such-and-such. The reality is that having and raising happy children means releasing selfishness, rigid schedules, and preconceived notions. It means letting go of some of the hopes and dreams you have for your children and allowing them to aspire to their own. Parenthood is about acceptance of the process, despite your confusion and frustration as to why your child isn't sleeping for a specific number of hours in a row, wanting to play a particular sport, or has a certain medical condition.

Releasing is not easy. It takes time, practice, and dedication. However, the rewards can be great. You will find that there is sweetness in the toddler snuggling in your bed, the girl who favors stained Beatles t-shirts over her sister's hand-me-down skirts, the child who decides ballet is not for her (making for an abundance of tutus and dance shoes in the dress-up bin) and the boy who prefers to sleep in a pink owl bed with his little sisters versus being alone. When you're able to let go of what you thought your children should be, you're able to love and accept them for who they are.

[Reprinted here with permission from enlightenedmama.com and with gratitude for all Liz Abbene and the enlightened mamas of Minnesota do for all of us!]

Everything You've Always Wanted to Know About Agpar Scores But Were Too Afraid to Ask

History

In 1952, an anesthesiologist named Virginia Apgar proposed a formula be devised that could be used by all medical professionals to assess the condition of a newborn infant. Up until that time anyone—doctor, midwife, nurse or anesthesiologist—could (and would) simply look at a baby during the time they remained in the delivery room and the conversation could go something like this:

Doctor: "He's a bit floppy, let's suction him again."
Nurse: "Maybe a bit of oxygen will pink him up a little, do you think blow-by would be enough?"
Midwife: "I'm going to rub him a bit with a towel here on Mom's tummy and get some better muscle tone."
Mother: "Isn't he too blue?"

Yes, he is blue and it is has been five minutes and someone could have/should have tried all of the above, but you get the idea that assessment of a newborn was haphazard at best, and could have been managed better. We have attempted to make alternative arrangements over the years in deciding who the decision-makers in the delivery or birthing room (or home) are going to be, but our wise friend Dr. Virginia Apgar gave us a tool to use that would become a universal way of guiding our protocols, which just means we now know what we should be seeing in a newborn, when we should be seeing it, and what to do about it if we don't. It was decidedly instrumental in taking an ambiguous concept and turning it into a workable framework in order to obtain an accurate reflection of the observations at present. Actually very simple, it works, and Apgar scoring has changed very little since its inception. I am including a short summary of the Apgar Score to give a little background for how this played into my own research and work in bonding.

What is the Apgar score?

Ninety percent of term infants make a successful and uneventful transition from living within the womb to the outside world. About ten percent will need some medical intervention and less than one percent will require extensive resuscitation. A reproducible and rapidly determined rating system is necessary for evaluation of the newborn infant. The Apgar score is a practical method for assessing a newborn.

How is the Apgar score done?

The Apgar score is a number calculated by scoring the heart rate, respiratory effort, muscle tone, skin color, and reflex irritability. Each of these objective signs can receive zero, one, or two points.

What does a high or low Apgar score mean?

A perfect Apgar score of ten means an infant is in the best possible condition. An infant with an Apgar score of zero to three needs immediate resuscitation. It is important to note that diligent care of the newborn is an immediate response to the current status of the infant. It is inappropriate to wait until Apgar scores are obtained to begin or continue to address the needs of the newborn.

Why was the Apgar score developed?

The score is named for the preeminent American anesthesiologist Dr. Virginia Apgar (1909-1974), who invented the scoring method in 1952. Having assisted at thousands of deliveries, Dr. Apgar wished to focus attention on the baby. Babies were traditionally dispatched directly to the nursery, often without much formal scrutiny after delivery. Apgar wanted the baby to be assessed in an organized and meaningful manner by the delivery room personnel. Dr. Apgar was the first woman to be appointed a full professor at Columbia University's College of Physicians and Surgeons.

Resources

Videos

Birth Story: Ina May Gaskin & the Farm Midwives, 2012, directed by Sara Lamm and Mary Wigmore. (DVD)

"Breast Crawl by UNICEF" http://www.breastcrawl.org/video.shtml A must see!

Breastfeeding: the Why-to, How-to, Can-do Videos—Vida Health communications. www.vida-health.com

The Business of Being Born with Abby Epstein and Ricki Lake. (DVD) (See also *More Business of Being Born*, the continuation of the series.)

"Christian Dads Experience What It Feels Like to Give Birth"—One for your partner! (YouTube)

Doula—about Loretha Weisinger's work with teens. (Netflix)

Doula: A Documentary—produced in 2012 by Childbirth Collective in Minneapolis and Emily Rumsey. http://www.emilyrumsey.com

"The Dramatic Struggle for Life"—very amazing footage from Bali. (YouTube)

Everybody Loves . . . Babies by Thomas Balmes. (DVD)

"Extraordinary Breastfeeding" A five-part online video series, these videos give real food for thought! (YouTube)

Guerrilla Midwife—Follow CNN Hero of the Year Ibu Robin Lim into the trenches of her work from Bali, where hemorrhage after childbirth is a leading cause of death, into the Tsunami disaster zone in Aceh, where her battle is fought with only one weapon, love. (Online video)

"Thalasso Bain Bebe par Sonia Rochel"—Baby bath by Brazilian midwife Sonia Rochel (YouTube)

Twin Vertex Birth—the birth of the author's twins at The Farm in 1982, with Ina May Gaskin. (DVD)

Internet Resources

AskDrSears.com—valuable advice on breastfeeding and parenting (my personal favorite)

Breastfeeding Resource Pages—La Leche League International. www.llli.org/nb.html

Caroline Flint, U.K. Midwife website: http://carolineflintmidwife.tumblr.com/

DONA International website: information on doula training, certification and *Doula* magazine. http://www.dona.org

Ina May Gaskin's homepage: http://inamay.com/

The Newman Breastfeeding Clinic, the Centre for Breastfeeding Education, and the Centre for Breastfeeding Studies: http://www.nbci.ca You can call them for help anytime, too: 416-498-0002. A connection to an amazing group in Canada with seemingly endless information—all excellent.

Ongoing blog: callthedoula.blogspot.com

Books

Attatchment Parenting: Instinctive care for your baby and young child, by Katie Allison Granju

Babies, Breastfeeding and Bonding, by Ina May Gaskin

Baby-Led Breasetfeeding, by Gill Rapley and Tracey Murkett

Birth Matters: A Midwife's Manifesta, by Ina May Gaskin

The Birth Partner—Revised 4th Ed.: A Complete Guide to Childbirth for Dads, Doulas, and All Other Labor Companions, by Penny Simkin

The Birth Partner: Everything You Need to Know to Help a Woman Through Childbirth, by Penny Simpkin

Birth—Through Children's Eyes, by Penny Simkin

Breastfeeding and Natural Child Spacing: How Ecological Breastfeeding Spaces Babies, by Sheila Kippley

The Breastfeeding Answer Book, by the La Leche League International

Breastfeeding Matters: What We Need to Know About Infant Feeding, Maureen Kathryn Minchin

Comfort Measures for Childbirth, by Penny Simkin

The Continuum Concept: In search of happiness lost, by Jean Liedloff

Do Birth: A gentle guide to labour and childbirth, by Carolyn Flint

Hold Your Premie, by Jill and Dr. Nils Bergman

Ina May's Guide to Breastfeeding, by Ina May Gaskin

Ina May's Guide to Childbirth, by Ina May Gaskin

The Labor Progress Handbook: Early Interventions to Prevent and Treat Dystocia, by Penny Simkin

Medications and Mothers' Milk, 14th ed., by Thomas W. Hale

Mothering the New Mother, by Sally Placksin

The NAPSAC Directory of Alternative Birth Services and Consumer Guide, by Penny Simkin

Natural Health after Birth, by Aviva Jill Romm

The Nursing Mother's Herbal, by Sheila Humphrey

Parenting Without Borders: Surprising Lessons Parents Around the World Can Teach Us, by Christine Gross-Loh

The Politics of Breastfeeding, by Gabrielle Palmer

Pregnancy, Childbirth and the Newborn, by Penny Simkin

Saving Babies? The Consequences of Newborn Genetic Screening, by Stefan Timmermans and Mara Buchbinder

The Simple Guide to Having a Baby, by Penny Simkin

The Spirit Catches You and You Fall Down: A Hmong Child, Her American Doctors, and the Collision of Two Cultures, by Anne Fadiman

Spiritual Midwifery, by Ina May Gaskin

The Tender Gift: Breastfeeding, by Dana Raphael

Testing Baby: The Transformation of Newborn Screening, Parenting, and Policymaking, by Rachel Grob

The Ultimate Breastfeeding Book of Answers: The Most Comprehensive, by Jack Newman and Teresa Pitman

When Survivors Give Birth: Understanding and Healing the Effects of Early Sexual Abuse on Childbearing Women, by Penny Simkin
The Womanly Art of Breastfeeding, by La Leche League International
Waiting With Gabriel: A Story of Cherishing a Baby's Brief Life, by Amy Kuebelbeck

Products

Beba Bean Pee-pee Teepee

"Birthing is the most profound initiation to spirituality a woman can have."
~Robin Lim

Acknowledgements

I must first honor here the very courageous Ethiopian and Somali women and men I have had the privilege of getting to know and love: Jamad Sheik Nur, Fatima, Jama, Farhia, Said, Fosiyo, Fowsiya, Meskia, Hikmet, Mahdi, Tigist, Mantegbosh, Mohammad, Abdighani, Yohannes, Keleme, Chala, Shamsudin, Hibo, Radiya, and so many, many others.

Next, for her courage, fearless outspoken wisdom, and insight, along with thousands of other midwives, doulas, and parents, I wish to thank Ina May Gaskin for her life's work, which has immeasurably blessed us all.

Special thanks goes also to those who believed in me when I didn't: eminent scholar and author, my father, Dr. Maurice L. Schwartz (1925-2014), who had ten books under his belt in his lifetime; David, my husband of thirty-eight years, who has encouraged me through every last step of the impossible paths I have chosen throughout our lives together—I will have you canonized yet! Our children: Abraham, Isaac, Ruth, Rachel, and Hannah who, each in her or his own exquisitely unique way, helped me grow and discover first who I am now and then what eventually became this book; and my sister Phebe Schwartz who is wandering around somewhere in Cambodia as I write this. Stay well and safe, my love!

My cousin Roslyn Sternberg-Willett—author, world traveler, feminist, and a rare woman of distinction and accomplishment, was the driving force behind getting me to ever bring my stories to a publisher in the first place.

For his tremendous support and invaluable advice throughout this entire project I wish to thank Mr. Nasibu Sareva, CFO and Executive Director of the African Development Center (ADC).

Ms. Ma Xiong holds a very special place in my heart, as does her family. Look for her forthcoming memoirs that I have been honored to work on with her.

Roberta Poirier, CNM, is my heroine and has been my mentor throughout my adult life, once I finally figured out what I wanted to be when I grew up. She has also been my midwife and friend. Hugs and many, many thanks, my dear!

And without my very own personal wizard-magician-computer-guru, Don Geronimo, I would not have gotten to first base, much less been able to let the rest of the world know about this book via our blog. (Did you know some people can talk to laptops? And they listen, too?) Thank you, dear Don. I owe you big time. Just say the word!

For all the mothers—Native, African, Indian, Asian, European, Arab, and American—who have permitted me to attend their births during the past thirty years, it is an honor that I don't take lightly. Each mama, each and every baby, and each partner make their birth unique. The time of that particular birth, that nanosecond within all the cosmos, makes that birth the most important single event in the universe that is happening at that moment, and you shared it with me. I am deeply grateful.

A huge thank you, too, goes to all of the midwives, doulas, nurses, and doctors who have shared their wisdom with me and supported me in my work, especially Debby Prudhomme, CD(DONA), Mary Williams, RN, CD(DONA), Catherine (Molly) Szondy, RN, CNM, and Valerie El Halta, CPM.

And for the real blood, sweat, tears, and prayers that birthed this book I have my very own doula, Tabatha Obert, to thank. (Starbucks helped!)

I also want to thank everyone at North Star Press: Corinne, Curtis, Anne, and everyone else who played a part, no matter how small, in the labor and birth of *Ma Doula*. I had no idea when I began this adventure how close we would become to one another. I could definitely not have done it without each one of you!

Last, but certainly not least, I must thank my agent/friend/editor Patricia Morris for her faith in my work and her unwavering support when I was ready to ditch the whole project. You are my fairy godmother! Who else makes dreams come true?